"Bishop Robert Barron is arguably the greatest Catholic communicator of our times. In *The Pivotal Players*, we meet the men and women whose lives animate Bishop Barron's words—and who can motivate each of us to live the adventure of our faith in new and unexpected ways."

> – **Arthur C. Brooks, PhD**
> Professor of Public Leadership, Harvard University, and bestselling author of *Love Your Enemies*

"This is a beautiful book. Peace and strength waft up from its pages as you read and turn them and gaze at the vivid, vibrant pictures. It is the fresh air of Catholic culture that you are breathing in, not as an abstract idea, but through the lives of the enlightened men and women who—differently but always freshly in every age—embody the exquisite truths of Jesus' Gospel."

> – **Abbot Jeremy Driscoll, OSB**
> Abbot of Mount Angel Abbey

"In this beautifully illustrated and captivating book, Bishop Barron draws our attention to twelve heroic figures, from St. Augustine to Flannery O'Connor. *The Pivotal Players* is a powerful and welcome reminder that the truths of the faith are not limited to the abstractions of theology and philosophy but have also been made manifest in the particular lives of our greatest theologians, artists, mystics, and saints."

> – **Jennifer Frey**
> Associate Professor of Philosophy, University of South Carolina

"The Pivotal Players in this book captivate the imagination, stir the heart, and inspire a life filled with love of God and love of neighbor. Bishop Barron's winsome text is accompanied by lavish art that brings to life twelve fascinating figures from diverse cultures and times. If I ran the world, this book of heroes would be required reading in every parish, in every classroom, and in every home. Get a copy for yourself and share a copy with a 'none' whom you love."

> – **Christopher Kaczor**
> Professor of Philosophy and author of *The Seven Big Myths about the Catholic Church*

"Bishop Robert Barron is a baseball fan, which is the ultimate demonstration that he's a very smart man. He's also a virtuoso evangelist and the best guide to the beauty and truth of the Catholic tradition I've ever known. This book is Barron in his element, so settle in and allow him to introduce you, or re-introduce you, to the Pivotal Players in the Catholic game. Play ball!"

– John Allen, Jr.
President of Crux and Senior Vatican Analyst for CNN

"In this book Bishop Robert Barron provides us with a wonderful introduction to a symphony of witnesses to Christ, each in their respective intellectual genius and spirituality. In doing so he gives a portal into the splendor of the truth of the Catholic faith as a religion of truth, beauty, and goodness."

– Fr. Thomas Joseph White, OP
Thomistic Institute, Angelicum

The Pivotal Players

12 HEROES WHO SHAPED THE CHURCH
AND CHANGED THE WORLD

ROBERT BARRON

Word on Fire, Park Ridge, IL 60068
© 2020 by Word on Fire Catholic Ministries
All rights reserved.

ISBN: 978-1-943243-67-9

Library of Congress Control Number: 2020915231
Barron, Robert E., 1959–

Printed in the United States of America

23 22 21   3 4

www.wordonfire.org

CONTENTS

Playing the Christian Game

BISHOP ROBERT BARRON

The book you are about to read is a slightly edited and elaborated presentation of the scripts for my film series *The Pivotal Players,* which is a follow-up to my earlier documentary *CATHOLICISM.* Many people who saw the first series remarked that their favorite episode was the one that presented biographies of four relatively contemporary saints of the Catholic Church. This very much confirmed my own conviction that the optimal way to present the truth of Catholicism is not so much through presenting abstract ideas but through showing concrete lives. Following the theologian Hans Urs von Balthasar, I have long felt that the best and truest theologians are those who embody the Christian thing and show the dynamics of the Christian life.

Accordingly, I endeavored in the second series to concentrate exclusively on telling the stories of great exemplars of Catholicism, many but not all of them canonized saints. I wanted to teach Catholicism precisely by looking at it in action. In choosing these figures, I concentrated on those who were truly pivotal—that is to say, those who made a significant difference, who set a new direction in the development of Christ's Mystical Body. Also, I wanted to include personages who decisively influenced not just the Church but the wider society too, for the ultimate purpose of the Church is to be salt and light for all the nations. A third consideration was this: I wanted to show men and women from across the two thousand years of Christianity, so that my viewer/reader might appreciate the persistence and consistency of the Catholic ideal even through myriad cultural shifts.

Hence we have, for instance, Augustine and Benedict from the ancient Church; Thomas Aquinas, Catherine of Siena, and Francis of Assisi from the Middle Ages; Bartolomé de las Casas and Ignatius of Loyola from the early modern period; and Flannery O'Connor and Fulton Sheen from our own time. A fourth preoccupation was to show forth the astonishing variety of dimensions and aspects of Catholicism. Thus Aquinas, John Henry Newman, and Augustine demonstrate the intellectual life; Catherine of Siena manifests mysticism; Francis of Assisi and Bartolomé de las Casas embody the Church's outreach to the poor and suffering; Michelangelo and O'Connor express artistic accomplishment; etc. A fifth consideration was to bring out the echoes, rhymes, and harmonies that obtain among the players. Therefore, the convert Augustine sings to the convert Newman; the Dominican Catherine's prayer is structured by her Dominican brother Aquinas' theology; the young Benedict retires to a cave to consider the purpose of his life, and a thousand years later, the young Ignatius goes to a cave to discern the divine will; Chesterton's lyrical theology informs the television preaching of Fulton Sheen.

Now, whenever one makes bold to compile a list—whether of the greatest singers of all time or the Pivotal Players within Catholicism—he opens himself wide, of course, to criticism: "How could you possibly have left out . . . ?" And so, obviously, I could/should have spoken of Irenaeus, John Chrysostom, Mozart, Bonaventure, Paul Claudel, Francis Xavier, and on and on. Guilty as charged, for they are all wonderful. One observation I might make in this context is that I had already covered, at least to some degree, a number of key figures in the *CATHOLICISM* series—Dante, Thomas Merton, John Paul II, and John of the Cross, to name a few—and I didn't want to repeat myself in this new documentary.

Which brings me to an elephant in the room: How come so few women are mentioned as Pivotal Players? There certainly should have been more, but I was hamstrung by my no-repetition principle, for I had purposely covered a great number of female figures in the *CATHOLICISM* series. In those films, you will find substantive treatments of Dorothy Day, Teresa of Avila, Bernadette of Lourdes, Edith Stein, Mother Katharine Drexel, Thérèse of Lisieux, Mother Teresa of Kolkata, as well as an entire episode dedicated to Mary, the Mother of God. If I hadn't made the first series, I would have chosen a number of these women as Pivotal Players.

The essays in this book, based as they are on scripts for roughly fifty-minute-long programs, are not in-depth treatments designed to be-guile the minds of academic specialists. They are sketches of the lives and thought of these twelve astonishing figures, and their intended audience is the educated laity. In addition to the main text, readers will find short sidebars throughout each chapter, featuring off-the-cuff Q&A asides that were captured during our filming. My fondest hope is that this book will inspire deeper study of these men and women and perhaps even deeper devotion to them.

Finally, why did I use the term "players" in regard to some of the most sublime and important figures within the Catholic tradition? Am I trivializing their achievements by using a word usually associated with games? Well, in regard to play, I'm an Aristotelian. Aristotle taught that play, precisely in the measure that it is sought for its own sake, is the highest form of activity. Indeed, art, philosophy, and the liturgy would count as forms of play in this sense. The men and women under consideration in this book are those who entered with particular creativity, intelligence, and abandon into the life of Christ—those who played the Christian game remarkably well.

CHAPTER 1

St. Augustine

THE TEACHER

Augustine of Hippo is not only one of the three or four most important players in the history of the Church; he is a pivotal figure in the development of Western civilization. He is the most significant bridge between the culture of ancient Rome and the Christian culture that would come to full flower in the Middle Ages.

As a master of the Latin language, he ranks with Cicero, Virgil, and Ovid; as a theologian and philosopher, he has practically no rivals, with the possible exception of Thomas Aquinas. Not only did he bring Trinitarian theology to its most articulate expression, he also managed to found the discipline of philosophy of history and basically to invent the literary genre of autobiography. And through it all, he lived a life of heroic sanctity, becoming one of the best-known and most influential saints in the history of the Catholic Church. Any one of these accomplishments would be sufficient to secure a lasting reputation. The combination of them in one man is nothing less than astonishing. Even the most gifted of his contemporaries have, for the most part, faded into obscurity; but Augustine, curiously, has exercised an influence and fascination generation after generation, very much up to the present day.

Why does Augustine come across as such a human figure?

It is most important to note that Augustine is not just a high-level philosopher and theologian—though he was indeed one of the greatest in the whole tradition—but he consistently gives you access to his heart. There are tears on almost every page of the *Confessions*. He opens himself in an honest, unapologetic way, which makes him appealing to people across the ages who can see themselves in him. It's fair to say that he wasn't someone who had it all together from the beginning.

THE *CONFESSIONS*

An exposition of the life and times of Augustine compels a consideration of his masterpiece, a spiritual and intellectual autobiography called the *Confessions*. Prior to this work, there had been, of course, histories and stylized biographies of great figures, but there had been nothing like the introspective analyses of mind, intention, and aspiration that we find in the pages of the *Confessions*. It is autobiography, yes; but perhaps more accurately, it is a self-portrait of a soul—or even more precisely, a "prayer overheard." For the entire text of the *Confessions* is addressed to God in attitudes of imploring, begging, cajoling, praising, and confessing sin. Through the consummate literary skill of Augustine, the reader is given the opportunity to listen in. What makes the *Confessions* extraordinarily rich is its combination of high intellectualism and profound emotion. There is no mistaking that this is the work of a man steeped in the most rarified academic culture of his time, but the pages of the book are replete with vividly remembered scenes and passionate feeling.

On the very first page of the *Confessions*, we find what to my mind is the best and most succinct statement of Christian anthropology ever formulated: "*Fecisti nos ad te, Domine, et inquietum est cor nostrum donec requiescat in te*"—"Lord, you have made us for yourself; therefore, our heart is restless until it rests in you." We are, in a word, hardwired for God, and our very desire proves it, for nothing in this world finally satisfies the restless longing of the soul. How eloquently Augustine evokes the universality of this aspiration by using the singular "our heart" rather than "our hearts." Despite all of our relatively superficial differences, we all come together in hungering and thirsting for God. In his very particular story, we are meant to see our own.

Augustine was born in 354 in the little North African town of Thagaste in the Roman province of Numidia. He was the son of a pagan man named Patricius and a Christian woman who would come to be known as St. Monica. Though he received a basic instruction in his mother's religion, he was not a committed Christian. Gifted intellectually and highly ambitious, he read the classical authors in the Latin tradition—Virgil, Cicero, Terence, and others—and longed to be, like them, a master of the spoken word.

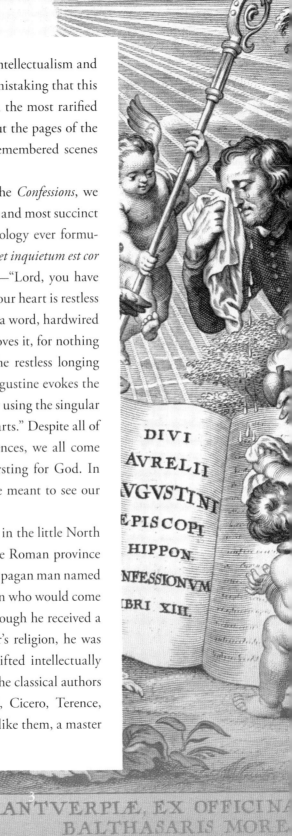

DIVI
AVRELII
AVGVSTINI
EPISCOPI
HIPPON.
CONFESSIONVM
LIBRI XIII.

ANTVERPIÆ, EX OFFICINA
BALTHASARIS MORE

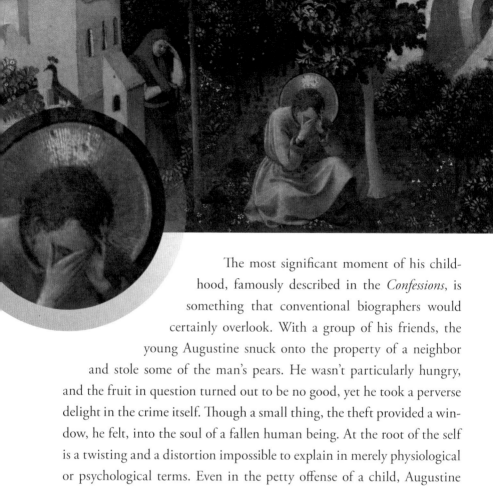

The most significant moment of his childhood, famously described in the *Confessions*, is something that conventional biographers would certainly overlook. With a group of his friends, the young Augustine snuck onto the property of a neighbor and stole some of the man's pears. He wasn't particularly hungry, and the fruit in question turned out to be no good, yet he took a perverse delight in the crime itself. Though a small thing, the theft provided a window, he felt, into the soul of a fallen human being. At the root of the self is a twisting and a distortion impossible to explain in merely physiological or psychological terms. Even in the petty offense of a child, Augustine could see the problem we all have: a perversion so profound that only the intervention of grace could adequately address it.

When he was a teenager, Augustine made his way to Carthage, the largest city in his part of the Roman world, in order to engage in the formal study of rhetoric. He refers to the city, punning in Latin, as a cauldron: *Carthago-sartago*. At the same time repelled and fascinated, Augustine threw himself into the sensual maelstrom of the place: "I was not yet in love, but I was in love with love. . . . My longing then was to love and to be loved. . . . I wore my chains with bliss but with torment too, for I was scourged with the red hot rods of jealousy, with suspicions and fears and tempers and quarrels." How contemporary and universal that sounds!

Soon after he began his studies in Carthage, when he was only seventeen, he commenced to live with a woman without marrying her, a common arrangement at the time. He stayed with her for fifteen years, and she became the mother of his only child, a son named Adeodatus (God-given). She is never named in the *Confessions*, and just before his formal conversion to Christianity, Augustine would, effectively, dismiss her.

During these crucial years, Augustine underwent two significant conversions, the first to philosophy and the second to Manicheism. The former was prompted by his reading of a book that has sadly been lost to posterity, Cicero's *Hortensius*, which was a sort of exhortation to live the philosophical life. The young Augustine drank this in, and it is fair to say that, until his dying day, he never lost the conviction that the best life is one dedicated to the pursuit of wisdom.

The latter conversion was equally decisive. Augustine became an enthusiastic companion of the Manichees, the followers of the third-century religious-philosophical teacher Mani. The Manichees presented an intellectually clarifying metaphysics, which presented the world as a battleground between good and evil, or, what amounts to the same thing, between spirit and matter. And they proposed a form of life in line with this vision, one that involved the escape of the soul from the body through a series of intellectual and ascetic disciplines. Augustine would remain a committed adept of this system for the next nine years of his life, finding in it, above all, a solution to the problem of evil and suffering. His conversion to this heretical sect was a shock to his mother and a source of deep sorrow to her. Monica's practice of praying for her son's return to the Catholic faith began in earnest at this time and lasted up to the moment of his Baptism.

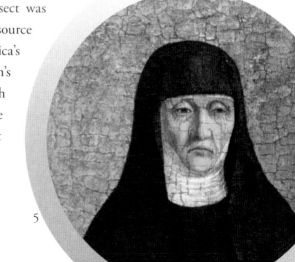

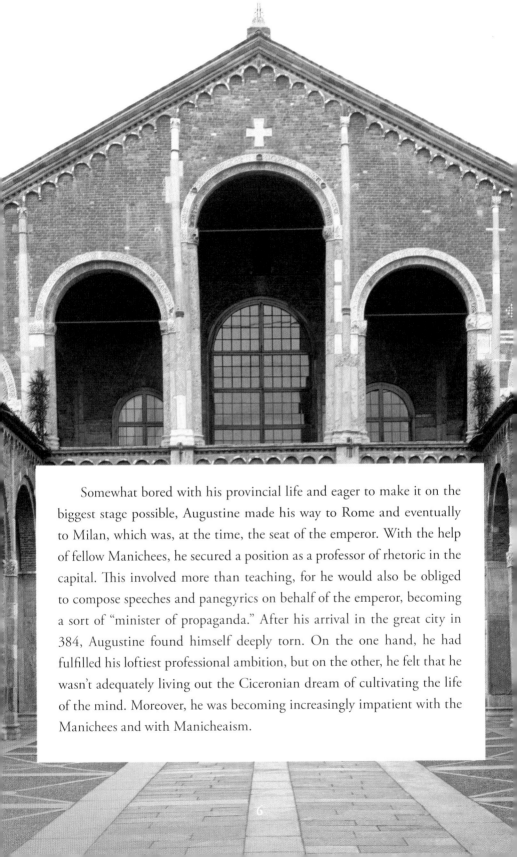

Somewhat bored with his provincial life and eager to make it on the biggest stage possible, Augustine made his way to Rome and eventually to Milan, which was, at the time, the seat of the emperor. With the help of fellow Manichees, he secured a position as a professor of rhetoric in the capital. This involved more than teaching, for he would also be obliged to compose speeches and panegyrics on behalf of the emperor, becoming a sort of "minister of propaganda." After his arrival in the great city in 384, Augustine found himself deeply torn. On the one hand, he had fulfilled his loftiest professional ambition, but on the other, he felt that he wasn't adequately living out the Ciceronian dream of cultivating the life of the mind. Moreover, he was becoming increasingly impatient with the Manichees and with Manicheaism.

At this crucial moment in his life, he met a man who would become a kind of spiritual father to him: the great bishop of Milan, Ambrose. Augustine had heard that the bishop was a fine preacher, and he initially came to take in the quality of his rhetoric. But he soon enough found himself entranced by the content of Ambrose's preaching. He was intrigued, first, by the Neoplatonic philosophy that clearly undergirded the thinking of Ambrose. Prompted by the bishop, Augustine commenced a careful reading of Plotinus and his disciples, which provided him with a far better theoretical framework for solving the problem of evil than the Manichees had proposed. The Platonic idea of evil as a type of nonbeing or privation allowed him to see that there was no need to posit a power of evil standing over and against the good. Secondly, he was fascinated by Ambrose's allegorical or symbolic manner of reading the Scriptures, especially the Old Testament. The subtle interpretations of the bishop showed Augustine a way beyond a literalism that made the God of the Bible repugnant to reason.

During this time of searching, Augustine had an experience of extraordinary power. While making his way to the place where he would deliver an encomium that he had written for the emperor, Augustine spied a man who was hopelessly drunk. Initially, he felt a sort of condescending pity for the poor fellow, but then he mused that, in the morning, the man would be sober, while he would still be drunk on ambition.

Inspired by Ambrose, Augustine turned for the first time to a serious study of the Bible, especially the writings of St. Paul and the Gospel of John. There he found philosophical depth, but also something new—namely, articulate speech about the Word of God becoming flesh for the sake of saving sinful humanity. At the same time, a Christian friend introduced Augustine to the story of St. Antony and the monks of the Egyptian desert. These tales of heroic asceticism stunned him. He said to his friend Alypius: "What is wrong with us? . . . The unlearned arise and take heaven by force, and here are we with all our learning, stuck fast in flesh and blood!"

All of this began to churn in him and push him toward Christianity, but still he hesitated. Finally, in the small garden of the house that he shared with Alypius, he entered into a real spiritual crisis, weeping, pacing up and down, tearing at his hair. "How long, how long shall I go on saying tomorrow and again tomorrow?" In the very midst of this turmoil, he heard the voice of a small child—a boy or a girl, he could not tell. But the voice was unmistakably saying, "*Tolle, lege; tolle, lege*" (Take and read; take and read). He immediately took up his book containing the Epistles of St. Paul, opened it up at random, and read the first line on which his eyes fell: "Not in rioting and drunkenness, not in chambering and impurities, not in contention and envy, but put ye on the Lord Jesus Christ and make not provision for the flesh in its concupiscences." It was enough to compel him to assent.

Augustine did not immediately seek Baptism, but rather, with a group of friends and disciples, including his mother and son, he retired to an estate not far from Milan called Cassiciacum. His purpose was to live a life of refined leisure, engaging in serious study, debate, and writing, developing a Christian philosophy in the company of like-minded companions. This period was indeed fruitful, for Augustine produced a number of memorable dialogues in the Platonic manner: *Contra academicos* (a refutation of radical skepticism), *De beata vita* (on the good life), and *De ordine* (on divine providence). Charmingly, Augustine's obviously brilliant son Adeodatus was a frequent interlocutor in these high-level philosophical conversations.

After a few months of this intense intellectual activity, Augustine—to the infinite delight of his mother, who had been praying for his return to the faith ever since he became a Manichee—actively sought Baptism, becoming a catechumen under the direction of Ambrose himself. He was baptized by St. Ambrose in the baptistery of the Milan Cathedral, during the Easter Vigil in the year 387. At this pivotal moment of his life, Augustine decided to abandon his career as a rhetorician, to return home to Thagaste, and to establish a Christian philosophical community, much like the one at Cassiciacum.

In order to get home, he and his group, including his mother and son, made their way to the Roman port of Ostia. While preparing to set sail, Augustine and Monica fell one evening into an intense conversation about spiritual things—more precisely, about the nature of the afterlife. In the course of that exchange, both felt a powerful attraction to heaven and a concomitant distaste for the things of this world. Just days after this shared mystical experience, Monica fell ill with a fever, and after dismissing concerns about where to bury her body, she died.

Augustine returned to Africa with Adeodatus and his small company of disciples and, for a short time, did indeed establish himself as head of a sort of Christian philosophical school in his native town. But while visiting the seaside city of Hippo Regius, Augustine was more or less pressed into service by the people to be their priest. After an initial tearful resistance, Augustine eventually gave in and dedicated himself to the careful study of the Scriptures, in order to prepare himself for this ministry. In short order, he gained a reputation as a master preacher and skillful administrator, and thus when the reigning bishop died, Augustine rather naturally became the leader of the Church in Hippo. He served as bishop of this comparatively small diocese from 395 until his death in 430.

He was, by all accounts, an aston-ishingly energetic bishop, adjudicating legal disputes, presiding at liturgies and preaching regularly, involving himself in the ecclesiastical affairs of neighboring churches, and producing a library of books and essays of the highest literary and theological quality. It is said that he did most of his writing in the evening hours and late into the night, after the regular work of the day was completed, like Thomas Aquinas often dictating to several secretaries at once. He commenced work on the *Confessions* shortly after he became Bishop of Hippo; he labored on his masterpiece, *The City of God*, between 412 and 426; and he wrote the seminal study on the Trinity, *De Trinitate*, between 400 and 428.

If his conflict with the Manichees specially concerned Augustine prior to his conversion, his battle with the Donatists and the Pelagians marked his post-conversion intellectual career. The Donatists claimed, to state it briefly, that the moral quality of the minister of a sacrament determined the validity of the sacrament. So, for example, a priest who had apostatized during time of persecution and had then returned to the faith would be deemed unworthy of functioning as a priest, and all of the sacraments received at his hands would have no power. Augustine took a far more objective position vis-à-vis the sacraments, maintaining that their efficaciousness is not a function of the minister's worthiness but of the grace of God gratuitously given. In making this clarification, he really saved the Church, for he traced its power not to fallible human beings but to the infallible God. The struggle with Pelagius and his followers would preoccupy Augustine in the last years of his life, and we will study it in some detail below.

St. Augustine died in 430 as the Vandals were laying siege to Hippo. They say that he spent his last days meditating on the psalms of repentance, which, at his request, were posted on the walls surrounding his bed.

What is Augustine's perspective on self-love?

The issue of desire is central to Augustine's thinking. He's a great philosopher and theologian of desire. He's not against desire; what he wants is properly ordered desire. One of his great definitions of sin is *incurvatus in se*—being caved in on oneself. When our desire turns in on ourselves, there's this shrinking, this closing. Think of a conversation between friends where, instead of getting lost in the flow of the conversation, one person is watching himself, the impression he's making, the cleverness of his remarks. Sin is something of a black hole, this turning in on oneself where no light can escape, where the press of the ego suffocates a person. Augustine wants to open up our desires since what we ultimately desire is God. And he is not just theorizing about this: he lived it. He knew what it was like to be trapped in sin, and he also knew the experience of liberation from this place.

THE CITY OF GOD

Augustine's massive work *The City of God*, which runs in most editions to around fifteen hundred pages, is the founding text of what would come to be called the philosophy of history. It is also a masterpiece of biblical interpretation, systematic theology, and theological anthropology. He himself referred to it as *magnum opus et arduum* (a big and difficult work). Most fundamentally, it is the master's definitive answer to a charge that troubled thoughtful Christians in the wake of the sack of Rome in 410. Many of the devotees of the old pagan religion had argued that Rome fell because it had abandoned the traditional piety of Cicero, Caesar, and Seutonius and had adopted the strange cult of Christianity. Augustine will contend that Rome fell, not because of Christianity, but precisely because of vices inherent to its own political and religious system. The basic problem, he said, is that Rome, like all other corrupt human institutions, was grounded in self-love. Augustine characterized a society produced by this inward-looking self-preoccupation as the *civitas terrena* or "the earthly city." If we seek the deepest roots of the problem, we will uncover false forms of worship.

Many first-time readers of *The City of God* are puzzled by the amount of time Augustine dedicates to a critique of the Roman gods and goddesses, but this analysis is basic to his argument. Rome is a compromised political order precisely because it

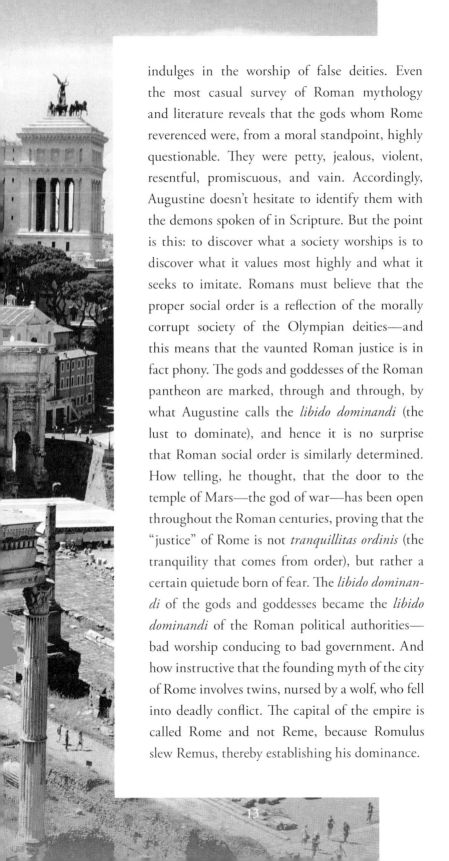

indulges in the worship of false deities. Even the most casual survey of Roman mythology and literature reveals that the gods whom Rome reverenced were, from a moral standpoint, highly questionable. They were petty, jealous, violent, resentful, promiscuous, and vain. Accordingly, Augustine doesn't hesitate to identify them with the demons spoken of in Scripture. But the point is this: to discover what a society worships is to discover what it values most highly and what it seeks to imitate. Romans must believe that the proper social order is a reflection of the morally corrupt society of the Olympian deities—and this means that the vaunted Roman justice is in fact phony. The gods and goddesses of the Roman pantheon are marked, through and through, by what Augustine calls the *libido dominandi* (the lust to dominate), and hence it is no surprise that Roman social order is similarly determined. How telling, he thought, that the door to the temple of Mars—the god of war—has been open throughout the Roman centuries, proving that the "justice" of Rome is not *tranquillitas ordinis* (the tranquility that comes from order), but rather a certain quietude born of fear. The *libido dominandi* of the gods and goddesses became the *libido dominandi* of the Roman political authorities—bad worship conducing to bad government. And how instructive that the founding myth of the city of Rome involves twins, nursed by a wolf, who fell into deadly conflict. The capital of the empire is called Rome and not Reme, because Romulus slew Remus, thereby establishing his dominance.

What Augustine proposes over and against Roman order is a different form of worship and a different form of government. Christians believe, he says, not in the dysfunctional and demonic deities of paganism, but in the one God of creation, who brings the world into being nonviolently. In the pagan stories, the world comes to be through a primal act of violence and conquest: Saturn devouring his children, or Jupiter conquering and killing his father and then parceling out earth, sea, and sky to his pliant siblings. But according to the Bible, the true God does not wrestle anything into submission when he creates, nor does he conquer any rival power. Rather, in a purely generous and nonviolent act of love, he brings the universe into existence. In a word, order comes through peace. Augustine insists that when such a God is worshiped, a fundamentally different kind of social order comes into being, one based upon compassion, forgiveness, and solidarity. This other city, this alternate form of political arrangement grounded in the love of God, is the *civitas Dei*, "the City of God." It is the earthly community that mirrors the heavenly *communio* of the angels and saints, gathered in worship around the throne of God.

The master establishes a brilliant correlation between the founding myth of Rome and the biblical story of Cain and Abel. In the account from the book of Genesis, Cain, in a fit of jealousy, slays his own brother and becomes, curiously enough, the founder of cities—and thus a kind of blood brother to Romulus. But whereas Romulus is clearly the hero of the Roman legend, Cain is cursed in the biblical story. What Augustine sees is that both Romulus and Cain are, through their violence, indeed progenitors of the *civitas terrena*, but the Bible is under no illusion that this manner of political arrangement is anything but criminal and unjust. In the Roman myth, the gods sanction the primal violence; in the biblical account, God sides with the murdered victim.

14

Augustine understands the whole of history as a sort of tensive struggle between the two cities, and his reading of that struggle is subtle indeed. For, on the one hand, the earthly city always seems to hold sway. Most nations, empires, institutions, and societies are expressions of the *civitas terrena*, and the *civitas Dei* is something like Noah's ark, floating on an immense sea of dysfunction and sin. On the other hand, the City of God is the bearer of the divine presence to the world and subsists under the divine providence, so that it strangely endures age after age, functioning as a challenge to the dominant social arrangement. In the struggles between Cain and Abel, the Egyptians and the Israelites, David and Goliath, the Roman Empire and the Church, Augustine sees the endless playing out of the primal contest between the two cities.

Though it often appears in the world as small, threatened, and powerless, the City of God is, in point of fact, the victor. And though I set the Roman Empire and the Church above as a stark contrast, it is most important to note that Augustine felt that the conflict between the two cities existed within the Christian community itself. It would not be correct to say that the City of God and the institutional Church are identical *tout court*. Moreover, elements of the City of God can indeed be found in the political and social orders of the world. The point is that the two are intertwined in complex ways, much like the wheat and the weeds in Jesus' famous parable. And thus, it would be altogether incorrect to read *The City of God* as advocating a flight from the world or a simple withdrawal from the earthly city to the

15

heavenly city. Rather, it should be read as a kind of guidebook for pilgrims (*pellegrini* [pilgrims] and *peligrinatio* [pilgrimage] are favorite words in this text). Augustine sees Christians as "resident aliens" within the societies of this world, or as travelers passing through to another country. He was fascinated by the advice that the Israelite prophets gave to their people during the exile in Babylon: they were not to succumb to the ways and religion of the Babylonians, to be sure, but they were also encouraged to obey the laws of their captors and to pray for their political leaders.

A particularly clear instantiation of this principle is Augustine's famous and controversial teaching on just war. As we have seen, the saint sees the *libido dominandi* as one of the essential features of the earthly city, and he denounces Rome over and over again for its violence. Therefore, he maintains an extremely strong prejudice against war. His moral acceptance of warfare under certain conditions should by no means, therefore, be construed as a "justification" of war, but rather as a concession to the sinful world, one way that citizens of the City of God make their way through the earthly city. Though we can find in Augustine's writing nothing of the systematic treatment of the issue that we find, for instance, in Thomas Aquinas, nevertheless, certain themes rather clearly emerge. A war is just only in the measure that it is fought for a morally praiseworthy cause, that it is declared by a competent authority, and that the combatants are fighting with the right intention. Far from "war-mongering," this is Augustine's sincere attempt to restrict war and to bring, in this arena of human endeavor, as much of the City of God into the city of man as possible.

We have seen that the master identifies the City of God with rightly ordered love. When everyone in a society gives God the highest praise, peace tends to break out. Another way to state the same idea is to say that gratitude is *the* mark of the

City of God. Members of that blessed community know that they are, in every way, dependent upon God and that whatever good they have is, therefore, received as a gift. Even the greatest achievements of the earthly city, in terms of art, architecture, religion, morality, etc., are marked by a self-regard and a self-reliance. Citizens of the City of God know that everything is grace. That insight—though of course never fully realized in fact—became the basis of a new civilization.

AUGUSTINE AGAINST THE PELAGIANS

The most significant battle of Augustine's later years—and one that has decisively influenced Christianity to the present day—was his struggle with Pelagius and his followers. Pelagius was, like Augustine, a provincial, hailing from Roman Britain. He came to the capital around the same time that Augustine did, but unlike his African counterpart, Pelagius remained in Rome for the rest of his life. A brilliant writer, teacher, and controversialist, Pelagius proposed an interpretation of Christian life that was, to many of his contemporaries and to many today, extremely attractive. To state it briefly, Pelagius held that moral perfection is something that human beings can achieve through the exercise of the will. He felt that God would never have given so many instructions and exhortations in the Bible unless he knew that men and women were capable of fulfilling them.

This can-do, optimistic theory ran counter to any idea of an "original sin," which would render human beings incapable of achieving moral excellence through their own effort. And it proved so appealing that Pelagian "cells" began to appear—first in Rome and then throughout the empire—made

up of disciples eager to spread their teacher's message. It should come as no great surprise that Pelagianism, in an even more radical form, is alive and well today. Not only do we think we are capable of perfecting ourselves; we are convinced we can determine the meaning of our lives.

Augustine sensed in this seemingly attractive proposal what Athanasius saw a century before in Arianism—namely, an assault on the very nature of Christianity. For if we are basically upright and just require some moral guidance, then we do not stand in need of a Savior. And in point of fact, on the Pelagian reading, Jesus is not a Savior at all, but rather a sort of ethical teacher, exhorting us to do our best. And if this is the case, then Christianity is a slightly modified version of all of the other programs of self-perfection on offer in the ancient world—and today. In their own ways, Plato, Aristotle, Cicero, and Seneca were urging human beings to realize their full potential through proper instruction and moral effort, just as philosophers, social theorists, psychologists, and self-help experts do in our context today. What Augustine saw with particular clarity is the biblical claim that there is something so fundamentally wrong with us, something so off-kilter and twisted, that we are incapable of saving ourselves, of simply righting the ship through heroic effort. And he saw the implication—namely, that we require much more than a teacher or guide; we require a Savior.

Augustine's view of sin is in line with much of our contemporary thinking about addiction and the role that unconscious and systemic factors play in our misbehavior. We are well aware that sin is the consequence of much more than simply our conscious and explicit choice. Rather, sin is more like a condition in which we find ourselves, a state of affairs in which we are always already implicated. Saying to a sinner, "Well, turn your life around!" is as simplistic as saying to a confirmed alcoholic, "Well, just stop drinking!" Something much more basic than free will has to be addressed and healed. The twelve-step context is actually quite illuminating in this regard, for an addict has to admit to his helplessness and indeed turn his life over to a higher power. This is very close to what Augustine meant when he spoke of sin as a state or a condition that has

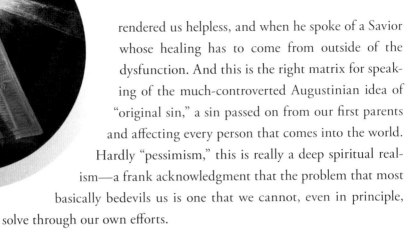

rendered us helpless, and when he spoke of a Savior whose healing has to come from outside of the dysfunction. And this is the right matrix for speaking of the much-controverted Augustinian idea of "original sin," a sin passed on from our first parents and affecting every person that comes into the world. Hardly "pessimism," this is really a deep spiritual realism—a frank acknowledgment that the problem that most basically bedevils us is one that we cannot, even in principle, solve through our own efforts.

WHY IS ST. AUGUSTINE A PIVOTAL PLAYER?

Through his literary genius and spiritual perception, Augustine has allowed numberless people over the centuries to see their own stories of sin and grace in his. His own restless heart has become the paradigm for spiritual seekers across the ages.

Writing at a moment when one of the great civilizations of the world was collapsing, he taught us that we are finally citizens of a higher society, one based on the right praise of God, and that we are, therefore, resident aliens in any of the earthly cities that we inhabit. This crucial distinction has helped the Church survive as worldly cultures have risen and fallen.

Finally, and perhaps most importantly, he reminded human beings of the intractability of the problem of sin, and thereby taught them to look not just for another teacher but for a Savior.

St. Benedict

THE MONK

In many ways, the figure we are about to consider is the most pivotal of all the Pivotal Players. For perhaps more than anyone else, St. Benedict of Nursia contributed to the saving of Christian culture in the West. At a time when Roman order had collapsed and barbarian invaders were picking through the rubble of a once great civilization, Benedict founded the religious community that would, in time, preserve the best of the old and allow for the emergence of a particularly Christian way of life. And so it is absolutely no exaggeration to say that without Benedict, there would be no Thomas Aquinas, no Catherine of Siena, no Ignatius of Loyola, no Michelangelo, and no John Henry Newman.

In fact, Newman paid particularly eloquent tribute to the manner in which Benedict and his sons rebuilt a civilization: "Silent men were observed about the country . . . digging, clearing, and building; and other silent men . . . were sitting in the cold cloister . . . while they painfully deciphered and copied and recopied the manuscripts which they had saved. . . . By degrees the woody swamp became a hermitage, a religious house, a farm, an abbey, a village, a seminary, a school of learning, and a city." Another of our Pivotal Players, G.K. Chesterton, reacting to critics in his own time who claimed that the Church represented a return to the Dark Ages, pointed out that the only real light during the Dark Ages was the Church. His reference was to the spiritual descendants of St. Benedict who relentlessly preserved Seneca, Cicero, Plato, Aristotle, Aristophanes, Caesar—in fact, practically everything of value that we have from the ancient world.

One of the most compelling questions today is whether a Benedictine moment might be upon us again—that is to say, a time when the best of the classical worldview must be preserved in the midst of a cultural crisis. The philosopher Alasdair MacIntyre famously opined: "We are waiting not for a Godot, but for another—doubtless very different—St. Benedict."

LIFE AND TIMES

Unlike St. John Henry Newman, St. Ignatius, or St. Augustine, who left us detailed spiritual autobiographies, the Benedict of history remains a relatively elusive figure. The principal source for his life are the *Dialogues* of Pope St. Gregory the Great, written about fifty years after the death of Benedict. In line with the custom of the time, Gregory's account is massively hagiographical and filled with stories of the fantastic and the miraculous. But from his narrative, we can cull a number of historically reliable details.

St. Benedict was born in the region of Nursia, north of Rome, around the year 490—which is to say, just fourteen years after the date generally accepted for the fall of the empire. One can only imagine the cultural and political chaos of that moment. It appears his parents were well-to-do, perhaps nobility, for they had the means to send him to Rome for formal studies. While in the Eternal City, sometime at the beginning of the sixth century, the young Benedict became disgusted with the corruption and lasciviousness of his fellow students. And so he fled from the city and

sought to "please God alone," retreating to the country and finding refuge in a cave on a cliffside near the little town of Subiaco, about forty-five miles east of Rome. There he lived as a hermit for three years.

It is fascinating to note that from the fourth through the sixth centuries, many of the best and brightest, in both the East and the West, took (quite literally) to the hills in order to live lives of austerity, poverty, and prayer, far from the corruption of "the world." One thinks of St. John Chrysostom, St. Jerome, St. Gregory of Nyssa, and of St. Augustine, whose dream, before he was pressed into service as Bishop of Hippo, was to establish a monastery where he and a few others could pursue a life of prayer and study. The spiritual father of all of these figures was St. Antony of the Desert, who, in the third century, abandoned his comfortable life,

gave all of his possessions to the poor, and established himself as a hermit in the Egyptian wilderness.

What was driving these men? It was a deep conviction that the authentic Christian life could not be lived coherently within the ordinary cultural framework of their time. Political confusion, barbarian invasions, and economic instability had a good deal to do with it, but it was also a function of the moral corruption of the period. They felt that they had to create the conditions for a new civilization, precisely by hunkering down, preserving and protecting a form of life that could, in time, influence the wider culture again. The biblical image for this is the ark of Noah, and we've seen this rhythm often in the history of the Church: retreat, preservation, reassertion. Perhaps the best example in our time is the hunkering down of the young Karol Wojtyła during a period of massive civilizational crisis, followed by the magnificent reassertion of the Catholic ethos by Pope John Paul II when the propitious moment finally arrived.

The three years that Benedict spent in the cave of Subiaco were a time of gestation and spiritual deepening. How like the period that St. Ignatius would spend in the cave of Manresa a thousand years later. Could a passing visitor, chancing upon the young hermit, ever have guessed that he was encountering the seed that would eventually grow into the Christian civilization of the West?

His reputation for sanctity was so great that soon other monks came to seek his advice and, in time, his leadership. Gregory tells the story of a group of monks who importuned the reluctant Benedict to become their abbot. The hermit gave in, but soon the little community was unhappy with his spiritually demanding leadership, and they attempted to poison him. When the saint asked a blessing over the poisoned drink, the cup shattered. In time, Benedict established a dozen small monastic communities around Subiaco and, in 530, founded the great house of Monte Cassino, a Benedictine monastery that endures to the present day, functioning as the motherhouse of the worldwide Benedictine family. During his years at Monte Cassino, Benedict labored on the rule for his communities, which in time would exercise a decisive influence on the development of monasticism in the West.

St. Gregory tells a charming story from this period of Benedict's life. It has to do with his twin sister, Scholastica, a woman deeply devoted to God. As was her custom, Scholastica came to visit her brother in a small building just outside the monastery. The two of them engaged in intense theological conversation long into the night. When Benedict announced that it was time for him to go, Scholastica begged him to stay. When he continued to insist that he return to the main house, his sister bowed her head in prayer. Immediately, a terrific storm blew up, which prevented Benedict from leaving. Smiling knowingly at Scholastica, he remained, and the two of them spoke of divine things until dawn.

Not long after this encounter, sometime around the year 547, St. Benedict died.

Why was Benedict so important for the survival of Catholicism?

Kenneth Clark, the great cultural historian, says that we made it by the skin of our teeth. It was people like Benedict who clung to the remnants of civilization and made the full flowering of Western civilization possible. In God's providence, people like Benedict appeared at the right time. It's the mustard seed principle that we see again and again in the lives of the saints. From a little beginning, from one young man withdrawing from society and retiring to a cave, came a great flowering.

THE *RULE* OF ST. BENEDICT

The vehicle by which Benedict was able to wield such decisive influence on the Church and on Western culture was the *regula* (the rule) that he crafted to guide the lives of his brothers in the monastery. Followed to this day by Benedictines the world over, the *Rule* obviously has relevance for those who adopt the monastic life, but it also had (and has) relevance to those interested in creating a more humane and better-ordered society. I will try to keep both of these points of reference in mind as I move through the *Rule*.

The *Rule* was not made up out of whole cloth, but rather emerged from a long tradition of monastic theory and practice. The personal example of Antony, the *Rule* of Augustine, the *Rule* of St. Basil, and the work of

John Cassian all shaped what Benedict formulated. But by far the greatest influence was the so-called *Rule of the Master*, written around the year 500 by an author whose name has been lost to us. Benedict took all of these sources, thought them through afresh, blended them with ample amounts of Scripture and the thinking of the Church Fathers, and produced something new and distinctive. And as history has clearly proved, the *Rule* is of enormous practical value. It's not just spiritually uplifting—it works.

The opening word of the *Rule* is of tremendous moment: "*Obsculta.*" It means, simply, "Listen." The use of this term has very deep roots in the biblical tradition. We recall that at the heart of the original sin was a refusal to abide by the divine Word. Assuming the prerogatives of God, Adam and Eve ate from the tree of the knowledge of good and evil. They made their own egos the criterion of what is right and wrong. This is why the history of salvation commences with someone—Abraham by name—who was willing to listen once more to the word of the Lord. At its best, Israel is a people who listen: "Hear, O Israel: The LORD is our God, the LORD alone," in the words of the She'ma prayer from the sixth chapter of Deuteronomy (Deut. 6:4). In the letter to the Romans, St. Paul says, simply enough, "Faith comes from what is heard" (Rom. 10:17). In the very first word of the *Rule*, Benedict is telling his monks to listen to a higher voice—and through them he would teach Europe again to attend to that same voice.

He goes on: "This message of mine is for you, then, if you are ready to give up your own will, once and for all, and armed with the strong and noble weapons of obedience to do battle for the true King, Christ the Lord." From a biblical perspective, the fundamental problem is always self-will, lack of obedience to "the power at work within us" that is "able to accomplish abundantly far more than all we can ask or imagine" (Eph. 3:20). Shifting metaphors, Benedict says, "Let us open our eyes to the light that comes from God." He is fighting against what the philosopher Charles Taylor calls "the buffered self," an ego that turns in on itself, refusing contact with a transcendent reality. He is saying to his brothers: "Let in the voice! Let in the light!" If they enter into this project with

Benedict, the master promises that they will constitute together "a school for the Lord's service." Once again, he will be teaching them the ways of the Lord, in the manner that a master teaches an apprentice, but through them he will be introducing the wider culture into this great classroom. How easy it is for individuals and entire societies to forget how to listen to the Lord and how to love him. Benedict's monastery will be a training ground.

Next, the master speaks of the various types of monks. This might seem a bit technical, perhaps of interest only to historians of monasticism, but a powerful spiritual teaching is on offer here. Benedict mentions first the "cenobites"—that is, monks who live in community. These are the monks that he rather clearly favors and of whom the *Rule* will principally treat. Next come the "anchorites" or hermits, those who, after a long training in the monastic life, set out on their own for the solitary "combat of the desert." It is intriguing that the recommendation here is the opposite of what Benedict himself lived. While he went from hermit to cenobite, he thinks the reverse movement is more spiritually responsible.

While these first two types of monks are altogether acceptable, the second two are decidedly not. Benedict speaks of the "sarabaites" and the "gyrovagues." The first are monks living in groups of three or four, without an abbot and free of any clear rule or monastic discipline. They take what they like from various traditions and live according to their own lights. In our terminology, they are "cafeteria" monks. The second reprehensible group—and by far the worst kind of monks—are the gyrovagues, those who literally wander around from community to community: "Always on the move, they never settle down, and are slaves to their own wills and gross appetites." It shouldn't be surprising that what concerns a spiritual teacher, writing at the beginning of the sixth century in Italy, is individualism, instability, lack of discipline. An entire society was unstable at the time; therefore, what was needed was a clear spiritual focus and an ordered community life. Wandering about, picking and choosing what one likes, eschewing any authority external to one's own will—these were both causes and effects of the cultural breakdown. Can we recognize

AUSCULTA PRÆCEPTA
O FILI MAGISTRI

something of the gyrovague mentality in the rootlessness and rampant individualism of our time?

After distinguishing the various types of monks, Benedict turns to a consideration of the abbot of the monastery. As many have pointed out, this section of the *Rule* amounts to a self-portrait of Benedict, the father not only of the monasteries that he personally founded, but of the entire monastic family in the West. It is crucial to note that the leader of the monastery is called an abbot, which is derived from the Hebrew *Abba*, the affectionate term for father, which Jesus himself used of God. He is not primarily administrator or bureaucratic director; he is the father of the community, and hence the monks are brothers to one another. This familial emphasis is on clear display throughout the *Rule*.

Departing dramatically from the social practice of the time, Benedict insists that the abbot should not be a respecter of persons, that he should not favor the landed, wealthy, and educated over the servile, but should rather be concerned only with the advancement of all in good works. This is a concrete application of St. Paul's principle that in Christ "there is no longer Jew or Greek, there is no longer slave or free, there is no longer male and female" (Gal. 3:28). Can we sense, at least within the confines of Benedict's monastic community, the beginning of a polity based on equality and the rights of all? Further, when considering a matter of great moment for the entire monastery, the abbot is obliged to consult all of the brothers, since "the Lord often reveals what is better to the younger." Also, the abbot, though he is the supreme legislator within the monastery, rules under the direction of God: "He will have to give an account of all his judgment to God." The monarchy of the abbot is situated within a context of checks and balances and under the rule of law.

After carefully delineating the Ten Commandments, the corporal and spiritual works of mercy, and many of the classical moral excellences, Benedict observes that the cloister of the monastery is a "workshop" of the virtues, and a place where one practices the "tools of the spiritual craft." Just as an apprentice learns the demands of his discipline under the supervision of his master, so the monk acquires skills in the moral arena under the tutelage of the abbot. This process of spiritual education is implied in the Benedictine vow of *conversio morum* (conversion of one's way of life).

Which of the virtues was most important to Benedict? Even the most cursory reading of the *Rule* would reveal the answer: humility. In fact, he delineates twelve degrees of humility, steps on the way toward a total surrender to God.

The first degree is to have before one's eyes at all times the fear of God. This means that one should always have as the top priority doing what God wants and avoiding what God prohibits.

The second degree follows immediately upon the first: not to love one's own will but that of God, imitating Jesus who said, "I have come down from heaven, not to do my own will, but the will of him who sent me" (John 6:38).

These first two recommendations become incarnate through the third degree of humility: always to submit to one's superior in obedience.

And the fourth makes this even more pointed: to obey in silence even when the burden placed on one is hard and unjust.

The fifth degree has to do with one's interior life: the willingness to confess to the abbot even those wicked thoughts that one has harbored privately, lest one's humility be but an external show.

The sixth degree is that the monk should be satisfied with his condition and his circumstances, even though they be base and vile. Think of how much time and energy we spend on making our homes and apartments "just so"—and how much inner and outer turmoil this causes.

The seventh degree is that the monk not only says with his lips that he is the lowest of all the brothers but that he actually believes it in his heart. This is not false humility, but rather the perception of self that naturally arises when one is directed toward the infinite goodness of God. This is why the greatest of the saints tend to refer to themselves as the worst of sinners.

34

The eighth degree is that the monk should never do anything unless it is explicitly prescribed by the *Rule* and ordered by the abbot. Self-assertion and the pursuit of one's own projects and plans are fruits of pride.

The ninth degree of humility is particularly difficult for people such as myself who like to talk! Benedict recommends that the monk be reluctant to speak, "not speaking unless asked a question." Think for a moment just how much mischief has been caused by speech, and how much better we'd all get along if we were more circumspect and reticent in what we say.

The tenth degree touches on a theme that surfaces frequently in the *Rule*—namely, laughter. In opposition to our predilection today, Benedict is rather down on levity. Do not, he says, be "given to ready laughter, for it is written, 'Only a fool raises his voice in laughter.'" Elsewhere he says, "We absolutely condemn in all places any vulgarity and gossip and talk leading to laughter." Well, was he just a killjoy? I don't think so. We must keep in mind that Benedict was forming his community during a practically unprecedented civilizational crisis. An entire culture had to be constructed; a new kind of person had to be fostered. It just wasn't a time for jokes. That said, I'm quite glad that there have been other figures in the spiritual tradition who were quite amenable to laughter; Francis of Assisi, Philip Neri, and G.K. Chesterton come readily to mind.

The eleventh degree of humility is much like the ninth, and counsels that "a monk speaks gently and without laughter, seriously and with becoming modesty, briefly and reasonably, but without raising his voice." Again, think of how many raised and intemperate voices must regularly have been heard in the chaotic wake of the fall of an empire. In place of a society of self-important shouters, Benedict wanted a monastery of humble and recollected monks.

Finally, we come to the twelfth degree of humility: in whatever he does—whether at work, or in choir, or in the fields, or on a journey—the monk should keep his head down and his eyes fixed on the ground, feeling at all times the weight of his sins. In almost any society—but especially our own—it is usually the case that the proud peacock makes the most headway and gets the most attention. But Benedict is not particularly interested in making headway on worldly paths; he wants monks who walk the road to heaven, and that is always the way of humility.

Having considered the types of monks, the role of the abbot, and the fundamental disciplines of the school of virtue that is the monastery, Benedict turns to what is the real heart of the matter: prayer—the lifting of the mind and heart to God. The life of a Benedictine monk revolves around and is conditioned by prayer. Following the example of the Psalmist, who said that he chanted the praises of God seven times a day, Benedict commands his monks to pray formally seven times each day: Lauds (Morning Prayer); then Prime, Terce, Sext, and None—that is to say, prayers at the first, third, sixth, and ninth hours of the day; then Vespers (Evening Prayer); and finally, Compline (Night Prayer) before retiring. Famously, Benedict tells his charges that "nothing is to be preferred to the Work of God," by which he means this steady rhythm of prayer. The monks are told to drop whatever they are doing and make their way to the place of prayer whenever the bell summons them. And at the heart of these seven sacred

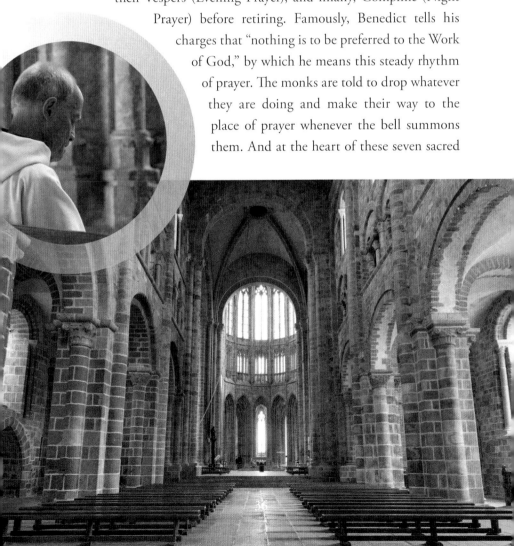

exercises are the Psalms, the great songbook of God's praise. The Psalms express the full range of human emotion, thought, and experience. The Psalmist cries; he sings; he laments; he exults; he hopes; he despairs; he wonders; he aspires; he doubts; and he professes faith. The monk is meant to enter into these prayers in such a profound and regular way that they become as natural to him as breathing.

Along with prayer, the other essential aspect of Benedictine life is work—hence the Benedictine motto, *Ora et Labora* (Prayer and Work). To be sure, work was and is essential for the maintenance of a monastery, but it also has a profoundly spiritual purpose. In the section of the *Rule* dealing with the qualities of the cellarer, Benedict says that "he will regard all utensils and goods of the monastery as sacred vessels of the altar." His point is that the ordinary work of farming, harvesting, writing, or cleaning is a means of offering praise to the Lord. Just as the monk enters daily into the rhythm of the Psalms, so he enters daily into the rhythm of his work on behalf of his brothers. In chapter 48 of the *Rule*, Benedict says, "Idleness is the enemy of the soul," and hence urges his charges to "have specified periods for manual labor as well as for prayerful reading." All the monks in the monastery—from the best educated and most noble to the simplest and most base—are required to work with their hands. Notice, too, that the study of divine things is construed by Benedict as a type of work. How wonderfully this anticipates the literally civilization-saving work—both in fields and scriptoria—that his sons would do over the course of many centuries.

We have already seen how Benedict privileges the cenobitic or community life over the eremitic or hermit's path. The stress on community can be found over and over again in the *Rule*. Brothers should learn to obey one another; younger monks should defer to older and seek their blessing; if anyone harms the community, he should immediately do penance; absent brothers should be prayed for; errant brothers should be corrected; respect should be shown to all. The godly life, for Benedict, is a life in common, and his family of God, properly ordered and disciplined, would in time become the foundation for wider communities, villages, towns, and cities.

Another key feature of the *Rule* is its stress upon radical poverty. Chapter 33, which considers the question whether monks ought to hold any private property, commences in this striking manner: "*Praecipue hoc vitium radicitus amputandum est de monasterio*"—"This evil practice [of private ownership] must be uprooted and removed from the monastery." He specifies that no monk should ever presume to give or receive anything without the explicit permission of the abbot, nor to possess anything as his own, "nothing at all—not a book, writing tablets or stylus—in short, not a single item." Indeed, everything should be held in common: "*Omniaque omnium sint communia.*" At the very end of his life, Thomas Merton commented that the communist ideal of common ownership is impossible to achieve at the political level, but remains a monastic ideal. Benedict seems to be following here the New Testament precept that the members of the early Christian community would place their wealth at the feet of the Apostles to be distributed to each according to need. Unless a civilization is grounded in something more substantial than moneymaking and the accumulation of material possessions, it will inevitably collapse. In stressing poverty so radically, the *Rule* opened the Western mind to the fundamental spiritual values that would alone sustain a culture.

One of the most remarkable features of the Benedictine life is an openness to the welcoming of guests. Chapter 53 of the *Rule* begins with this straightforward remark: "All guests who present themselves are to be welcomed as Christ." Benedict says that the moment a visitor is announced, the superior and the brothers should hasten to greet him and to show him every mark of respect. Throughout the guest's stay, the brothers should indicate to him, by a nod of the head or a prostration of the body, that they are adoring the Christ that they see in him. The superior or one of the brothers whom he designates should accompany the visitor at prayer, and the monks should break their own fast so as to eat hospitably with the guest. Moreover, the abbot himself should wash the hands of a visitor and, aided by the entire community, wash the visitor's feet. A monk should be specially designated as guestmaster so as to assure that there is adequate lodging for visitors.

I can personally testify that these rules are still followed. I have been received in Benedictine houses all over the world with extraordinary hospitality—and when I arrived at the great monastery of Citeaux in France, the abbot indeed washed my hands in the presence of the entire community. As many have indicated, this almost exaggerated openness to visitors is what has prevented Benedictine life from turning in on itself, becoming withdrawn and sectarian. Even as they cultivated a distinctive and radical form of Christianity, Benedictines knew from the beginning that their life was for the world. Set apart, yes—but precisely on behalf of the wider community. It is absolutely no accident, therefore, that the Benedictine monasteries became, in time, centers of civilization, and not simply places of retreat.

Benedict saw his brotherhood as, in one sense, looking backward, and in another sense, looking forward. The radical way of life encouraged by the *Rule* was meant to echo the manner of life described in the Acts of the Apostles, and it was meant to anticipate the fullness of community that will be found in heaven. Poor, humble, obedient, prayerful, welcoming, radically devoted to God, the Benedictine monk was (and is) a light to the world and an ambassador of God.

WHY IS ST. BENEDICT A PIVOTAL PLAYER?

As I mentioned at the outset, Benedict of Nursia is arguably the most pivotal of all of the figures we are considering in this book. St. Paul took advantage of the Roman roads to preach the Gospel in the first century; the earliest popes used the administrative and legal structure of the Roman Empire to give stability to the Church; Tertullian, Jerome, and Augustine took advantage of the Latin language and the philosophical clarity that Rome inherited from ancient Greece in order to think through the Christian mysteries. There was, therefore, the very real danger that, with the collapse of Roman order, Christianity would simply implode.

But Benedict and his brothers managed to save what was best in the classical culture and use it as a matrix for the further development and propagation of the Christian faith. At one of the most crucial moments in history, Benedict preserved a form of life that would eventually shape the civilization of the world. It is unquestionably true that anyone who reverences Socrates, Demosthenes, and Pythagoras—and anyone who calls with confidence on the name of Christ—owes an enormous debt to St. Benedict of Nursia.

St. Francis of Assisi

THE REFORMER

Is there a more winsome and beguiling figure in the entire history of the Catholic Church than Francis of Assisi? Even for nonbelievers, Francis seems to sum up what is best in the Christian tradition, and it would be difficult to find anyone—even the most ardent of atheists—who would stand against him. *Il Poverello*, the little poor man—simple, humble, close to nature, deeply in love with God—continues to sing across the ages to our own cynical time.

It remains, however, a serious temptation to romanticize Francis, to turn him into a harmless religious symbol, much like the little statues of him that accompany bird baths in suburban backyards. In his own time, Francis was a deeply troubling and unnerving figure. Initially, most people took him for a madman, and his first followers were derided, mocked, and regularly chased out of town. And once we delve more deeply into the historical record, we see that the charming troubadour of God was also a fierce ascetic who disciplined his body, poured ashes on his food, and practiced radical self-denial. Like almost all of the saints, Francis of Assisi was a sign of contradiction—and he remains so to the present day. During a time when many in the Church had drifted into indifference or moral corruption, Francis represented a back-to-basics evangelicalism, a return to the radicality of the Gospel. This is what makes him a permanently relevant figure in the life of the Church.

Francis was born in 1182 in the lovely Tuscan town of Assisi, situated on a spur of Mt. Subasio, hovering above the vast plain extending from Perugia to Spoleto. His father was Pietro Bernardone and his mother was called Pica. Pietro was one of the leading cloth merchants in the town, and he was often obliged to travel in connection with his business. While he was on a trip to France, a son was born to him, who was christened Giovanni. Later on, the boy was nicknamed Francesco (Francis), perhaps because of his father's affection for France.

Young Francesco would have received a basic instruction in reading and writing, though it is clear from the few autographs we have that he never became a particularly proficient writer. What most fascinated him as a young man were the songs of the French troubadours, which were all the rage at the time. Wandering through the towns of Tuscany were *jongleurs* who sang in a sort of French-Italian argot of Charlemagne, the Knights of the Round Table, and especially of beautiful ladies to whom the singer was willing to pledge his heart. Throughout his life—even after his conversion to radical Christianity—these songs stayed close to Francis' heart. Indeed, he would become, in time, a sort of troubadour of God, assembling around himself his own round table of ardent disciples, and promising his fidelity to Lady Poverty.

Francis went to work in his father's shop and soon enough became enamored of fine clothes and the latest fashions. He was a skilled businessman who excelled in making money and, in the words of one of his

earliest biographers, even more so at spending it. He loved to carouse with his friends, prowling the streets of Assisi and serenading the pretty girls. He wasn't exactly a bad person—just superficial and a tad self-absorbed. Like many young men before and since, Francis wanted to be famous, and the quickest route to fame at that time was through victory in warfare. And since the city states of Italy were in a constant state of conflict, the opportunities to distinguish oneself in battle were many. In 1202, Francis participated in a battle between Assisi and Perugia. By all accounts, he fought bravely, but he was taken captive and spent several months in a filthy Perugian prison. Upon being released, he returned to his life of business and pleasure. Still longing for military distinction, he set off on another expedition, this one in support of the papal armies. On his way, he stopped in Spoleto, where he experienced a powerful dream: A voice said to him, "Francis, from whom can you expect most, the servant or the master?" When Francis responded, "The master," the voice said, "Then why follow the servant, instead of the master?"

Upon returning to Assisi, he experienced a kind of dryness: the things that used to excite him now seemed empty. And he began to be entranced by spiritual things, by the invisible presence of God. When asked whether he was still hoping to be married, he said, "I am thinking of marrying! And the girl to whom I intend to plight my troth is so noble, so rich, and so good that none of you ever saw her like!" Francis began to give alms to the poor, and if he had no money for them, he would hand them his cap and his cloak. While on a pilgrimage to the shrine of St. Peter in Rome, Francis hurled all of his gold pieces toward the altar and then exchanged clothes with a destitute beggar. On his way back to Assisi, he confronted a man suffering from a severe case of leprosy. In his previous life, Francis admitted, nothing filled him with greater disgust than a leper. But

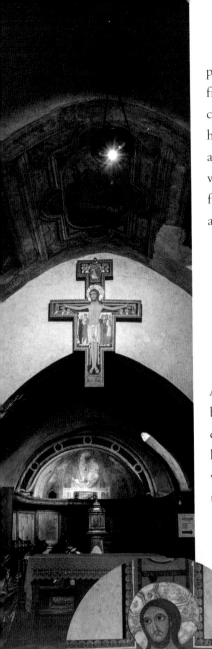

prompted by the Spirit, Francis came down from his horse, embraced the man, and pressed coins into his misshapen hand. Immediately, he said, he was filled with a happiness unlike any he had experienced before. Something was stirring in Francis: a radical detachment from the goods of the world and a passionate attachment to the purposes of God.

THE RESTORER OF CHURCHES

About three quarters of a mile south of Assisi, built on a hillside from which the whole plain can be viewed, there stands, to this day, a little church called San Damiano. In 1206 it was essentially a ruin, but Francis came there to pray. He was kneeling before a serene Byzantine crucifix when suddenly the figure of Christ sprang to life and from his lips came these words: "Francis, go repair my house, which is falling in ruins." There is no way to communicate adequately the impact these words had on Francis. Suffice it to say that they confirmed and focused all of the religious energies that had been stirred up in him—and he immediately

went to work. He took a number of bales of cloth from his father's shop and sold them to eager customers. He then presented the money to the itinerant priest who cared for San Damiano. When Pietro Bernardone heard of this, he (understandably enough) flew into a rage and demanded retribution. Francis agreed to have the case adjudicated before the local bishop.

The trial took place publicly, probably in the square in front of the episcopal residence. Bishop Guido determined that Francis' motives were pure but that his actions were rash, and that he should return the money to his father. In answer, Francis said, "Gladly, my Lord, and I will do still more. . . . Up to now, I have called [Pietro] Bernadone my father! But now that I propose to serve God, I give him back not only this money . . . but all the clothes I have from him." With that, he stripped himself and cried, "I can advance naked before the Lord, saying in truth no longer: my father, [Pietro] Bernardone, but: our Father who art in heaven!"

He who once loved the finest clothes now donned a hermit's garb: a tunic secured at the waist by a leather belt, sandals on his feet, and staff in hand. Still hoping to restore San Damiano but in possession of no money, Francis commenced to beg, going into town and asking for stones and provisions. When someone would give him alms, Francis would break into song in praise of God—usually in French, the language he typically used, an early biographer tells us, when he was filled with the Holy Spirit.

For the next three years, Francis went about the work of restoring San Damiano and other local churches, including one situated deep in the woods near Assisi called the Portiuncula. While attending Mass there, Francis heard the Gospel passage wherein Jesus told his disciples to preach the message of the kingdom of God and to take no money or sandals or staff for the journey. Total trust in God's providence while preaching repentance for the sake of the kingdom became Francis' program, and it filled him with joy. He realized that the commission given to him at San Damiano was not simply about restoring church buildings, but building up the life of the Church itself. Accordingly, he threw away his staff, took off his sandals, replaced his leather belt with a simple cord of string—and set off to preach. His style was winsome and positive, unlike that of many of the penitential preachers of the time.

Though at first many thought the young ascetic was mad, he won them over through the joy that so obviously filled his heart. And soon, followers came. One of them, Bernardo, was a wealthy man, but he was so impressed by Francis' way of life that he resolved to give away everything he owned. Standing on a street corner in Assisi, he handed out fistfuls of money to the poor. When his arms grew tired, Francis helped him. Francis gave this original band some basic spiritual formation and then, incredibly, sent them out on mission, as far as St. James of Compostela. He told them to preach, to beg, to offer the peace of God, and not to defend themselves if attacked, trusting radically in God's providence. Some listened to them and gave them alms, but many laughed at them and threw mud at them; still others took their clothes or dragged them by their hoods through the fields.

Who was Clare of Assisi?

Clare, a young woman from a wealthy family in Assisi, became intrigued by Francis and eschewed her former life and joined him and became the mother of all female Franciscans up and down the centuries. She founded a community of intense contemplatives and ascetics that remains present to this day. We see at different times throughout Church history these cases where a male and female saint come together in a powerful work. St. Francis and St. Clare are one of the best examples of that.

THE ESTABLISHMENT OF THE ORDER

It is fair to say that Francesco of Assisi never intended to found an order. But when followers came to share his life, he saw it as the will of the Lord. And so, in May of 1209, Francis and his twelve disciples made their way to Rome to the see of Pope Innocent III, one of the most powerful and fascinating figures of the Middle Ages. Innocent reigned at a time of remarkable corruption in the Church. Many bishops, priests, and religious had become landed gentry, far more concerned with maintaining their property than fulfilling their pastoral responsibilities. Most of the clergy were poorly educated in the faith and rarely preached, and many were given over to lives of debauchery and sensuality. Furthermore, the buying and selling of Church

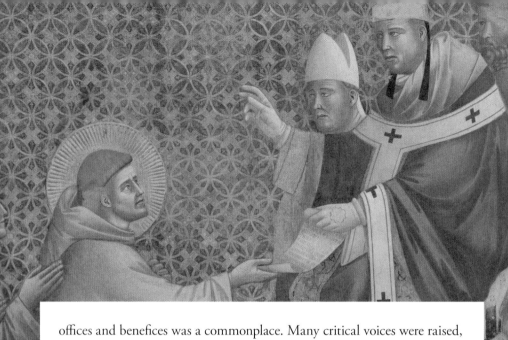

offices and benefices was a commonplace. Many critical voices were raised, and many penitential movements emerged. All the reformers were calling for a cleansing of the Church, but some went too far, advocating the total eradication of Church property and, in some extreme cases, the killing of bishops and priests deemed too worldly. Trying to hold the Church together during this tumultuous time was the central concern of Pope Innocent, a canny politico and a spiritually alert man.

There is a wonderful contemporary account of Francis' first meeting with the great pope. Entering the Lateran palace boldly, Francis came directly into the presence of Innocent III. He looked so shabby with his tattered tunic, unruly hair, and great black eyebrows that Innocent pretended to take him for a swineherd: "Leave me alone with your rule," he said. "Go find your pigs instead. You can preach all the sermons you want to them!" With evangelical simplicity, Francis did what he was told. He went straightaway to a pigsty, smeared himself with dung, and reappeared before the pope! But when Francis laid out his program of radical poverty, simplicity of life, reliance upon begging for alms, the preaching of repentance, and total trust in divine providence, some of the pope's advisors saw another heretical proposal for the dismantling of the institutional Church, and the pope himself wondered whether the successors of this zealous band could ever live up to the ideal that Francis proposed. But one of the cardinals observed trenchantly, "If we reject this poor man's request on such a pretext, would not this be to declare that the Gospel cannot be practiced, and so to blaspheme Christ, its Author?" Legend has it that when Pope Innocent saw Francis, he recognized him as a figure from one of his dreams. The pope had dreamt the Church was collapsing and that a small figure in ragged clothes came to hold it up. That man was Francis of Assisi. In any case, Innocent approved the little band of brothers as a religious order attached to his own person, and he gave them the task of preaching penitence.

Upon their return, they took up residence in an area near Assisi called Rivo Torto. Here they lived the radical Franciscan life of poverty, obedience, simplicity, and purity. At Rivo Torto, Francis resolved to call his community the "Friars Minor," or the little brothers, because they were to be the least—not only materially but psychologically as well, taking the lowest place and eschewing all honor or privilege. The Friars Minor actively sought out places where they were not well known so that they might experience rejection and insult, practicing "holy patience." They were devoted to hard work as well, especially the care of lepers. Once, Francis felt that he had not sufficiently respected one of the patients in a leprosarium and he accordingly ceded his own place to the poor sufferer and ate his dinner from the man's plate and used his utensils. But the special mark of Francis' community was joy. On one occasion, a brother came back from begging with a song on his lips. Francis ran to greet him, kissed him, and said, "Blessed be that brother who goes forth to beg without being urged and comes back home in such good spirits!" He said that "spiritual joy is as necessary to the soul as blood is to the body." For Francis, a gloomy man was "hardly a citizen of the city of God."

The sojourn at Rivo Torto ended in a curiously Franciscan way. One day, while the friars were assembled for prayer in a simple hut, a peasant arrived with his donkey, hoping to find shelter for the animal. Pushing the animal into the space, he said, "You can see that we couldn't find a better place anywhere than this." With that, the Franciscan brotherhood got up and humbly ceded the place to the animal and his owner!

What can we learn from the growth of the Franciscan order?

The Gospel principle is the mustard seed principle, which we saw above in the life of St. Benedict. Things begin very small and grow into something impressive. Francis, as a young man, heard the voice of Christ, calling him to "rebuild my Church." Francis began collecting stones and rebuilding a particular church. But out of this initial response to the call of God, the Franciscan order developed and has now stretched across the centuries to our present day. Saints make an act of trust; they do what God asks of them and allow God to provide the growth. Like the feeding of the five thousand, the saints give Jesus the little they have, and Jesus multiplies it for the feeding of the world.

THE GROWTH OF THE ORDER

The order that Francis never really intended to found grew, in the early days, by leaps and bounds. It is as though Francis and his band had awakened a latent spiritual hunger in the people of that time and place. As he and his brothers made their way around Italy, they inspired hundreds and then thousands to join them.

On one of his journeys, he preached one of the most famous sermons in Christian history. Francis always had a profound affection for all of

God's creatures. Quite correctly, he saw them as his brothers and sisters, since they had come from the same Father as he. Not far from Bevagna, Francis arrived at a place where the trees were filled with what seemed like thousands of birds. Marveling at this, Francis said to his companions: "Stay here by the road and wait for me, while I preach to our sisters the birds." They say that the birds gathered around him in great numbers as he spoke to them. He told them to rejoice in their beautiful plumage and in their freedom to fly where they wish—and to thank God for the food that he provides them and for the streams from which they drink. "God sustains you without your having to sow or reap." With that, the legend says, they burst into a joyous song.

The second most famous story dealing with Francis and animals has to do with the saint's interaction with the wolf of Gubbio. While on his way to Gubbio, Francis was stopped by some of the townspeople, who told him of a particularly ferocious wolf who terrorized the town, eating not only animals but men and women as well. Even heavily armed soldiers were afraid to venture outside the walls of the city. Francis blithely responded, "What have my donkey and I ever done to my brother [wolf]?" He agreed to confront the wolf and speak to him. As the people climbed on roof and rampart to watch the spectacle, Francis went forth from the city gate. They watched in horror as the wolf lunged at the saint with gaping jaws. With a simple sign of the cross, Francis stopped the wolf's advance: "Come here, brother wolf! In Christ's name, I forbid you to be wicked." The animal meekly lay down at Francis' feet, and the saint continued, "I understand why the people of Gubbio detest you, but I want to reconcile you with them." When the wolf made signs of acquiescence, Francis went on: "If you agree to make peace, brother wolf, I will tell the people to feed you as long as you live, for I know that it was hunger that drove you to commit so many crimes." The wolf put his paw in Francis' hand, and then the saint led the now placid animal into Gubbio. In the town square, Francis urged the people to do penance for their sins, and then he said, "My brother wolf here promises never to harm you again if you will promise to feed him as long as he lives." And this they did for the next two years, until the animal died.

Did these things really happen? Well, there are dozens of such stories about Francis. They say that he preached to the flowers; that he moved tiny worms off of the path lest they be crushed; that out of love for "brother fire," he would not allow candles to be snuffed out; and that he once gave his cloak to redeem two sheep being led off to slaughter. Indeed, we find many similar accounts in the lives of holy people. Could it be that saints have a special instinct for the ties that bind us, through God, to every other creature?

MISSIONS NEAR AND FAR

Within a few years of its founding, the Franciscan order had grown to several thousand members. At a General Chapter meeting in 1217, it was determined that some Franciscans should be sent on mission to Christian lands in order to practice a sort of "new evangelization." In the spirit of Francis, they set off without knowing the languages of the lands to which they were journeying and without receiving any prior permission from the bishops into whose territories they were traveling. Predictably, trouble ensued.

In Hungary, the brothers were taken for religious charlatans who had come to exploit the common people. Accordingly, they were driven from the cities, and in the country, farmers hustled them off their land using pitchforks. In many cases, the unfortunate friars were stripped naked and publicly mocked. But things proved even worse in Germany. None of the friars spoke a word of the native language, except for "Ja." When they were asked whether they were the heretical band that had already wreaked havoc in Italy, they innocently responded, "Ja." At which point they were bound naked to pillories and flogged. The mission to England, however, was more immediately successful. Franciscan brothers, as early as the 1220s, had established houses in Oxford, London, and Canterbury. There is a story told of a high-ranking prelate who had decided to abandon his position and become a friar minor. When the priory at Oxford was being constructed, this man labored alongside the simplest workers, "carrying stones and mortar like a mason's apprentice."

In time, Franciscans set out for missions in non-Christian territory. Five brothers ventured into Muslim Morocco, where they were immediately arrested and brought before the magistrate. When asked what they believed in, the brothers began to recite the Creed, at which point they were handed over to torturers, who did their very worst. The next morning, they were asked whether they persisted in their Christian faith. When they replied affirmatively, they were immediately beheaded. When this news was communicated to Francis, seeing the genuineness of their faith even to death, the saint replied, "Now I can truly say that I have five Friars Minor." Francis himself, still enamored of the chivalric ideal, endeavored to join the Crusaders in the hopes of converting Muslims to Christianity. He went to the Christian forces at Damietta in the Nile delta. He had a powerful impact on the soldiers themselves, many of whom joined his company. But he also made bold to evangelize the Sultan and his court directly. Making his way toward the enemy lines, he was captured and then brought into the presence of Al-Malik al-Kamil. A noble and chivalric figure himself, the Sultan was charmed by Francis and deeply impressed by his courage, for the Christian saint volunteered to undergo a trial by fire to prove the truth of his religion. Acknowledging that he could never convert without alienating his people,

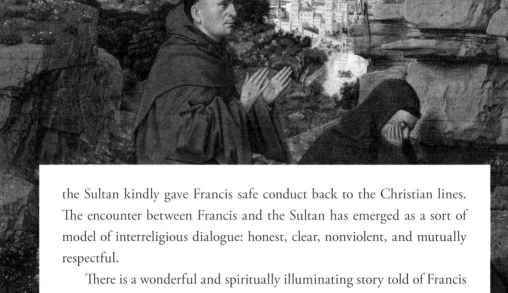

the Sultan kindly gave Francis safe conduct back to the Christian lines. The encounter between Francis and the Sultan has emerged as a sort of model of interreligious dialogue: honest, clear, nonviolent, and mutually respectful.

There is a wonderful and spiritually illuminating story told of Francis during this period of the order's worldwide expansion. Speaking to one of his favorite colleagues, Brother Leo, the saint said:

"You are going to write what perfect joy is. [Suppose] a messenger told us that all of the doctors of Paris have entered the order. . . . Write that this would not give us perfect joy. And supposing that the same messenger were to tell us that all the bishops, archbishops, and prelates of the world, and likewise the kings of France and England, have become Friars Minor . . . that would still be no reason for having perfect joy. And supposing that my friars had gone to the infidels and converted them to the last man . . . this would still not be perfect joy.

"Father," asked Brother Leo, "what is perfect joy?" Francis responded: "Supposing that in winter, coming back from Perugia, I arrive in pitch darkness at the Portiuncula. Icicles are clinging to my habit and making my legs bleed. Covered with mud and snow, starving and freezing, I shout and knock for a long time. . . . [The porter asks who it is, and I respond], 'Brother Francis.' But he doesn't recognize my voice. 'Off with you, prankster . . . this is no time for jokes.' . . . And, grabbing a knobby club, he jumps on me, seizes me by the hood, and drags me through the snow, beating me and wounding me with all the knobs in his cudgel. . . . Well, Leo, if I am able to bear all this for love of God, not only with patience but with happiness . . . write down that at last I have found perfect joy!"

STIGMATA AND DEATH

Just a few weeks after attending the General Chapter of 1224, Francis left the Portiuncula and traveled with a handful of his companions about a hundred miles north of Assisi to an isolated mountaintop called La Verna. He entered there into a profound spiritual retreat, eating little and praying constantly. Brother Leo has conveyed to history some of what happened to Francis on that holy mountain. Leo claims that Francis did serious battle with the dark spiritual powers but also experienced moments of intense communion with God, once even levitating far above the ground while rapt in prayer.

On September 14, 1224, the feast of the Triumph of the Cross, just before sunrise, Francis was kneeling in prayer. He pleaded, "O Lord, I beg of you two graces before I die—to experience in myself in all possible fullness the pains of your cruel Passion, and to feel for you the same love that made you sacrifice yourself for us." St. Bonaventure, in his classic account of this miracle, writes, "Suddenly, from the heights of Heaven a seraphim with six wings of flame flew swiftly down." He bore the likeness of a crucified man. Staring at Francis, he imprinted on the saint's flesh the marks of crucifixion. Bonaventure notes that the marks on his hands and feet were not so much wounds as vestiges of nails: "His hands and feet appeared as though pierced with nails, with round black heads on the palm of the hands and on the feet, and with bent points extruding from the back of the hands and the soles of the

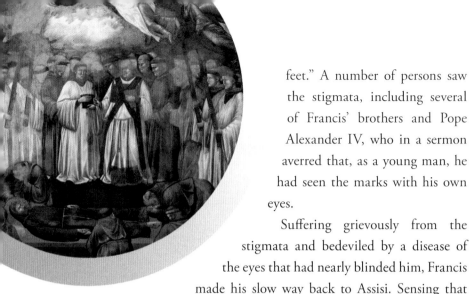

feet." A number of persons saw the stigmata, including several of Francis' brothers and Pope Alexander IV, who in a sermon averred that, as a young man, he had seen the marks with his own eyes.

Suffering grievously from the stigmata and bedeviled by a disease of the eyes that had nearly blinded him, Francis made his slow way back to Assisi. Sensing that death was fast approaching, he asked to be brought to a little hut for the infirm, just beside the Portiuncula. As he prepared for death, he had the brothers sing to him his own festive composition, "The Canticle of the Sun." Some of the brothers were scandalized that he seemed so joyful as death approached. When his suffering was most acute, he asked to be lowered naked to the ground so that he could die in utter poverty. Along with his brothers, he began to intone Psalm 141: "Bring me out of prison, so that I may give thanks to your name. The righteous will surround me, for you will deal bountifully with me" (Ps. 141:7).

He died singing.

WHY IS ST. FRANCIS OF ASSISI A PIVOTAL PLAYER?

A permanent temptation is to see Christianity as a beautiful but impossible ideal, a pleasant fantasy that could never take root in the real world. After all, we say to ourselves: How could we possibly love our enemies, or bless those who curse us? How, in the face of violence, could we possibly turn the other cheek? How could we live in utter reliance upon divine providence, trusting that God will take care of us? How could we really embrace a crucified man as the source of salvation?

As G.K. Chesterton famously said, "The Christian ideal has not been tried and found wanting. It has been found difficult; and left untried." Francis of Assisi vividly reminded his contemporaries—and vividly reminds us—that the Christian ideal *can* be realized. And he showed, furthermore, that the realization of that ideal unleashes enormous transformative power. Though real Christians will always be seen as a little eccentric, they will, in time, always prove to be the true center and produce fruit—thirty, sixty, and a hundredfold.

St. Thomas Aquinas

THE THEOLOGIAN

Thomas Aquinas' contribution to the Church and to Western culture in general has been so massive that it is exceedingly difficult to get a grip on him. He was a philosopher, a scientist, a Scripture commentator, a theologian, a mystic, and in all things, a saint. It is this last description that is, at the same time, the most overlooked and the most illuminating. When one interprets Aquinas merely as a rationalist philosopher, one misses the point of everything he wrote, for Thomas was a saint, deeply in love with Jesus Christ. He was a spiritual master, and his writings were designed to lead people on the road to Christ.

Toward the end of his life, after having struggled to compose a text on the Eucharist, Thomas, in an act of spiritual bravado not keeping with his generally taciturn nature, hurled his book at the foot of the crucifix and asked for judgment. According to the well-known account of this episode, a voice came from the figure of Christ: "You have written well of me, Thomas. What would you have as a reward?" Then came the response: "*Non nisi te, Domine*" (Nothing but you, Lord). With all his heart, Thomas Aquinas wanted nothing other than Jesus, nothing more or less than Jesus. Grasping this is the key to grasping all that he wrote.

Thomas Aquinas was born in either 1224 or 1225 in the family castle of Roccasecca, near the town of Aquino, situated about midway between Rome and Naples. His mother, Theodora, was descended from Norman and Neapolitan gentry, and his father, Landulf, was a minor nobleman. Thomas' family was caught up in the confusing and shifting politics of the day, which pitted the pope against the Holy Roman Emperor.

When Thomas was only five years old, he was sent to the Benedictine monastery of Monte Cassino, not too far from his home. He would stay among the Benedictines for nine very formative years. Far too many commentators have overlooked the importance of Thomas' sojourn in the Benedictine world. At Monte Cassino, he would have learned the rudiments of the contemplative life, and he would have fallen in love with the Scriptures, especially the Psalms. In his maturity, Thomas would understand theology as essentially an elaboration of the *sacra pagina* (the holy page).

There is a delicious story told concerning Aquinas at this early stage of his development. After hearing his teacher discourse on God during an elementary catechism class, young Thomas reportedly said, "But master, what is God?" He never stopped asking that question his whole life long.

When he was around fifteen, Thomas left Monte Cassino for
political reasons and took up what we would call under-
graduate studies at the newly founded University of Naples. While in Naples, the teenager became a double
radical. Under the influence of his professor Peter
of Ireland, Thomas became a devotee of the
Greek philosopher Aristotle, whose writings
had been condemned by a number of popes.
Though some of Aristotle's texts were well
known in Christian Europe, the bulk
of his corpus—including treatises on
metaphysics, the existence of God, and
the nature of the soul—were just coming into circulation at this time. Many
serious Christians felt that the ancient
philosopher's views were at odds with
Catholic orthodoxy. But others—Peter
of Ireland among them—felt that Aristotelian philosophy represented a breath
of fresh air, a new approach to religious
questions more grounded in this-worldly
reality. In a word, Aristotelianism was an
exciting and rather dangerous movement in
the Christendom of the mid-thirteenth century,
and Thomas Aquinas would become one of its
most enthusiastic adepts.

But the Aristotelian radical would become even more countercultural when he embraced the other great revolution of his time: the mendicant movement. While he was still a university student in Naples, Thomas took the habit of the preaching friars of St. Dominic. Like his contemporary Francis of Assisi, Dominic de Guzman felt that Christianity needed to be revitalized through a return to the radicality and simplicity of the Gospel message, and so he gathered around himself a band of brothers dedicated to lives of preaching, poverty, and radical trust in God. For some, the presence of Franciscans and Dominicans was a sign of renewal in the Church, but for many others, it was a scandal.

Thomas' parents wanted him to be the abbot of Monte Cassino—a respected position at an established institution. The last thing in the world they wanted—or expected—was that he would join this strange and upstart group of beggars. So on his way to Paris to begin his Dominican formation, Thomas was waylaid by his own brothers, who had been sent by their mother to stop him. Though they tried to tear his Dominican habit from his back, the young Aquinas clung to it desperately until they stopped. They then locked him away in the family castle at Roccasecca in the hopes of dissuading him. But it only caused his resolution to deepen. During his time in seclusion, he studied the Bible intensely, memorizing large portions of it. According to a famous legend, his brothers introduced a comely prostitute into Thomas' chambers, hoping to coax him from his celibate commitment. The young Dominican chased the girl from the room, shouting and brandishing a torch. Eventually, his family relented and allowed him to go his way.

Thomas traveled with his Dominican companions to the intellectual capital of the Christian world at that time: Paris. In the middle of the thirteenth century, Paris was a magnet for

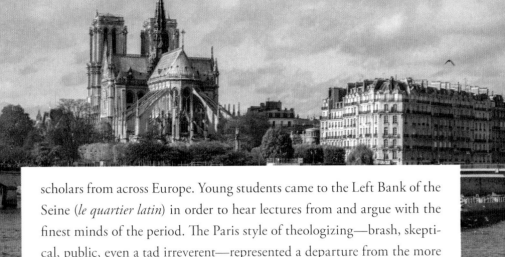

scholars from across Europe. Young students came to the Left Bank of the Seine (*le quartier latin*) in order to hear lectures from and argue with the finest minds of the period. The Paris style of theologizing—brash, skeptical, public, even a tad irreverent—represented a departure from the more conservative monastic approach. When he arrived in the New Athens of Paris in 1245, Thomas found his intellectual home, and he also found his greatest mentor in Albert, the Dominican scientist and philosopher who, even in his own lifetime, was called *Magnus* (the Great). Under Albert's tutelage, Thomas continued his underground study of Aristotle.

In 1248, he followed his mentor to Cologne, becoming the great man's apprentice. While a student there, Thomas—taciturn, self-effacing, and by no means slender—was given the nickname "the dumb ox of Sicily." When Albert heard of this, he remarked, "We call him the dumb ox, but he will make resound in his doctrine such a bellowing that it will echo throughout the entire world." Thomas Aquinas was ordained a priest in Cologne, in a predecessor church to the great *Kölner Dom* that stands to this day. In 1252 he returned to Paris in order to commence what we would call today doctoral studies, and in 1256 the twenty-nine-year-old Aquinas became a *magister* of theology and began to lecture. A magister's tasks were laid out clearly. First, he was to preach, for primarily he was a *magister sacrae paginae* (master of the sacred page). Preaching would conduce naturally toward biblical commentary, and biblical commentary would lead to the searching out of complex theological questions.

These questions—the medievals called them *quaestiones disputatae* (disputed questions)—were not entertained abstractly or exclusively in the pages of books. Rather, they were addressed in the context of a lively public debate. A master such as Thomas would publicize an upcoming public disputation, and a crowd of students, faculty, and interested outsiders would gather. The initial discussion would be led by a *baccalaureus*, what we would call today a doctoral student. He would entertain arguments, questions, and objections from the floor, trying as best as he could to respond to them. The master would preside over this entire process, but without speaking a word. The next day, the master would return, the crowd would assemble once more, and he would then give his magisterial resolution of the matter, followed by his response to what he deemed the best of the questions and objections. Thomas Aquinas' *Summa theologiae*, generally regarded as his masterpiece, is a literary rendition of a series of these *quaestiones disputatae*. A typical article in the *Summa* begins with the statement of the issue (like the summoning of the *quaestiones disputatae*); that is followed by a series of objections (like the comments and questions from the floor); and that is followed by the magisterial resolution of the matter, and finally by an answer to the objections. It is so important that we remember the lively background for Thomas' texts as we make our way through them.

Is Thomas a philosopher or a theologian?

This is a complicated issue that has been answered in opposite ways. Bertrand Russell, in his book *History of Western Philosophy*, includes Aquinas as a minor character, seeing him as little more than a competent commentator on Aristotle. At the same time, there are some on the Catholic side who would so elevate Aquinas as to say that he is not only a philosopher but the greatest philosopher of all time. But Thomas is best read as a theologian who wanted to use philosophy at the service of a higher end—namely, to move people toward Christ. The effort to isolate some of his writings as philosophical violates his own spirit. But however we understand him, Thomas Aquinas certainly ranks as one of the four or five greatest thinkers in the Western tradition.

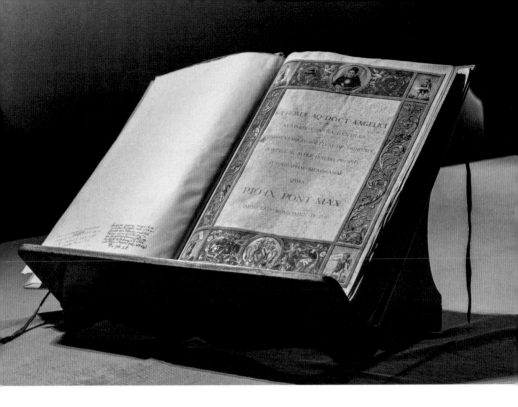

SCHOLAR AND SAINT

Aquinas' literary career lasted only about twenty-five years, but his productivity was nothing short of staggering: his collected works fill fifty double-columned folio volumes. Thomas was obviously a genius, but he was also a man of extraordinary order and discipline. His day began with two Masses: one that he celebrated and a second at which he assisted. And it continued almost without interruption as a cycle of reading, teaching, and writing. It is said that he dictated different works to as many as three secretaries at once, turning from one to the other. He would take a brief nap in the middle of the day and would frequently dictate arguments in his sleep. He was famously absentminded. They say that a brother Dominican was assigned to sit next to him at meals to make sure that he didn't put anything inedible in his mouth!

One of the best-known anecdotes about Thomas concerns a dinner he attended at the table of King Louis IX (St. Louis) of France. In the midst of a raucous conversation, Aquinas sat in abstracted silence, as usual lost in thought. Then suddenly, to the surprise and embarrassment of the other diners, Thomas brought his fist down on the table, upsetting the plates and glasses. He said, "That will settle the Manichees." He had come up with an argument to defeat the dualistic heresy of Manichaeism. One of his Dominican brothers reminded him rather sternly that he was at the king's table, but the king himself, more concerned with truth than decorum, ordered that a scribe be sent to write down the friar's argument lest he forget it.

No account of Thomas Aquinas' life would be complete without a reflection on the events immediately preceding his death. On the feast of St. Nicholas, December 6, 1273, Thomas was celebrating Mass in the presence of his friend Reginald. Something extraordinary happened during that Mass, for afterward, Thomas broke the routine that had been his for twenty-five years. According to one source, "he suspended his writing instruments," refusing to work, write, or dictate. When pressed, he said simply, "I cannot do any more. Everything I

have written seems to me as straw in comparison with what I have seen." What happened to Thomas? After filling tens of thousands of pages with words about God, the great master fell abruptly silent. Had he suffered a stroke? There is some evidence for this: in the wake of the experience, his sister referred to Thomas as *stupefactus* (stupefied). Or had he seen something?

Thomas died at the Cistercian monastery of Fossanova, while on his way to attend the Council of Lyons.

THOMAS' DOCTRINE OF GOD

We recall the question raised by the very young Aquinas: "Master, what *is* God?" Answering that question remained, throughout Thomas' life, his principal obsession. One of the curious features of Aquinas' treatment of God is how agnostic it is: he is much more apt to tell us what God is not than what God is. Though he wrote, as we said, thousands of pages about God, he honored St. Augustine's great dictum: *si comprehendis, non est Deus* (if you understand, it is not God).

The great temptation is to turn God into a supreme version of a creature, to think of him as one being, however exalted, among many. Thomas clarifies that God is not a being; he is not in any genus, even that most generic of genera—namely, existence. Rather, God is, in Thomas' pithy Latin phrase, *ipsum esse subsistens* (subsistent being itself). God is not an item in the universe or alongside it; rather, he is the reason why the contingent and evanescent universe exists at all. Atheists both old and new rather consistently miss this point. When they find no "evidence" for this supreme being, they confidently declare that there is no God. But they are mistaking God, as Thomas understands him, with the gods: supreme items within the realm of nature. God is the answer to the question, "Why is there something rather than nothing?"

Aquinas sums this up by applying to God an attribute that belongs to him alone—namely, simplicity. We would tend to understand this term in precisely the wrong way, taking it to mean elementary or undeveloped. Thomas means that God is not this or that kind of being, neither here nor there, neither great nor small, but rather the act of being itself, without distinction or specification or condition. In every creature, there is a difference between essence (*what* the thing is) and existence (*that* it is). But no such distinction obtains in God. I am a human being; the keyboard on which I am typing is a being of a very definite technological type; a tree is a being of a botanical type; etc. But to be God is "to be to-be." Can you see how this is simply a philosophically precise restatement of God's answer to Moses when the great patriarch asked for God's name? "I am who I am" (Exod. 3:14). As the simple reality, God is that whose being is unconditioned, unrestricted, unlimited. This is why Thomas speaks of God as infinite, without borders. It is also why he is described as immaterial. It is not as though he is less than material; rather, his being transcends the limits inherent in a material manner of existence. This is also why God is referred to as eternal. Time conditions material things; God stands outside of time. Thomas also speaks of God as immutable or unchangeable. This has nothing to do with impassivity in the psychological sense. It means that God cannot "improve," or move from an inferior to a superior state. Instead, he is utterly perfect and fulfilled in his manner of being.

Perhaps you've noticed by now that this procedure is largely negative—Thomas telling us what God is not rather than what God is. What does it mean to be immaterial, eternal, infinite, immutable? Well, we really don't know, for nothing in our ordinary experience is like that. Nevertheless, some very real spiritual insights can be gained from these reflections. Since God is immutable, he is reliable. He doesn't pass from one emotional state to another; he doesn't fall in and out of love with the universe that he makes. Since God is eternal (not stuck in any particular moment of time), he can be present to every moment of time. Since he is immaterial, he is not required to be in any particular place, but can be present in and to every place.

But is the God of Thomas Aquinas personal? Yes. Since he is in possession of all the perfection of existence, he must have mind, will, and freedom. God knows and loves himself first—and then knows and loves all that participates in his being. His knowledge of the world is not passive and derivative but rather creative. Things exist because God knows them into being. This is why Psalm 139 is right: "O Lord, you have searched me and known me" (v. 1). God's love follows from his knowing, for to know something *as* good is *ipso facto* to will it, to rest in it, to savor it. God loves his own perfection with an absolutely perfect love. This love is so intense that it spills over: creation is nothing but the fruit of this effervescent love.

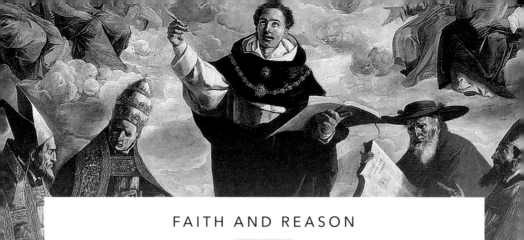

FAITH AND REASON

What makes Thomas Aquinas perhaps most relevant to our time is his approach to the issue of faith and reason. For many rationalists today, faith is simply credulity or superstition or gullibility, believing things on the basis of no evidence. It would certainly be anachronistic to say that Enlightenment-style rationalism was in vogue in the thirteenth century; nevertheless, a form of rationalism was indeed prevalent in the Paris of Thomas' time—namely, Latin Averroism. This was a Westernized version of the theory of the Islamic philosopher Averroes, who had argued that theology represents relatively primitive thought appropriate for the unsophisticated, whereas philosophy is the speech of sophisticates. What this gave rise to, in its Latin, Western form, was a "double truth" theory, whereby something can be true theologically and false philosophically, and vice versa. We can find traces of this view to the present day, for a consequence of Latin Averroism is that faith and reason finally have nothing to do with each other. Faith, at the end of the day, is irrational. This is precisely what Immanuel Kant and his Enlightenment colleagues thought, and why they urged people of faith to grow up.

Well, Thomas Aquinas was having none of this. He stood passionately and resolutely against Latin Averroism and the double-truth theory, insisting that faith and reason cannot come into conflict with one another, precisely because they come from the same source: the God who is Truth itself. For Thomas, faith is not below reason (infrarational); rather, it stands above reason (suprarational). It is not opposed to reason but goes beyond it. Its darkness comes not from an insufficiency of light but from an excess of light. But this means that reason can explore the faith with complete freedom. There is no *sacrificium intellectus* (sacrifice of the intellect) involved in authentic religious faith.

Are faith and reason opposed?

Thomas Aquinas, more than anyone else in the tradition, boldly asks all of the questions, including the fundamental question of whether there is a God. If this question is open, any question is open. The great harmony between faith and reason that was instantiated in the writings of St. Thomas assures us that reason poses no threat to religion where reason and religion are authentically understood.

THE HUMAN PERSON

One of the most remarkable contributions that Thomas Aquinas made was in the area of theological anthropology (to give it its formal description)—or, more simply stated, his understanding of the human person.

What is perhaps most striking about Thomas' approach is how anti-dualist it is. Aquinas is much more at home with the biblical understanding of the human being as a unity than he is with the Platonic dualism that had dominated much of Christian theology before him. For Thomas, the soul is not an alien power standing over and against the body, nor an unhappy spirit imprisoned in the body; rather, it is the form of the body, the energy that makes a body distinctively human. This statement from the *Summa* is typical: "The whole human soul is in the whole body, and again, in every part, as God is in regard to the whole world." Also this: "The soul is in the body as containing it, not as contained by it." One upshot of this unifying view is that the body should be reverenced: "The nature of our body was created, not by an evil principle . . . but by God. . . . Consequently, out of the love of charity with which we love God, we ought to love our bodies also."

But doesn't Aquinas think that the soul survives the body? He does indeed, for the intellectual capacity of the soul—its ability to engage in properly abstract thinking—is an indication of its immateriality. But the soul is destined to be reunited with the body: "At the resurrection the soul will not resume a celestial or ethereal body, or the body of some animal. . . . No, it will resume a human body made up of flesh and bones." Heaven is not a Platonic realm of pure spirit; it is an embodied place, for a human soul is incomplete apart from a human body.

Another key dimension of Thomas' anthropology is his biblically based conviction that the human being is made in the image and likeness of God. This has nothing to do with physical resemblance, for God is not material; it has to do with the curiously infinite capacity of the mind and the will. The mind is never satisfied by any of the particular truths of the sciences or philosophy. It wants to know the Truth itself. The will is never satisfied by any particular good; it wants the Good itself. In a word, both mind and will are ordered to God. By nature, we are ordered to something beyond nature—and from this paradox flows much of the drama and poetry of the human condition. The human being is made for ecstasy, for the journey into God.

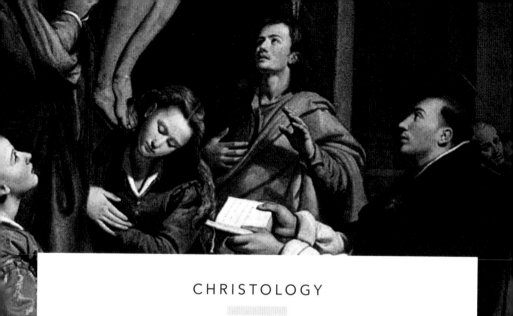

CHRISTOLOGY

Though this is overlooked in most treatments of Thomas Aquinas, the great Dominican saint is best characterized as someone deeply in love with Jesus Christ. We can sense this love in his devotion to the Mass and the Eucharist, as well as in his more remarkable mystical experiences. But we can also see it in his writings concerning Jesus, which are the lynchpin of his work.

There is a text from the third part of the *Summa theologiae* that I have always found both moving and extremely clarifying. The topic under consideration is the appropriateness of the Incarnation. Thomas tells us that something is appropriate or fitting if it corresponds to nature. Thus, it is fitting that human beings engage in speech, for we are, by nature, rational animals. But the very nature of God is to be good, and as the ancient adage has it, *bonum diffusivum sui* (the good is diffusive of itself). When you are in a particularly good mood, you don't withdraw into yourself; rather, you effervesce, you overflow, you move *out*. God's supreme goodness can be seen accordingly in the wild variety and fecundity of creation. God didn't remain shut up in isolated self-regard; rather, he *expressed* himself. But if God is the absolutely highest good, then it would follow—it would be *conveniens* or fitting—that God would give himself in the fullest possible manner; and this, says Thomas, takes place when God joins to himself a created nature, becoming one with creation. The Incarnation is therefore the surest and purest indication of God's goodness.

We could sum this up by saying that the good God is ecstatic: he tends to stand out from himself, to move toward the other in love. But this fits perfectly with Thomas' reflections on the human person, for we saw earlier that human beings, by their nature, tend outward and upward, ecstatically reaching out toward the good and the true. Jesus Christ—the coming together of divinity and humanity—is accordingly the meeting of two ecstasies, a divine ecstasy that reaches down and a human ecstasy that reaches up.

With the icon of Jesus Christ in mind, we can also understand with greater clarity one of Thomas' master ideas—namely, that the true God and humanity are not in competition with one another. Aquinas says, with the mainstream of the Catholic tradition, that Jesus is the hypostatic or personal union of two natures, divine and human, which come together without mixing, mingling, or confusion. Jesus is not quasi-divine and quasi-human (like Hercules or Achilles), nor is he merely human (like a saint) or purely divine (as the Docetists would have it). Rather, he is truly human and truly divine, neither nature having to give way to accommodate the other.

But do you see how this coheres with (indeed gives rise to) Thomas' understanding of God as *ipsum esse*? A supreme being, however great, would still be one finite nature among many and hence would compete with any other finite thing. A supreme being, therefore, could not become incarnate without compromising itself or the integrity of the creature to whom it is united. The God who does indeed give himself away utterly, becoming a creature but without undermining himself or the creature he becomes, cannot be one being among many. What a beautiful and illuminating coincidence of teachings!

WHY IS ST. THOMAS AQUINAS
A PIVOTAL PLAYER?

Thomas Aquinas showed as completely and passionately as anyone in the tradition that Christians could think deeply about their faith. For him, no question, even the most fundamental, was off-limits. He demonstrated thereby that faith and reason are not in opposition to one another; that being a believer involves no *sacrificium intellectus*. In our time, when so many hold that religious people are simpletons, and religious faith only a crude superstition, Thomas Aquinas remains more relevant than ever.

He is also pivotal because he beautifully exemplified a truly catholic mind—by which I mean, a mind open to every and any influence, willing to embrace the truth wherever he found it. Thomas was primarily inspired of course by the Bible and the great Christian theological tradition. But he also read and cited with enthusiasm the pagan philosophers Plato, Aristotle, and Cicero; the Jewish rabbi Moses Maimonides; the Muslim scholars Averroes and Avicenna. Even when he disagreed with a thinker, as he did with Origen and Siger of Brabant, he always did so with respect and without polemics. In this, he's a wonderful model for our time, when the religious conversation is sadly so marked by rancor and vituperation.

Finally, he's pivotal in his understanding of God as noncompetitively transcendent. The God of Thomas Aquinas is not a threat to human freedom and human integrity, but the very ground of that freedom and that integrity. Thomas Aquinas would agree with St. Irenaeus that "the glory of God is a human being fully alive." At a time when so many people see God's existence as undermining the human project, how liberating and clarifying this doctrine is. The God of Thomas Aquinas is the God of the burning bush, that power whose proximity makes the world more beautiful and more radiant without consuming it.

St. Catherine of Siena

THE MYSTIC

Caterina Benincasa, known to the world as Catherine of Siena, is one of the strangest and most intriguing of the Church's saints. An uneducated woman from an ordinary family, she became, in the course of a very short life, an object of fascination to thousands and a counselor to kings, queens, and popes.

Though she never studied theology and never learned formally to read or write, she came to be recognized as a Doctor of the Church and a master of the spiritual life. Her mystical connection to the higher world—she spoke to Christ, Mary, and the other saints as casually as one friend talks to another—constitutes a powerful challenge to the flattened-out secularism of our time. She also witnesses to the deeply biblical truth that the higher world and this world are not separated by a terrible gulf, but rather interact and interpenetrate. Jesus' great prayer includes the petition: "Your kingdom come. Your will be done, on earth as it is in heaven" (Matt. 6:10). Catherine knew that truth in her bones.

Like St. Augustine, St. Bonaventure, St. Teresa of Avila, and St. John of the Cross, Catherine profoundly understood the subtle process by which one rises from the degradation of sin to the ecstasy of union with God. Her descriptions—which are among the most striking and beautiful in the spiritual tradition—help all of us who seek to walk the way of the Lord.

LIFE AND TIMES

Catherine was born in Siena on March 25, 1347, the twenty-fourth child of Jacopo Benincasa and his wife, Lapa. By all accounts, she was a beautiful, lively, and fun-loving child. When she was a girl of six or seven, Catherine had an experience that changed her forever and provided the interpretive key for much of what she would say and do in the course of her life. While returning home from a cousin's house and standing in the middle of a busy thoroughfare, Catherine suddenly saw in the sky a vision of Christ surrounded by other saints and Apostles. What was most remarkable was that Jesus was robed in the vestments of the pope. She was utterly captivated by the vision, feeling herself drawn into a higher and more beautiful world. That she would serve Christ precisely in and through serving Christ's vicar the pope was clearly signaled by this experience.

Sometime after receiving this vision, Catherine took a vow of perpetual virginity and frustrated thereby her family's attempts to find her a husband. In her early teens, she retreated to a small room in her family's home and took up the vocation of a *reclusa*, a holy woman dedicated to prayer, the Mass, and fasting. Catherine's practice of fasting would intensify in the course of her life, culminating in an asceticism so radical that she ate practically nothing.

Around the year 1369, Catherine joined a group called the *mantellate*, women—mostly widows—dedicated to prayer and service and associated with the Dominican tradition. In making this move, Catherine was passing from a purely contemplative form of life to an active engagement with the wider world. She began to attract an extremely devoted group of followers, a *familigia*, to whom she was *Mama*. What drew them to her was the intensity of her prayer and the radicality of her commitment to service.

When Catherine prayed, she would move into a state of ecstasy, shutting her eyes and clenching her fists. While she was in this condition, she was unresponsive, even to the sharpest needles. When she came out

of her ecstasy, she would share the most wonderful
stories of encounters with Jesus, Mary, St. Dominic,
and many other heavenly figures. In one of her most
famous encounters, Jesus took her as his bride and gave
her a ring to seal their relationship. On a pastoral trip to
Pisa, Catherine had a powerful mystical experience. After attending Mass
celebrated by Raymond of Capua, her spiritual director, she fell into a
trance and assumed the attitude of the crucified Jesus. She reported an
encounter with Jesus, who communicated his wounds to her, though the
marks remained invisible to others.

There are an equal number of remarkable stories dealing with Catherine's
care for the sick and the poor. Keep in mind that her life unfolded at the very
height of the Black Plague, which devastated Europe, killing as much as one
third of the entire population. Catherine cared for countless plague victims,
heedless of the danger. One of the most touching stories of her ministry
to the sick involves a cranky and difficult *mantellate* named Andrea, who
was dying of breast cancer. Despite Catherine's relentless kindness, Andrea
was consistently cruel and unappreciative, often criticizing Catherine and
spreading gossip about her. One day, Catherine bathed Andrea's ulcerated
breast and found the process utterly revolting. But she was inspired to drink
the filthy water in her basin as a sign of humility and dedication. Afterward

she reported her thirst was simultaneously quenched and reawakened, a mystical commonplace suggesting that the experience of God is inexhaustible. The point is that she found Christ precisely through an act of self-forgetting love.

A second striking pastoral encounter was with a young man from Siena named Niccolo di Toldo, who had been condemned to death by beheading. Catherine came to see him in prison and comforted him before his execution, encouraging him to see his death as a mystical marriage to Christ. Then she accompanied him to the scaffold and, in the midst of mystical prayer, placed his head on the block and subsequently received it after the decapitation. As the young man died, Catherine saw his soul being received into the hands of Christ—and this is why she was reluctant to wash the blood that had splashed onto her habit.

One of the major motifs in Catherine's writing is blood. Blood is life, food, drink, bath, communion, mortar, ransom, key, door, grace, and much more. The word appears over eighteen hundred times in her work. She has even been called "the apostle of the blood of Christ." It seems to be, in sum, Catherine's favorite symbol for the mercy of God, the lifeblood of God.

The truly public dimension of Catherine's ministry commenced around 1375, when she was all of twenty-eight years old. The dominant issue, both for her personally and for the Church at large, was the so-called Avignon captivity of the papacy, the exile of the popes from Rome to a city under the sway of the French king. The popes—for the most part French—wanted to stay close to home and to avoid the fierce internecine politics of the Eternal City. During this "captivity," the Church fell into remarkable corruption, both financial and moral, and Catherine and others, including St. Brigid of Sweden, saw the return of Peter's successor to Peter's city as the key to reform.

In the summer of 1376, Catherine made the journey to Avignon in the company of several members of her *familigia* and confronted Pope Gregory XI directly. That an uneducated woman even got an audience with the pope, much less the opportunity to challenge him to his face, witnesses to the extraordinary reputation that Catherine had by this time. That the pope agreed to quit Avignon and take up residence in Rome witnesses to the stunning persuasive power that the saint must have had. When Gregory died just a year after returning to Rome, he was succeeded by Urban VI, but Urban's intransigence and hostility to his enemies led to the election of an anti-pope, who promptly took up residence in Avignon, thus commencing the Great Western Schism.

Catherine stood stubbornly with Urban and against the Avignon pope. At Urban's urging, she came to Rome in 1378 and remained there until her death in 1380. Every day, she made her way across the city of Rome to attend Mass at St. Peter's, even as her health severely declined. Her last words, according to some accounts, were "*Sangue, sangue, sangue!*" (Blood, blood, blood!).

Did Catherine of Siena have power in the Church?

We tend to associate power and prestige with the priesthood. But it's interesting that, in the Middle Ages, a figure like Catherine was recognized as having great spiritual power. There were priests and bishops who called her "Mama"; they were extremely devoted to her as their spiritual teacher. Catherine managed to get an audience with the pope and convince him to leave Avignon and return to Rome. How did she do it? Think about the figures we lionize in society today: actors, actresses, musicians, athletes, politicians, successful businesspeople. In the fourteenth century, in a culture that was deeply Christian, a figure like Catherine of Siena was viewed in this way. Though she was of a rather low social status, uneducated, and basically illiterate, her ecstatic contact with a higher world made her something of a celebrity (to use a crude term) in her own time. Power is not merely holding office; there is a great spiritual power that comes from holiness of life and a radical living of the Gospel.

CATHERINE'S TEACHING: GOD AND THE SOUL

That Catherine is a true theologian is evidenced in Pope St. Paul VI declaring her a Doctor of the Church in 1970, but her theology is not of the usual scholastic or academic type. Rather, it unfolds through a series of images and metaphors, some staples of the mystical tradition, others remarkably original and unusual. Her theology can be distilled from her incredibly vivid letters and also from her great treatise, referred to as *The Dialogue*, which is essentially a conversation between herself and God.

Who is the God who emerges from Catherine's writings? In an early revelation to her spiritual director Raymond of Capua, the young Catherine reported this divine word: "Do you know, daughter, who you are and who I am? . . . You are she who is not and I AM HE WHO IS." This should not be read as a denigration of the self; rather, it is an accurate account of how God and the world relate to one another. As we have seen in Thomas Aquinas, God is that reality that exists through the power of his own essence, whereas all creatures exist only in the measure that they participate in God: "In him we live and move and have our being" (Acts 17:28). She speaks of the divine essence as a *mare pacifico* (a peaceful sea) and of us as "fish in the sea." The metaphor is a good one, since it shows that God and creatures are not in a competitive relationship; rather, creatures live and exist precisely through God and his mercy. This is why Catherine can compare God to a mirror in which the soul sees her own dignity and value. She also speaks of God as Beauty itself, which is reflected in the beauty of creatures.

The God that she loves is not an abstraction or a distant principle. Rather, God is intimately involved in the world that he continually sustains in existence. She goes so far as to refer to him as *pazzo d'amore* (crazy in love) with the world. Whatever this providential God does or permits is done or permitted out of love, not hatred—and seeing this is key to the Christian life. In point of fact, God loved us into being, for he loved us before we came to be.

The problem, of course, is sin, which Catherine compares to the waters of a raging river that have drawn us under. Only through recourse to the bridge, which is the body of our crucified Savior, can we be saved. Just as sin is corporate, so salvation is corporate. We are saved in and through the Mystical Body of Jesus. Catherine makes this more specific, referring to the kneading together of divinity and humanity in Jesus. And her imagery is quite distinctive: God the Father speaks to her, saying, "In the union of these two natures I received and accepted the sacrifice of my only begotten Son's blood, steeped and kneaded with his divinity into the one bread." In other words, the Incarnation affects a weaving together, indeed a baking together, of the divine and the human. The traditional term for this process is "deification" or even "divinization," the making divine of the human. The process stands at the heart of Catherine's understanding of the Incarnation. In the *Dialogue*, the Lord says to Catherine: "So as I told you, I became a man and humanity became God through the union of my divine nature with your human nature." This union, once again, happens through the blood of Jesus.

What is the Church, according to Catherine? It is the Mystical Body of Jesus, extended through space and time, and hence the vehicle by which the blood of Jesus works its saving power. This is why, in a delicious image, Catherine refers to the pope as the "cellarer" with the "keys of the blood" of Christ. The sacraments are the concrete, indeed embodied, application of the power of Christ. And this is why she compares them over and again to food.

CHRIST THE BRIDGE

One of the most powerful and memorable of Catherine's images is that of Jesus as a bridge. In order to understand this properly, we have to hold in our minds the kind of bridges that she would have known in the cities of the Middle Ages. Perhaps the Ponte Vecchio in Florence would give the best indication. These were complex structures, marked by a variety of levels and filled with buildings, shops, and even residences. Jesus referred to himself as "the way, and the truth, and the life" (John 14:6). This implies that he is not simply a teacher to be attended to and not simply a moral instructor to be imitated, but the very divine life itself, someone to be entered into, participated in, *walked on*. In the *Dialogue*, God the Father tells Catherine about this bridge: "The bridge that stretches from heaven to earth by reason of my having joined myself with your humanity. . . . This bridge [is] my only begotten Son." The bridge, the Father goes on, has three levels or "stairs," which correspond to three states of soul.

The first level or stair is walked by beginners in the spiritual life, those at the "mercenary" stage. These are people who have given up on sin primarily out of fear of divine punishment. They have indeed climbed out

of the rushing water of the sinful world, but their motivation is relatively primitive. They are at the servile stage, fearing God as a slave fears his master. Mixing her metaphors, as she is wont to do, Catherine sees this level as corresponding to the feet of Christ nailed to the cross. Just as a slave kisses his master's feet, so the beginner kisses the feet of his Lord.

The second stair is walked by those who have transcended servile fear and have learned to love God. But their love is based upon the pleasure they have in the relationship, upon spiritual benefits—consolations, as Ignatius of Loyola would call them. One can see this dynamic in many who have begun the spiritual journey in great excitement but who have yet to encounter real obstacles and suffering. In line with the mixed metaphor already mentioned, this stair corresponds to the open heart of the crucified Jesus. One has moved beyond fear and has come to real friendship with the Lord, a heart-to-heart communion.

The third stair is walked by those who have become sons and daughters of God, those who have found "filial" love. This is a friendship with God based not on good feelings or "rewards" or consolations. It is simply love for the sake of love. The purest sign that one has moved from the second to the third stair is that one is willing to accept any suffering, any failure, any pain, precisely out of love for God. This is the total abandonment to God that results in real deification, an identity between the divine will and one's own will.

This corresponds to the mouth of the Redeemer. "Let him kiss me with the kisses of his mouth!" says the bride in the Song of Solomon (Song of Sol. 1:2). Both St. John of the Cross and St. Bernard saw the kiss of Christ's mouth as the culmination of the spiritual life. For people in this state, "every time and place is for them a time and place of prayer." Intimacy with God gives rise to a lightness of being, an elevation of the soul upward to God. In Catherine's case, this sometimes took the form of literal elevation. Those in this state of union experience an illumination of the mind, which enables them to interpret the Scripture aright. This is how Catherine understood the extraordinary capacities of Jerome, Augustine, and Thomas Aquinas: they were not simply learned, for many learned people don't know how to read the Bible. They were elevated, lifted up to real union with God. But this intimacy with God always flows over into active service. This is the Christian difference that separates Catherine from, say, Plato or Plotinus. The highest ascent is always accompanied by the most humble descent into love of one's neighbor.

Another image that Catherine uses in the *Dialogue* in order to illustrate spiritual progress is that of tears. Here she distinguishes five types of tears: the bitter tears of damnation shed by those in hell; the tears of fear shed by those at the very beginning of the spiritual journey; the tender tears of those who are beginning to love God; the tears of the perfect, who have attained to real union with God; and the "sweet tears shed with great tenderness" that are shed by those utterly given over to the Lord.

Since the great saint of Siena mentioned the tears of the damned, I should like to say a word about Catherine and hell. In the *Dialogue*, we find the report of a conversation between Christ and Catherine that is especially illuminating. Fired by the hope that all people might be saved, Catherine said to Jesus, "How could I ever reconcile myself, Lord, to the prospect that a single one of those whom you have created in your image and likeness should become lost and slip from your hands?" The answer that the Lord gives her, confided to her spiritual director Raymond of Capua, is breathtaking: "Love cannot be contained in hell; it would to-

tally annihilate hell." In other words, the love that Catherine
is exhibiting, precisely through her hope that all be saved,
functions as an antidote to the poison, or according to her
own metaphor, an obstacle to the entrance of hell. She tells
her Lord, "If I could remain united with you in love while,
at the same time, placing myself before the entrance of hell
and blocking it off in such a way that no one could enter, that
would be the greatest of joys for me."

With the mainstream of the Catholic tradition, Catherine holds that the spiritual life cannot begin apart from grace. No one can save himself from the predicament of sin. Grace comes first, but grace can be integrated and cooperated with through action.

A first step is intense self-knowledge, which Catherine compares to a retreat into a monastic cell: "To attain charity you must dwell constantly in the cell of self-knowledge." This reveals both our degradation and our dignity as children of God. Mixing metaphors, she says that the cell is also a well, "where there is earth as well as water"—that is to say, the knowledge of sin and the knowledge of grace, awareness of our nothingness and of God's fullness. Anticipating Ignatius by two centuries, Catherine refers to this process as "discernment."

Like all of the other saints and spiritual masters, Catherine appreciates humility as the foundation for all spiritual progress, for it is the undoing of Adam's pride. Closely tied to humility is obedience—to one's superiors in the religious life, and to the commandments and evangelical counsels for anyone seeking perfection. "Obedience has a wet nurse, true humility, and the soul is as obedient as she is humble and as humble as she is obedient."

But at the very heart of the spiritual life is charity or love, for love is what God is. When the human will is rightly ordered to God, it marvelously expands: "You make [the heart] so big . . . so big that it has room in its loving charity for everyone: with well-ordered charity, it seeks everyone's salvation." Very much in the tradition of St. Augustine, Catherine sees a well-ordered love as loving God first and then all things for the sake of God and in the manner of God. What does this look like concretely? First, we should refrain from judging one another and leave judgment completely to God. Whether someone is saved or lost is none of our business. Rather, our business is to act for everyone's good. Second, we should pray and work for the salvation of all. Third, we should never seek any reward or recompense for our love, for love is willing the good of the other. Period. There is a terrible corollary to this law of love, and it is the law of suffering. Since love is the surrender of self, it will always involve a certain pain of loss. This is why the Lord tells Catherine, "I have already told you that suffering and sorrow increase in proportion to love: When love grows, so does sorrow." Christians, of course, readily recognize this as a participation in the crucifixion of Jesus, which was the supreme act of love.

Finally, we must speak of prayer. Catherine uses the word *orazione* over five hundred times in her writings. The saint distinguishes between an inner prayer, which is constant and born of a deep appreciation of God's relation to the soul, and an outer prayer, which is identical to the particular acts of prayer recommended by the Church. The two are in a reciprocal and mutually supportive relationship. Inner prayer, which is an awareness of the divine love, should give rise to particular prayers and in turn be awakened by them.

VISIONS AND ECSTASIES

There is no doubt that Catherine of Siena experienced extraordinary visions, locutions, and ecstasies—vivid encounters with the heavenly realm. But like John of the Cross and so many other mystics down through the ages, she remained extremely wary of clinging to such things. Those who become attached to mystical experiences can fall into extreme bitterness and weariness when they cease. Better in all cases to remain humbly dependent upon God's will.

One of the great marks of the mystical state, for Catherine, is what Gregory of Nyssa called *epektasis*: the coincidence of supreme enjoyment of God and a further hunger for God. It is a sense of the infinite surplus of the divine reality: the more we have, the more we want to have. Here are Catherine's own words: "Yet your consuming does not distress the soul but fattens her with insatiable love. . . . The more she possesses you the more she seeks you and the more she seeks and desires you the more she finds and enjoys you, high eternal fire, the abyss of charity."

The mystical experience is, above all, an experience of union. The word *unione* appears frequently in Catherine's writings. We have, she thought, a fundamental oneness with God, simply in the measure that we are creatures. But the more love grows in us, the more this oneness intensifies, the more thoroughly we are "kneaded into" God. Once more, this process is grounded in Christ, who is the personal union of divinity and humanity: the more we participate in his love, the more we grow into God, becoming, in her words, "one thing" with God.

Catherine's vision is dynamic and evolutionary: we are either moving forward in appropriating the divine love, or we are moving backward. This is why the soul can never be content with the level of union it has attained; rather, it should always be restlessly seeking. The key is the death of the selfish will and the emergence of the will that is identical with the divine will. This marriage of the two wills is "drunkenness," "fire," "ecstasy," "a kiss," and "a baby at his mother's breast."

How do we know that Catherine's ecstasies were not just a psychological malady?

In our post-Freudian era, we are quick to dismiss someone like Catherine of Siena as insane. But even in her time, people understood madness. To discern the difference, we have to look at the integrity of her life as a whole. Catherine had great intelligence, a sense of purpose, a gift for friendship, and was an inspiration to people around her—hardly the marks of an insane person.

WHY IS ST. CATHERINE OF SIENA A PIVOTAL PLAYER?

In a particularly vivid and even startling way, Catherine of Siena witnessed to the existence of a dimension beyond this one. She lived, as we have seen, in steady and deeply personal contact with the saints, with the Virgin Mary, with Jesus Christ, and with the persons of the Trinity. In our age, so marked by a secularist ideology, this sort of talk is dismissed as fantasy or mere imagination. But the sheer power and integrity of her life argues against this sort of reductionism. She reminds us, as Hamlet said to his friend: "There are more things in heaven and earth, Horatio, / Than are dreamt of in your philosophy." She signals to us that the world of our ordinary experience, though real to be sure, is but a shadow and image of a world more fully real.

She's also pivotal because of the intensity of her love. Precisely because Catherine was so immersed in the realm beyond this one, she was able to function as a conduit of grace and mercy to this suffering world. She herself was a kind of bridge between heaven and earth. She herself was a kind of Jacob's ladder.

She also exemplifies Thomas Aquinas' great principle: that when it comes to the theological virtues, no excess is possible. It's impossible to have too much faith, too much hope, or too much love. When a person falls in love with Christ as deeply as Catherine did, she loves excessively, completely, utterly—even unto the giving away of her own life.

Michelangelo

THE ARTIST

In the eighth century, a controversy broke out in the Christian world over the issue of the legitimacy of using icons in worship. On one side of the dispute were the iconoclasts (the smashers of icons), who argued that the use of pictorial representations of sacred things ran contrary to the Old Testament prohibitions against making graven images. To picture God, angels, or saints struck the iconoclasts as tantamount to idolatry. On the other side of the argument were the iconophiles (the lovers of icons). They argued that God had made an icon of himself in the humanity of Jesus, for Paul referred to Christ as the *eikon* (image) "of the invisible God" (Col. 1:15). Hence, when human artists make pictures of Christ and his saints, they are simply prolonging the Incarnation.

One of their most articulate and energetic spokespersons was a monk named John of Damascus, who lived and worked in an isolated monastery near Jerusalem. Though hardly a household name, John was one of the most influential, indeed pivotal, figures in the history of the Church. For in waging the ultimately victorious struggle against iconoclasm, he made possible the unsurpassingly rich tradition of visual arts within Catholicism. If there were no John of Damascus, there would be no Ravenna, no Arena Chapel, no Sainte Chapelle—and no *Pietà*, no *David*, no Sistine Chapel ceiling. I highlight these last three references, for in many ways,

Michelangelo represents the full flowering of the Catholic artistic tradition, which found its origin in John of Damascus' victory. Can beauty be a route of access to God and a means of evangelization? John of Damascus said "Yes!" And no one ratified that affirmation more stunningly and completely than Michelangelo.

Called in his own lifetime *il Divino* (the divine one), Michelangelo is generally regarded as the greatest artist that Western culture has produced. How wonderful that the subject matter of this most sublime of artistic geniuses was almost exclusively the Christian religion. His work—in painting, architecture, and sculpture—is rightly characterized as representing the high point of the Renaissance, but it should also be appreciated as one of the signal contributions to the Catholic tradition, easily ranking with the work of Aquinas, Augustine, Mozart, and Dante.

What about Michelangelo's art was so transformative?

A large part of the impact of Michelangelo's art was its anatomical realism. We take this for granted today, but he was one of the first artists to render such vivid depictions. Michelangelo had a gift that allowed him to imagine figures in three dimensions in a way that most people can't. But beyond the anatomical realism, there is also the spiritual power and energy of his sculptures and frescoes.

LIFE AND TIMES

Michelangelo Buonarroti was born in 1475 in the little village of Caprese, about sixty miles east of Florence. His father was a small-time Florentine banker who had fallen on hard times and had taken an administrative position in the small town. Just a few months after the boy's birth, the family moved back to Florence. When Michelangelo's mother became quite ill, the baby was given to a wet nurse from the town of Settignano, set near the quarries from which the finest marble in Italy was derived. This is why, years later, the artist could say, "I sucked in with my nurse's milk the chisels and hammer with which I make my figures." Michelangelo would always consider himself a sculptor first and last.

When he was still a young child, Michelangelo apprenticed to the Florentine painter Domenico Ghirlandaio, who had worked, along with Botticelli, on decorating the walls of the Sistine Chapel in Rome. Under his tutelage, the young artist learned the fresco technique that he would employ years later in his own work in the Sistine Chapel. In time, he was taken in by the de facto leader of Florence, Lorenzo the Magnificent, who was a great patron of the arts and who maintained a sculpture garden on the grounds of his palace. There, Michelangelo learned the art and technique of sculpture, and he listened to the philosophers and poets whom Lorenzo had gathered around him. Just two years after taking Michelangelo under his wing, Lorenzo died, and his family was swept from power.

The vacuum was filled by one of the most extraordinary figures of the period, the Dominican preacher Girolamo Savonarola. Fired with an apocalyptic vision, Savonarola preached against what he took to be the vanity, materialism, and superficiality of Florentine society. He became convinced that the beginning of the sixteenth century would signal the end of the world, and he conveyed that conviction to a surprising number of his contemporaries, including the painter Botticelli, who, under Savonarola's influence, cast some of his own paintings on the fire.

In rather short order, Savonarola's reign ended with his public execution in the main square of Florence, but the fiery preacher's influence on Michelangelo should not be underestimated. Even as an old man, Michelangelo wrote that Savonarola's voice still echoed in his mind. What did the artist take from the apocalyptic Dominican? Perhaps something to balance the sunny humanism of Lorenzo's court: a keen sense of human frailty and of the never-ending struggle between good and evil that takes place in every heart.

In the summer of 1496, two years before the fall of Savonarola, Michelangelo left Florence for Rome, and it was in the Eternal City that he first made his reputation. He received a commission from a French cardinal for a Pietà, which would function as an altarpiece. Ironically, that cardinal never lived to see the completion of his commission, which turned out to be one of the most beloved and admired sculptures ever created. After five years in Rome, Michelangelo returned to Florence, in the spring of 1501, and almost immediately accepted a remarkable challenge. In the Cathedral of Florence there was a gigantic but oddly shaped block of marble that had been acquired forty years earlier in the hopes that it might be carved into the figure of a prophet. But the stone had defeated every sculptor who tried to wrestle something from it. Within three years, Michelangelo turned the misshapen stone into a consummate masterpiece: the *David*.

Not long after completing the *David*, Michelangelo was employed by the newly elected Pope Julius II, nephew of the man who built the Sistine Chapel. Pope Julius, who embodied the quality the Italians call *terribiltà*, first

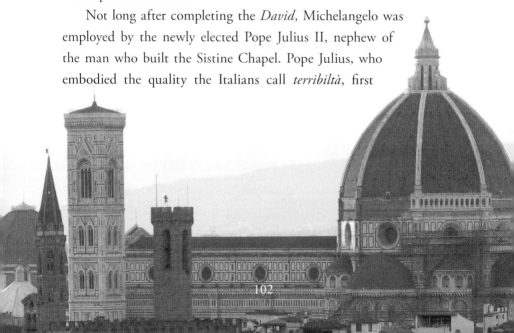

asked Michelangelo to create a tomb for the pope that would rival the tombs of Augustus and Hadrian. The colossal project, involving upwards of fifty massive sculpted figures, appealed immediately and deeply to Michelangelo. Over the course of many decades, long after Julius died, the master labored at this Herculean task, but for many reasons—political, financial, personal—it never came close to completion, though elements of it emerged, including the haunting *Captives* on display today in the Louvre and most famously the stunning sculpture of Moses that rests today in the church of San Pietro in Vincoli.

Julius diverted Michelangelo's attention from the tomb—and thank God he did—because he wanted the master to decorate the ceiling of the Sistine Chapel. We will consider this work in some detail in due time; suffice it to say for the moment that he labored on the ceiling from 1508 until 1512. In 1535, at the behest of Pope Paul III, Michelangelo returned to the Sistine Chapel in order to commence work on *The Last Judgment*, which fills the entire altar wall.

In 1546, Michelangelo was appointed chief architect of the new St. Peter's, a project originally started during the papacy of Julius II. The master revived and improved the original plan of the architect Donato Bramante, and added to it one of the most magnificent domes in the history of architecture. Based upon Filippo Brunelleschi's dome for the Cathedral of Florence, Michelangelo's construction is a masterpiece of balance, harmony, integrity, and decoration.

The master died in 1564, at the age of eighty-eight. That very year, Shakespeare was born.

THE *PIETÀ*

A serious problem in approaching any of Michelangelo's great works is that they have become so familiar, so iconic, that we convince ourselves too easily that we already know them. We have to defamiliarize them and look at them with fresh eyes.

In regard to the *Pietà*, we should look, first, at Mary. For five centuries now, scholars and admirers have remarked the serenity and youthfulness of her face. Mary, we presume, would have been at least forty-five or fifty at the time of the Crucifixion, and yet Michelangelo depicts her as a young woman, perhaps in her early twenties. Was he remembering his own mother, who died when she was quite young? Perhaps. But a far more compelling interpretation is a theological one. When asked about Mary's appearance, Michelangelo himself remarked, "Do you not know that chaste women retain their fresh looks much longer than those who are not chaste?" How much truer, one would imagine, of the Immaculate Virgin, conceived without original sin and hence evocative of Eve before the fall. What Michelangelo is showing us is not only the "historical" Mary, but Mary as New Eve and ever-young Mother of the Church. Michelangelo was, throughout his life, a great devotee of the poet Dante. At the end of the *Divine Comedy*, we find a famous line placed on the lips of St. Bernard as he sings the praises of the Mother of God: "Virgin Mother, daughter of your Son, humbler and loftier past creation's measure." Since Mary's Son according to the flesh is also the divine Word through whom all things are made, Mary is both mother and daughter of Christ. Is Michelangelo suggesting this absolutely unique relationship in the youthfulness of Jesus' mother?

One of the most extraordinary features of the *Pietà*, from a purely structural or compositional standpoint, is how Michelangelo managed to make the figures of Jesus and Mary look so natural and elegant together, despite the fact that what is being presented is a woman supporting the body of an adult man on her lap. In fact, Mary's body is significantly larger than that of Jesus. She contains him. In the wonderful words of Sr. Wendy Beckett, she is like a great mountain, and his body is like a river flowing down. The Fathers of the Church compared Mary to the ark of the covenant, the receptacle of the Ten Commandments, which the ancient Israelites appreciated as the dwelling place of God. So Mary, who carried the incarnate Word in her very womb, becomes the Ark of the Covenant *par excellence.*

According to the Gospel accounts, Mary, having given birth to Jesus, placed him in a manger, the place where the animals eat. At the climax of his life, Jesus would become food for the life of the world. Therefore, Michelangelo depicts Mary's left hand in a gesture of offering, as though she is presenting him as a gift; her right hand supports him but touches him only indirectly, through her garment. Both are Eucharistic references. The Church continually offers the Body of Jesus under the forms of bread and wine, and when the priest shows the Blessed Sacrament, he touches the monstrance only through a veil.

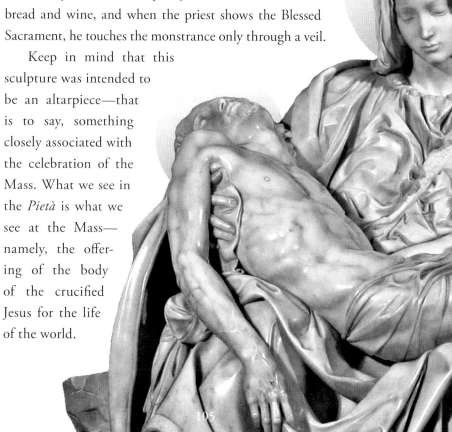

Keep in mind that this sculpture was intended to be an altarpiece—that is to say, something closely associated with the celebration of the Mass. What we see in the *Pietà* is what we see at the Mass— namely, the offering of the body of the crucified Jesus for the life of the world.

THE *DAVID*

When the great art historian Kenneth Clark presented Michelangelo's *David* for the first time in his series *Civilisation*, he said simply, "What a man!" The *David* does in many ways represent the highwater mark of Renaissance humanism, the celebration of the glory and beauty of the human being. Going beyond even the most skilled of his classical forebears, Michelangelo here depicts the symmetry, harmony, athleticism, and sheer grandeur of the human body. However, it would be wrong indeed to see Michelangelo as simply a talented imitator of classical forms and this magnificent statue as simply a splendid updating of the classical ideal. The *David* must be read Christologically if we are to uncover its deepest meaning.

In the pages of the New Testament and in the writings of the Church Fathers, David is consistently presented as a type or foreshadowing of Jesus. Jesus is born in David's city of Bethlehem; throughout the Gospels, he is referred to as the son of David; the angel tells Mary that Jesus will assume the throne of his father David and that his reign will be without end. As David went out naked against Goliath, relying only on the power of the Lord God, so Jesus went naked into battle on the cross, facing down the powers of sin and death and putting his absolute trust in the Father.

With this comparison in mind, we can look at David's physical perfection with deeper perception. Christ is the son of David and he is the New Adam, the realization of what God has always intended for humanity. Think of the risen Jesus as the fulfillment of every possible human potential, spiritual and physical. Christianity does not advocate the escape of the soul from the body—as do Platonism and Gnosticism—but rather the resurrection and transfiguration of the body. Now Kenneth Clark's "What a man!" takes on a fuller resonance. Looking at Jesus, Pontius Pilate said "*Ecce homo*"—"Here is the man" (John 19:5). With unconscious irony, Pilate was holding up the man he was condemning to death as the archetype of humanity. In this unparalleled sculpture of David, prototype of Christ, Michelangelo is saying much the same thing.

THE SISTINE CHAPEL CEILING

The Sistine Chapel was built by—and named for—Pope Sixtus IV. It was completed in the year 1481 and thus was a relatively new building when Michelangelo began his work on the ceiling in 1508. Reflecting its importance as the papal chapel and the site of the conclave to elect the pope, the Sistine Chapel was constructed to mirror the temple of Solomon as described in the first book of Kings: its length twice its height and three times its width. Just as the temple was covered in cedar and gold, so the chapel was meant, from the beginning, to be decorated with the finest paintings. Just after the chapel's completion, Sixtus engaged the services of three of the leading Italian artists of the time: Perugino, Signorelli, and Botticelli. Their fresco cycles cover the walls of the chapel.

It fell to Sixtus' nephew, Pope Julius II, to commission the decoration of the ceiling, and for this task, the pope turned to Michelangelo. The pope's initial idea was to fill the ceiling with portraits of the twelve Apostles, but the artist saw this as unimaginative. He proposed something much more ambitious: nine scenes from the opening chapters of the book of Genesis, dealing with creation and the fall, surrounded by depictions of the prophets and sibyls who had foretold the coming of Christ, as well as smaller portraits of the ancestors of Jesus mentioned in the Bible. Julius accepted the proposal, and Michelangelo commenced the project with the help of only a small team of assistants.

It is most important to note, as we begin our analysis, that the entire masterpiece is centered on Christ, though Jesus is explicitly depicted only once in the enormously complex composition. The Scriptures tell us that creation took place precisely through the Word of God and that Adam is a prototype of Jesus. Moreover, the fall is the reason why the Incarnation came about: "O happy fault that earned so great, so glorious a Redeemer." Finally, all of history—in both its secular and sacred dimensions—should be appreciated as a preparation for the coming of the Word made flesh.

To get a handle on the overall design, it might be best to divide the nine central scenes into three triads: the first dealing with the creation of the world, the second with the creation and fall of human beings, and the third with the stories of Noah, which show the degrading effects of sin on the human race.

In the first panel, depicting the separation of light and darkness, God is portrayed as an energetic male figure, his arms upstretched and his torso twisting upward and away from the viewer. This conveys the primordial spiritual activity of the Creator. There is certainly a good deal of manly power in the portrayal, but as Andrew Graham-Dixon points out, there is something of the feminine as well, suggested by God's pectoral muscles, which seem as rounded as a woman's breasts. His primal act of creation also appears to be an act of division. This reflects the Genesis account: God distinguishes night from day, the sky from the earth, the dry land from the sea, the man from the woman, etc. And it anticipates what God would do throughout the Bible, separating Israel from the other nations, the wicked from the righteous, the new creation from the old. And all of it points, therefore, to the great fresco on the wall of the Sistine Chapel: the Last Judgment, God's final act of separation.

The second panel in this opening triad has to do with the creation of the sun, moon, planets, and the earth. God is depicted twice: first focusing as he brings forth the sun and moon, and second scurrying off to produce the earth and its vegetation. I have always found wonderful the look of awe, even terror, on the face of the accompanying angel as he takes in what God has done. According to an ancient tradition, the sun is associated with Christ, and the moon—reflected light—with the Blessed Mother. Thus we have an anticipation here of the one who would bring creation to its fulfillment and who would describe himself as the light

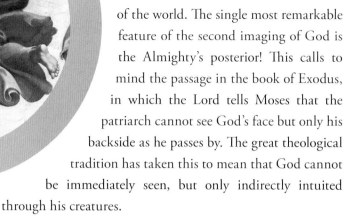

of the world. The single most remarkable feature of the second imaging of God is the Almighty's posterior! This calls to mind the passage in the book of Exodus, in which the Lord tells Moses that the patriarch cannot see God's face but only his backside as he passes by. The great theological tradition has taken this to mean that God cannot be immediately seen, but only indirectly intuited through his creatures.

The final panel in the opening triptych is a composition of extraordinary gracefulness and serenity. With a gentle gesture of benediction, God, in the company of his angelic retinue, hovers over the surface of a placid sea. This could be a reference to the very beginning of the book of Genesis, where we hear that the Spirit of the Lord brooded over the sea, but it is more likely that Michelangelo is staying with the narrative progress of Genesis and that this scene represents the act by which God brings forth a multitude of sea creatures that swarm the ocean. How wonderful that this colossal act of creation is only hinted at, for we can't see what God is making happen under that placid surface.

The second great triad of images, forming the center of the ceiling's overall composition, deal with the creation of man and woman. The first image is, arguably, the most famous picture in the history of Western art. It is, as Kenneth Clark said, at once sublimely great and universally

accessible. Once again, the familiarity of the image can block our appreciation of its meaning. First, we should note the absolute novelty of the depiction of God. The Creator had been presented before as a hand coming from a cloud or as a staid standing figure; but to show him as an energetic, athletic man literally flying through the air was unheard of. One is put in mind of Thomas Aquinas' description of God as *actus purus* (pure act or energy). Adam is portrayed as a paragon of physical beauty, as striking and perfect as the *David*, as balanced and harmonious as the *Vitruvian Man* of Leonardo da Vinci. This is a representation of humanity as God intended it.

In one of the most creative and eloquent inventions in the history of art, Michelangelo shows the energy of God flowing—a bit like an electrical current—from the finger of God to the finger of the reclining Adam. This is the communication of the soul—the seat of intelligence, will, imagination, and freedom, those spiritual qualities that constitute the image and likeness of God. There is an ancient Christian association between the Holy Spirit and the finger of God. St. Augustine, for example, says, "The Holy Spirit, through whom charity is shed abroad in our hearts,

is also called in the Gospel the finger of God. . . . The finger of God is God's spirit through whom we are sanctified." The same Spirit of God that hovered over the waters now communicates life to human beings.

Interestingly, the face of the Creator, creased in concentration, is staring not at Adam but at his own finger, the vehicle of spiritual communication. Just as the finger of God wrote the Ten Commandments, so here the finger of God is imparting to the first man an awareness of the divine law, the capacity for responsible thought and action. In his biography of Michelangelo, Ascanio Condivi, who knew the artist personally, confirms this interpretation: "God is seen with arm and hand outstretched as if to impart to Adam the precepts as to what he must and must not do."

Above God's left shoulder are cherubim and seraphim, high angels making up the heavenly court. Under the crook of his left arm is a beautiful female figure, her eyes wide as a doe's, staring with fascination and a hint of dread at Adam. She is undoubtedly Eve, the mother of all the living, whose fate will be closely tied to that of Adam. Next to her is a child who bears a strong facial resemblance to Adam. God's left index finger rests on the child's shoulder, even as his right index finger reaches out to Adam, establishing a dynamic connection between the two. This, of course, is Jesus Christ, the new Adam, already present in the mind of God in the very act of creation. Speaking of the mind of God, in very recent years, a suggestion has been made that the drapery whirling around this heavenly group calls rather vividly to mind the contours of a human brain. We know that Michelangelo was doing serious anatomical studies at the time, and that he was acutely aware of the biblical idea that God made the world through his Logos or mind. Therefore, this interpretation might not be illegitimate.

The next scene—the creation of Eve—stands at the very center of the entire composition. The reason, I believe, is that this is the moment when matter and spirit cross, or better, find their harmony. It is no accident that the words "matter" and "mother" are close relatives. The woman's body, especially in its connection with childbirth, has been symbolic, across the cultures, of earth, nature, and materiality. Notably, the Creator God is grounded in this scene, in such stark contrast to his flying personification in the previous panel. Eve comes forth from the side of Adam into the light and into the astonishing presence of God. Her gesture is eloquent indeed, for it signals the purity of our first parents prior to the fall. Her folded hands evoke prayer and adoration, the spiritual stance humanity was intended to assume from the beginning. Before the tumble into sin, Adam and Eve were a balance of matter and spirit, of earth and heaven.

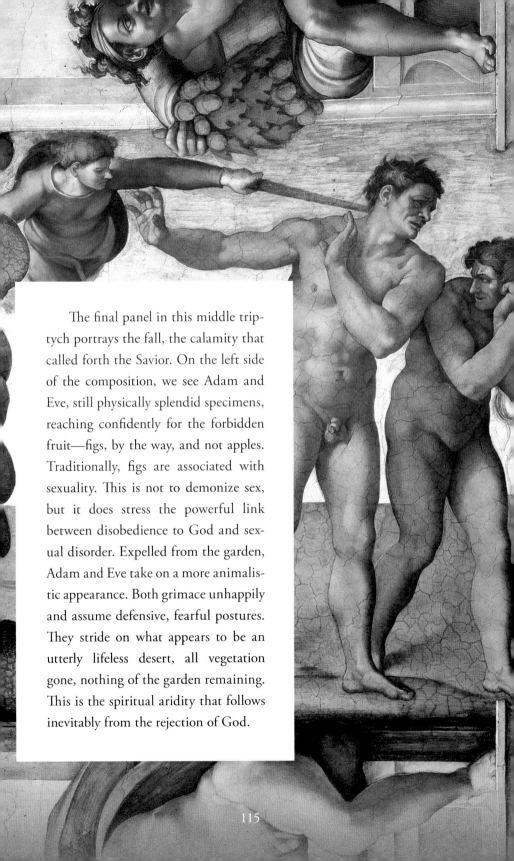

The final panel in this middle triptych portrays the fall, the calamity that called forth the Savior. On the left side of the composition, we see Adam and Eve, still physically splendid specimens, reaching confidently for the forbidden fruit—figs, by the way, and not apples. Traditionally, figs are associated with sexuality. This is not to demonize sex, but it does stress the powerful link between disobedience to God and sexual disorder. Expelled from the garden, Adam and Eve take on a more animalistic appearance. Both grimace unhappily and assume defensive, fearful postures. They stride on what appears to be an utterly lifeless desert, all vegetation gone, nothing of the garden remaining. This is the spiritual aridity that follows inevitably from the rejection of God.

The final three panels deal with the effects of the original sin, the steady decline of the human race into dysfunction. The central scene in this last group is actually the first panel that Michelangelo painted. It shows a crowd of desperate people fleeing the great flood and seeking the last high ground that remains. Carrying their possessions, clinging to one another, and weeping openly, they represent the flotsam and jetsam of the human race. In the far left corner of the composition, we find a woman whose breasts have dried up and can give no nourishment to the child who cries at her shoulder. On the other side of the panel, we see a young man in the attitude of a river god from antiquity, curled up against a wine-keg; but instead of offering an abundance of intoxicating wine, he is preparing for a watery death. Noah's Ark, depicted in the distance, looks not so much like a boat but a church, indeed like the Sistine Chapel itself. This, of course, is not accidental, for the ark was seen by the Church Fathers as a type or anticipation of the Church, the place of haven and safety in the midst of a sinful world. In one of his most famous sermons, delivered in 1494, Savanarola had warned of a second flood that would destroy the lascivious society of his time, and he encouraged the people to take refuge in the Florence Cathedral, which he explicitly compared to the ark of Noah. Could that sermon have been echoing in Michelangelo's mind as he composed this scene?

On one side of this central panel, Michelangelo depicted the sacrifice of Noah, which portrays the patriarch in an entirely priestly attitude. Offering the holocaust, surrounded by his family and by a multitude of animals, he anticipates the sacrifice of Christ on the cross as well as the sacrifice offered at the Mass. This is just one of the many indirect allusions to Jesus and his work on the Sistine ceiling.

On the other side of the central scene is the final chapter in the narrative that Michelangelo has composed. It represents, accordingly, the full expression of sin and dissolution, the triumph of matter over spirit. We see a depiction of the drunken Noah being discovered, in his nakedness, by his sons—and hence doubly humiliated. Purely worldly "spirits" have robbed Noah of mind, will, and responsibility, and hence have made him a parody of what human beings are supposed to be. This declension is beautifully suggested in the pose of Noah, which is a pathetic imitation of the pose of Adam at his creation.

Though this cycle ends on a negative note, we are not meant to be discouraged, for the entire purpose of the narrative is to make sense of the coming of the Savior, who by his Incarnation would reconcile matter and spirit and thereby repair the damage done by sin. Christ the New Adam would come to undo the effects of the fall.

What is the significance of The Last Judgment?

The first thing to point out in Michelangelo's masterpiece *The Last Judgment*, which covers the altar wall of the Sistine Chapel, is the depiction of Christ, which is very unusual. It was at this time that the heliocentric view of the galaxy was coming into vogue—the idea that the sun is at the center of the solar system. Notice that the compositional heart of the picture is a sunburst behind Jesus, and he looks not like the typical depiction of Jesus but like Apollo, the god of the sun in the ancient world. The idea here is that just as the solar system revolves around the sun, so all of time and space revolve around the person of Jesus Christ. And now it comes to its culminating moment: the last judgment. On Jesus' right, we see those figures who have been found worthy rising into heaven. To Jesus' left, we see those who have not descending into hell.

There are two key figures surrounding Jesus. Mary stands to the right of Jesus and is turned away from those who are descending, for she is no longer able to intercede for them; she withdraws her hands as though she is allowing Jesus' hand of judgment to rise. On the other side, St. Peter is presenting the keys of the kingdom to Jesus. Jesus gave the keys to Peter within space and time, but now, at the end of space and time, Peter returns the keys to Jesus. Other striking figures include

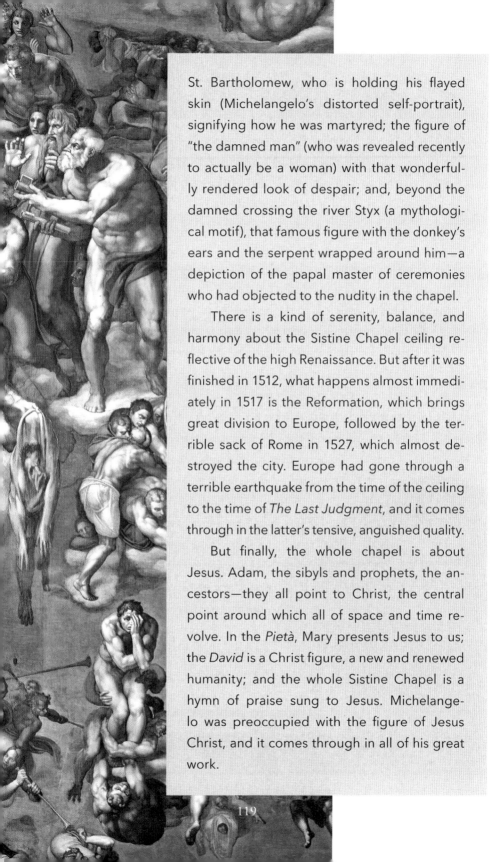

St. Bartholomew, who is holding his flayed skin (Michelangelo's distorted self-portrait), signifying how he was martyred; the figure of "the damned man" (who was revealed recently to actually be a woman) with that wonderfully rendered look of despair; and, beyond the damned crossing the river Styx (a mythological motif), that famous figure with the donkey's ears and the serpent wrapped around him—a depiction of the papal master of ceremonies who had objected to the nudity in the chapel.

There is a kind of serenity, balance, and harmony about the Sistine Chapel ceiling reflective of the high Renaissance. But after it was finished in 1512, what happens almost immediately in 1517 is the Reformation, which brings great division to Europe, followed by the terrible sack of Rome in 1527, which almost destroyed the city. Europe had gone through a terrible earthquake from the time of the ceiling to the time of *The Last Judgment*, and it comes through in the latter's tensive, anguished quality.

But finally, the whole chapel is about Jesus. Adam, the sibyls and prophets, the ancestors—they all point to Christ, the central point around which all of space and time revolve. In the *Pietà*, Mary presents Jesus to us; the *David* is a Christ figure, a new and renewed humanity; and the whole Sistine Chapel is a hymn of praise sung to Jesus. Michelangelo was preoccupied with the figure of Jesus Christ, and it comes through in all of his great work.

WHY IS MICHELANGELO
A PIVOTAL PLAYER?

Over and against the puritanical, iconoclastic strain, which infects Christianity at different points throughout its history, Michelangelo proves that the sensual, the artistic, and the beautiful can be a vehicle to the spiritual. He confirms, more convincingly than any other figure in the Catholic artistic tradition, the great incarnational principle.

Like Dante, Chesterton, and Aquinas, Michelangelo was also a splendid Christian humanist. He recognized and then expressed artistically the fact that Christianity, which proposes the divinization of men and women, is the greatest humanism possible. In the godlike perfection of so many of his creations, Michelangelo shows that the ultimate destiny of human beings is infinitely beyond anything proposed by the worldly humanisms of both antiquity and modernity. The Church Fathers loved the adage *"Deus fit homo ut homo fieret Deus"* ("God became human so that humans might become God"). No one expressed this principle in a more visually compelling way than Michelangelo Buonarroti of Florence.

Bartolomé de las Casas

THE ACTIVIST

Bartolomé de las Casas is one of the most powerfully prophetic figures in the history of the Catholic Church, a man who, like Jeremiah, Ezekiel, and Isaiah, called attention to great injustice and courageously spoke up on behalf of voiceless victims. His advocacy of the cause of the indigenous peoples of the newly discovered Americas made him, also, a forerunner of the political movements of the eighteenth and nineteenth centuries, which emphasized the dignity of the individual, fundamental human rights, and government by the consent of the governed.

Exposed as a very young man to the terrible abuse of the Indians, Las Casas remained his whole life long a passionate activist, a firebrand, a thorn in the side of the complacent. He was a man who moved easily among both the simplest peasants and the denizens of royal courts, encouraging the former and lighting a fire under the latter. By all accounts, he was irascible, prickly, difficult to get along with—but even those less than attractive qualities were put in service of his mission. A Dominican, he had a good deal of the tenacity and determination of his Dominican sister Catherine of Siena, and he relied heavily on the intellectual work of his Dominican brother Thomas Aquinas.

He is a powerful reminder to us today that an essential component of the Gospel life is love for the poor and a commitment to fight injustice wherever we find it. In his passion to set things right, Las Casas is a worthy successor of the Israelite prophets, of John Chrysostom, and of Ambrose of Milan, as well as a precursor of William Wilberforce, William Lloyd Garrison, Martin Luther King, Oscar Romero, and John Paul II.

LIFE AND TIMES

Bartolomé de las Casas was born in Seville, Spain, probably in 1484, making him a slightly younger contemporary of Michelangelo. He was around nine years old when Christopher Columbus returned from his epoch-making voyage to the New World and paraded through the streets of Seville in the company of some natives whom he had brought back with him. Las Casas' father accompanied Columbus on the Admiral's second voyage to the Indies, and young Bartolomé himself came to the New World in 1502, when he was around eighteen years of age. He landed in the port of Santo Domingo in what is now the Dominican Republic. Most of those travelling with him were hungry for gold, and it is probably fair to say that wealth and worldly success were foremost in the mind of the young, intelligent, and energetic Las Casas.

But what he found in these early Spanish settlements appalled him. The native people were treated essentially as slaves, as nonpersons, and as such, they were treated with stunning brutality. Most of the Indians were gathered into work camps, which the Spanish called *encomiendas*, and were compelled to labor, day and night, in unsanitary conditions. When the native people rebelled against this injustice, they were put down mercilessly, the far superior weapons of the Spaniards overwhelming the primitive defenses of the Indians. Las Casas was an eyewitness to a number of these conflicts and provided details that chill us across five centuries. The *conquistadores* pursued not only the warriors but the women and children as well, putting all of them to the sword: "'The Spaniards bragged on

their various cruelties, each trying to top the others on novel ways to spill blood.' Three Indians were tied together and slowly strangled 'in honor of Christ, our Redeemer, and of his twelve Apostles.'" Some of the killers wanted to test their cutting skills and so pierced the Indians with reverse strokes, "opening them from chest to groin, their entrails spilling out." Here is Las Casas: "I saw all this, and more, so foreign to human nature. I shudder to tell it. Perhaps it was a nightmare. I can hardly believe it myself."

At this point in Las Casas' life, the historical record becomes a bit murky, but we know that he returned to Spain in 1506 and was ordained a deacon in his native Seville. He then journeyed to Rome with some members of Columbus' family, and was probably ordained to the priesthood, perhaps by the pope himself, Julius II, when he was there. He then returned to Hispaniola in July of 1509, a divided figure. On the one hand, he had not forgotten the atrocities perpetrated upon the Indians; on the other hand, he was very much part of the Spanish establishment, controlling an *encomienda* and supervising a number of slaves.

Things became clearer for him when, in 1510, a group of Dominican friars arrived on the island. It did not take these bright and perceptive men long to see the same injustices that Las Casas had noticed. On the Fourth Sunday of Advent, 1511, one of the friars, Fr. Montesinos, delivered—with the full support of his brothers—a scathing sermon, which was heard by the entire Spanish leadership in Santo Domingo. "There is a sterility of conscience among you on this island," he began, "and a blindness in which you live. You are in mortal danger of condemnation, not realizing the grave sins you are committing with such insensitivity. . . . By what right and by what law do you hold these Indians in such cruel and horrible servitude? . . . Let me be perfectly clear. You are killing them to get the gold you so crave!" The sermon was a bombshell and prompted fierce protests on the part of the Spanish leadership, who conveyed their concerns as far as the court of the king and queen of Spain. But the Dominican held firm. Las Casas himself remained divided. Stung by the sermon but still unwilling to let go of his plantation, he presented himself to one of the Dominicans for confession, only to be told that he could not receive absolution until he released those innocent people he was holding captive.

In 1514, Las Casas joined an expedition to Cuba, whose purpose was the evangelization and "pacification" of the island. Though he himself was kind to the Indians under his control, the Spanish *conquistadores* were customarily brutal. Las Casas was an eyewitness to one of the greatest atrocities committed during the conquest: the slaughter at Caonao. A large contingent of Spanish soldiers under the command of General Narvaez entered the town, where more than two thousand Indians were gathered. What set things off isn't entirely clear, but Las Casas reported that, "in the span it takes to say two *credos*, [the Indians] were all killed." He goes on: "They fell upon those sheep and lambs, slashing, disemboweling, and killing them." How to explain this? "I think the devil got into them," wrote Las Casas. In the wake of this crime, Las Casas could lead his double life no longer. He freed all of the Indians in his *encomienda*, and he began, in the spirit of the Santo Domingo Dominicans, to preach against the system of oppression that the Spanish had put in place. The power establishment was appalled and offended, but Las Casas had set his face like flint.

In 1515, filled with prophetic zeal, he returned to Spain to engage the king, the aging and ailing Ferdinand, directly. Though the royal court was filled with people who directly benefitted from the *encomienda* arrangement, Las Casas got a hearing. But Ferdinand was too weak and sick to do anything substantial, and he died in January of 1516. Undeterred, Las Casas sought to influence Charles, the new king of Spain and one of the most powerful figures in European history, since he was the Holy Roman Emperor as well. For the next several years, Las Casas insinuated himself in the court of Charles as it traveled through Spain. Over and again, he presented his arguments and eyewitness testimony, often in an aggressive way. Many, including the young king, were sympathetic, but others found him annoying and tiresome.

In 1519 Las Casas, in the company of many of the leading men of Spain and New Spain, had the opportunity to present his case before the king. By all accounts, the young sovereign listened intently. Here is how Las Casas began:

My Very High and Powerful Lord and King, I am one of the veterans who went first to the Indies. I lived there many years. I have seen with my own eyes, not read things in histories which may be untrue. I have touched with my own hands. I have witnessed those gentle and peaceful people suffer monstrous cruelties.

. . . And I ask why, Your Majesty? *Why*, without cause or reason, was hell brought alive to these people? Greed, Your Majesty, unvarnished greed. The thirst and hunger for gold.

The king gave Las Casas the extraordinary permission to realize a dream that the reformer had cultivated for some time—namely, the establishment of a new order in the Indies, whereby simple Spanish farmers would be able to cultivate the land without exploiting the Indians, while Christian evangelists would peacefully go about their work of bringing Christ to the native people. The king had ceded to Las Casas the northern shore of what is now Venezuela for this experiment. In 1521, Las Casas and his settlers arrived in the Indies and were met with skepticism and opposition. They made a valiant effort to establish their ideal community, but it was undermined from the beginning and, like many other attempted utopias, ended in disappointment, violence, and recrimination.

Chastened, Las Casas returned to Santo Domingo, where he was warmly welcomed by the Dominican community. In the course of many months of prayer and reflection, and under the influence of his hosts, he decided to join the brotherhood of the Dominicans. In his early months as a Dominican, Las Casas immersed himself in prayer and study and acquired the erudition that enabled him to make his case for the rights of the Indians with greater authority. He became a student especially of the Bible and of St. Thomas Aquinas, the great Dominican master.

Las Casas was throughout his life a man of action, never one to remain ensconced in libraries or lecture halls. Accordingly, once established in the spiritual and intellectual tradition of the Dominicans, he set out as a missionary. At a time when travel was exceedingly dangerous, he made journeys to Panama, Peru, Nicaragua, and Mexico. He had a special affection for Nicaragua, whose physical beauty overwhelmed him. But he was also impressed by the small number of Indians in that country. It became clear to him that many had been enslaved and exported to Panama and Peru to work in the mines. The Protector of the Indians rose up in righteous indignation and challenged the colonial leadership: "Where in the law, or in Rights, natural, human, or divine, is it a given that these people should be plunged into a service so awful for the sake of Spaniards?" At first, the governor tried to mollify Las Casas, but when it became clear that this strategy would not work, he actively expelled the pesky friar from the country. The intrepid Dominican then made his way to Guatemala and Mexico, evangelizing, teaching, and defending the Indians whenever he could. At a gathering of bishops and other ecclesial leaders in Mexico City, Las Casas made the acquaintance of the Franciscan Bishop Zumarraga, the bishop to whom Juan Diego revealed the image of Guadalupe.

In 1540, Las Casas returned to Spain in order to recruit new Dominican friars for work in the New World, but also to lobby for a definitive remaking of the laws governing the relationship between the Spaniards and the Indians. These so called "New Laws," promulgated in 1542 by King Charles, represent in many ways the high point of Las Casas' career, the culmination of all that he had labored for over the years. They were the practical embodiment of the principles closest to his heart. He fought for them in the course of two years: writing, researching, arguing, lobbying, moving between university lecture hall and royal court, withstanding all the time fierce opposition from those whose livelihoods depended upon the degradation of the Indians.

The New Laws called basically for the undoing of the standard system put in place from the time of Columbus, and they were predicated upon four assumptions: first, the Indians enjoyed dignity as subjects of the Spanish crown; second, Indian slavery should be eliminated; third, the *encomienda* system was fundamentally unjust and should be eliminated; and fourth, future wars of conquest were prohibited. The promulgation of these laws set off a firestorm of protest both in Spain and in the New World—and much of the negativity was focused on Las Casas. At this decisive moment, he was appointed Bishop of Chiapas in the southern region of what is now Mexico. He was consecrated bishop in his hometown of Seville and then returned to the Indies, this time with the practical authority to enforce the laws necessary to protect his beloved Indians.

Did Las Casas support the slavery of Africans?

Las Casas continues to be, five centuries later, a very controversial figure. The most troubling aspect of his legacy is his suggestion to the Spanish establishment that, in order to defend the rights of the Indians, they should bring in African slaves to work on the plantations. This is, of course, a gross inconsistency and a black mark on Las Casas, but to his credit, he admitted as much later in his life. Further, it is easy for us, five hundred years later, to look back critically on Las Casas, but we should realize that at that time virtually everybody supported the enslaving of Indians and Africans. In fact, well into the nineteenth century in many places—certainly the United States—people were still justifying slavery. And these were not marginal figures but many of the leading figures of the political and ecclesial establishment. Las Casas was extraordinarily before his time, extraordinarily prophetic—even though, by his own admission, he certainly got some things very wrong.

It would be an understatement to say that his reign as Bishop of Chiapas did not go particularly well. From the moment of his arrival, he was opposed by the establishment figures, and Las Casas was never known for his diplomatic skill. He lashed out at his opponents, excoriating them in sermons and official statements and, most devastatingly, refusing to give them absolution, even on their deathbeds, unless they released all of their slaves. Riots ensued, and there were threats on the bishop's life.

Frustrated with the situation on the ground and convinced that he could advance the cause of the Indians more effectively in the courts of the king in Spain, Las Casas returned to the Old World in 1547 and found himself almost immediately embroiled in controversy. The king had established a Council of the Indies, based in Valladolid, to determine policy regarding the native peoples of the New World. Las Casas entered

into the lists with enthusiasm. After a few smaller skirmishes, he found himself face-to-face with Juan Ginés de Sepúlveda, one of the leading philosophers and theologians of the time.

THE GREAT DEBATE

Though we have hinted at the arguments that Las Casas used to defend his point of view, we can best present them in a developed way in the context of analyzing his confrontation with Sepúlveda, which took place when Las Casas was at the height of his powers. The central issue that Las Casas and Sepúlveda debated was whether Spain's conquest of the New World was in fact just at all—Las Casas arguing the negative and Sepúlveda the positive.

Sepúlveda based his argument largely on Aristotelian grounds—Aristotle still being, at the time, the leading intellectual authority in Europe. The ancient philosopher had maintained that there are certain people who, due to their lack of intelligence or moral integrity, are destined to be ruled. To acknowledge the rights of such people, or to put them in positions of authority, would be detrimental—not only to society at large but to them. This was the argument employed for centuries to justify slavery. Sepúlveda rested his case on the fact that the Indians "are by nature a servile and barbarous people."

Sepúlveda pressed the issue, insisting that aggressive war could be waged against the naturally inferior Indians in order to compel them, for their own good, to convert to Christianity. Here is a direct quote from Sepúlveda: "And, if they are made submissive, it is easier and more expedient to preach the faith." Moreover, since the natives of the New World engaged in the abominable practice of human sacrifice, the use of force against them was even more justified. In order to bolster this last point, Sepúlveda reached beyond Aristotle to the Old Testament, which indicates that God gave the Israelites free rein to exterminate those who were practicing idolatry and child sacrifice. The Spaniards weren't wiping out the Indians—only compelling them to convert. Because of "the injuries they cause each other, killing men for sacrifices and even to cannibalize them," the Indians should be put down by force.

To answer Sepúlveda's first point, Las Casas dug deeply into the work of his Dominican forebear St. Thomas Aquinas, especially Thomas' rich and complex treatise on law. The great medieval master had argued that there are three types of law existing in a sort of nesting relationship. Positive law—the particular and concrete statutes by which a city or nation is governed—nests within the natural law, which is a set of fundamental moral precepts and instincts, such as to foster life, to seek community, to cultivate friendship, to do justice, etc. The natural law, finally, nests within what Thomas calls the eternal law, which is identical to the structure of the divine mind. What follows from this schema is that a rightly ordered society is one whose positive laws are ultimately reflections of the will and purpose of God. And from this idea both Thomas himself and many of his disciples concluded that even pagan societies, in the measure that they

promulgate just laws, can be recognized as at least implicitly in line with Christian civilization.

Las Casas pressed this point vigorously in regard to the Indians of the New World. Their social structures and political organizations revealed, he insisted, a keen sense of the moral law. Moreover—and here he relied on his intimate, first-hand knowledge of the Indians—the natives of New Spain were skilled in architecture, painting, needlework, and song. Directly addressing Sepúlveda, Las Casas said, "So these men are not stupid, Reverend Doctor. Their skillfully fashioned works of superior refinement awaken the admiration of all nations, because works proclaim a man's talent, for, as the poet says, the work commends the craftsman."

Though he does not cite it, Las Casas would undoubtedly have rejoiced in the judgment of the great European artist Albrecht Durer who, upon seeing artifacts from the New World, commented, "But I have never seen in all my days what so rejoiced my heart as these things. For I saw among them amazing artistic objects and I marveled over the subtle ingenuity of the men in these distant lands. Indeed I cannot say enough about the things which were there before me." Indeed, Las Casas extolled the musical and linguistic skills on display in the Indian cultures: "In  the liberal arts that they have been taught up to now, such as grammar and logic, they are remarkably adept. With every kind of music they charm the ears of their audience with wonderful sweetness. They write skillfully and quite elegantly." Again, he backs this up with the authority of an eyewitness: "I shall explain this at greater length . . . not by quoting the totally groundless lies of the worst [deceivers] . . . but the truth itself and what I have seen with my eyes, felt with my hands, and heard with my own ears while living a great many years among these peoples."

We recall that Sepúlveda's second argument had to do with the necessity of evangelizing at the point of a sword, provided that the evangelist is dealing with primitive and/or violent people. With this Las Casas took vigorous exception. Taking Christ himself as his model, he argued that authentic evangelization takes place only in a peaceful context and through the use of words, ideas, and good example. What in fact has blocked the successful evangelization of the Americas, he insisted, is the violent and hateful comportment of the Christians themselves. Comparing the campaign to convert the Indians to equally fruitless campaigns in other parts of the world, Las Casas comments: "There is no other reason why Saracens, Turks, and other unbelievers refuse to embrace our faith than the fact that we deny them with our conduct what we offer them with our words." He goes even further, insisting that nonbelievers are in fact justified in using force to repel their invaders, even when those aggressors are bearing the Christian religion. His conclusion: "Christ gave His apostles permission and power to preach the

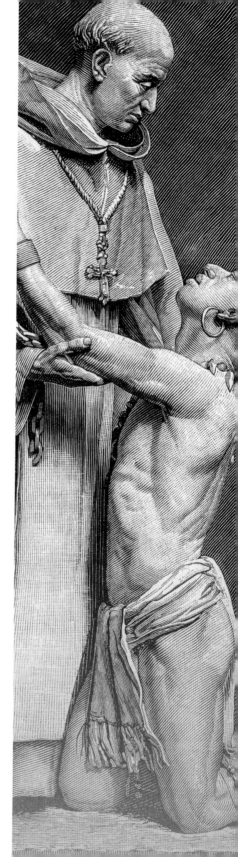

gospel to those willing to hear it, and that only! Not power to punish the unwilling by any force, pressure, or harshness. He granted no power to apostle or preacher of the faith to force the unwilling to listen, no power to punish even those who drove the apostles out of town." How indeed to preach—through the threat of death—the one who said, "I came that they may have life, and have it abundantly" (John 10:10)? A fine rhetorical question. "What does the gospel have to do with firearms? What does the herald of the gospel have to do with armed thieves?"

Las Casas goes so far as to say that the "idols" of the Indians ought not to be destroyed. Rather, the Indians should be allowed to set them aside once they have grasped the truth of the Christian religion. Or better, they should be permitted to integrate them into Catholic belief and worship—as the pre-Christian peoples of Europe did so often upon being evangelized. Drawing once again upon his Dominican brother Thomas Aquinas, Las Casas speaks of the obligation to follow even an erroneous conscience. Thomas had maintained that one is obliged to abide by one's conscience, even if it has been inadequately informed. Thus, Las Casas concludes, the Indians, worshiping false gods in good faith, cannot be compelled by force to change their religious practices. Only when they come to understand the true God are they morally obliged to let go of their idolatry. Here Las Casas proved remarkably prophetic, for it was not until 1965, with the promulgation of the document *Dignitatis Humanae,* that the Catholic Church in its official teaching adopted substantially this same position.

By common consensus, Sepúlveda's strongest counterargument had to do with the Indian practice of human sacrifice. In the face of such a clear violation of natural law, hadn't the Spaniards the right to put down the practice by force? Indeed, Thomas Aquinas and others had argued that one of the justifications for warfare is the righting of moral wrongs. Could there be anything more morally repugnant than the sacrificing of human beings? And therefore, could there be any violence more justified than that of the Spaniards against the Indians?

In defending the native peoples against this charge, Las Casas went to extremes, and it is doubtful whether anyone, either in his own time or today, would find his argument convincing. Though he admitted that, objectively, the practice was abhorrent, within the framework of the Indian religious system it represented the greatest possible service that could be rendered to the divine. Hence, read from a purely natural perspective, Las Casas contended, it proved the high culture and civilization of the Indians. Again, I don't think even he was convinced by this argument, but it demonstrated something that is on display in the entire debate with Sepúlveda—namely, Las Casas' tremendous, and for his time unprecedented, attempt to see things from the standpoint of the other. It is this extraordinary capacity for empathy that makes him a precursor to the abolitionists, the civil rights activists, and all those who over the past several centuries have advocated for the voiceless.

It appears that Sepúlveda and Las Casas were never in the same room when they articulated their arguments before the council in Valladolid, and no official "winner" emerged from the debate—though both of the players claimed victory. Although Las Casas' arguments weighed heavily on the conscience of the religiously sensitive emperor, Charles did not dissolve his empire or return his conquered lands in the New World to the native peoples. It would, in fact, require several centuries before the arguments formulated by Las Casas gave rise to revolutionary change. But it is no small thing that they were first heard, in the middle of the sixteenth century, from the mouth of this intrepid Dominican friar.

FINAL YEARS

Las Casas never returned to his beloved Indies. He spent the last fifteen years of his life as an historian, chronicling the Spanish conquest of the Americas and defending the prerogatives of the Indians. From time to

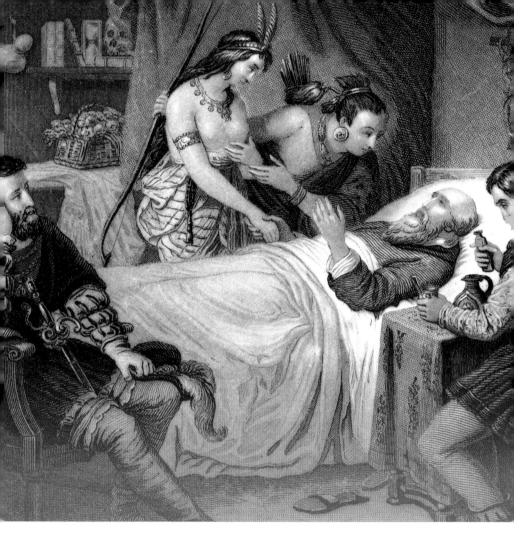

time, he embroiled himself in controversies at court and at the universities, and one time, he ran afoul of the Spanish Inquisition, which accused him of denying the sovereignty of the Spanish monarch. Through it all, he remained feisty, defiant, unconquered. After sojourns in both Valladolid and Toledo, he finally found his way to Madrid, where in 1564 he drew up his last will and testament. In it he instructed one of his Dominican colleagues to assemble all of his writings on the New World so that, "if God determines to destroy Spain, it will easily be determined that justice was being rendered on account of the destruction of the Indies." Scrappy to the end.

During the hot summer of 1566, Las Casas was on his deathbed. But he sent two of his Dominican brothers to bring a last petition before the Council for the Indies. After the presentation, the president of the Council sighed and said, "We shall see" about it. It is fair to say that the world has been debating Las Casas' proposals ever since.

He died on July 18, 1566, and was buried in the main chapel of the monastery of Nuestra Señora de Atocha. No one is certain where his remains lie today.

Why are there so few depictions of Las Casas in artwork or statues?

Las Casas' legacy is not that of an immediately warm and attractive figure like Francis of Assisi or even Ignatius of Loyola, who both have a broad popular appeal. By all accounts, Las Casas was a prickly, difficult figure, reminiscent more of someone like St. Jerome, who was famously hard to get along with. But his life reflects Hans Urs von Balthasar's great line that the saints disappear into the mission of the Church. Las Casas saw his great mission as being the defender of the Indians, and he would have been happy to know that this is what people remembered of his life—that the rights and dignity of the Indians were defended. Having said all that, if you look at people who seriously study the Church's tradition around human rights and the social teaching of the Church, Las Casas is taken very seriously indeed as a prophetic figure.

WHY IS BARTOLOMÉ DE LAS CASAS
A PIVOTAL PLAYER?

Bartolomé de las Casas shows, as vividly as any figure in the great tradition, that a commitment to justice is an essential dimension of Christian discipleship. You simply cannot claim to be a follower of Jesus and remain indifferent to suffering and injustice. Even when many of the leaders of both Church and state were more than content to countenance the oppression of the Indians, Las Casas, in the name of Jesus, said no.

Secondly, he not only had the prophetic capacity to identify with the perspective of the other; he had the distinctively Christian capacity to identify that other with the suffering Christ: "Just as you did it to one of the least of these who are members of my family, you did it to me" (Matt. 25:40). When so many in Europe were more than willing to see the conquered Indians as little more than pack animals to be exploited and enslaved, Las Casas insisted that the rights of the Indians be respected and their dignity upheld. And this conviction was not simply expressive of a deeply felt humanism; it was the fruit of Christian mysticism and spirituality.

Thirdly, Las Casas anticipated, by four centuries, many of the key features of Catholic social teaching: the dignity of each individual, a people's right to self-determination, the moral superiority of democracy, and the prohibition against all forms of coercion in matters of religion.

His shout against injustice still echoes in our consciences to this day.

Ignatius of Loyola

THE FOUNDER

Ad maiorem Dei gloriam (To the greater glory of God) is the motto associated with St. Ignatius of Loyola and the religious order that he founded, the Society of Jesus. *Semper maior* (Always more, always greater) is a pithier version of the adage. Both capture the spirit of Ignatius: restless, moving ever onward, unsatisfied with the quality of his relationship with the Lord, always convinced that the divine love could be answered by a more expansive fidelity on his part. His passion to become a dashing courtier, a courageous and celebrated soldier, and an advisor to royalty became, under the influence of grace, a passion to serve Christ—all the way, holding nothing back.

Though superficially his life seemed of comparatively little moment, he has had an impact greater and more lasting than some of the best-known of his contemporaries: Charles V of Spain, Henry VIII of England, even Martin Luther and John Calvin. He effected this influence first through the establishment of the Jesuit order, which even in Ignatius' lifetime had become a powerful force in Europe and beyond and which today spans the globe; and second, through his masterpiece *The Spiritual Exercises,* which for the past five centuries has taught people how to commune with God and to find true freedom.

A soldier dedicated to achieving his own glory became a soldier fighting for the glory of God—and that conversion changed the world.

LIFE AND TIMES

Íñigo de Loyola was born in 1491, the year before Columbus sailed, in the Basque region of far northern Spain, near the French border. He was the youngest of thirteen children, and his parents were minor nobility. Both his mother and father died before Íñigo was sixteen. Around that very impressionable age, he journeyed to Arévalo, where King Ferdinand was holding court. At this center of Spanish politics and culture, the boy became a sort of junior page and soon became entranced by the beautifully dressed and well-mannered people that clustered around the king.

After some years at court, the young man conceived the desire to become a soldier and commenced to study the martial arts: sword play, the firing of pistols, and the deft use of the lance. And he sought to dress in the dandyish style of the other courtiers: tight-fitting hose, soft leather high boots, a suit of gaudy colors, jaunty cap, and his hair worn long and flowing. The very first sentence of his autobiography, written well after his conversion, summed up these first months in Arévalo: "[I was] given over to the vanities of the world" and had a "great and foolish desire to win fame." In his early twenties, he was arrested in his hometown for "atrocious crimes carried out . . . with premeditation and involving ambush and treachery," in the words of the official police report. What precisely he did remains a mystery, and he got off after a brief imprisonment. But he remains perhaps the only saint who has a formal police record!

Still seeking military glory, Íñigo joined the army of the Viceroy of Navarre, who was engaged in a war with the French. During a battle at Pamplona, Íñigo was seriously injured in both legs by a cannonball. On the spot, French surgeons set the bones of his right leg, but they did so clumsily, and when the young man returned home, his own surgeons had to break the leg and reset it. Nevertheless, the bones did not knit together properly, and Íñigo was left with an unsightly bump on his leg. Still desiring to look the part of the elegant courtier, he told the surgeons to saw it off, which they did—without anesthetic, of course. In the *Autobiography*, he referred to all of this, with admirable laconicism, as "butchery."

During his long convalescence in the summer and autumn of 1521, Íñigo endeavored to read in order to pass the time. He loved perusing tales of knights and chivalrous soldiers, but no books of that type were on offer. All that he could find were a life of Christ and tales of well-known saints. As he studied these books, something extraordinary happened: what would usually bore him commenced to fascinate him. He found himself wondering whether he might imitate the exploits of great saints such as Dominic and Francis. He also discovered that whereas his customary reading excited him at first but then left him feeling empty and despondent, reading the lives of Jesus and the saints produced a lasting sense of peace. This was the first instance of what he would later call "discernment of spirits."

How significant was Ignatius' injury to his life?

Ignatius' injury was the turning point of his life. There is a lesson here for us as well. So often, in the midst of tragedy, injury, or trauma, we ask, "Where is God?" or "How could God let this happen?" But now look at Ignatius. What appeared to be a great tragedy—every dream he had as a young man was shattered by this incident—became the occasion for new life in Christ. God was closing a door and opening an entirely new door that led to this extraordinary spiritual revolution. God used this experience to clean out his attachments to his own ego, to his pursuit of a noble career and the pleasures of the world. This was aggressively knocked out of him so that something new and deeper could emerge. It helps us to see how to read the negative experiences in our lives; God is present in all things, even our negative experiences. Had Ignatius pursued the life he intended, no one—not even a specialist historian of the period—would remember Íñigo of Loyola. But by opening himself to God's grace in the midst of his suffering, he began the journey that led him to become a great saint, from whom graces continue to pour into the world. When we find ourselves on a bed of pain, instead of reading it as dumb suffering, we can remember that God is in all things, and pray for the strength to respond to his ever-surprising grace.

Once back on his feet, Íñigo determined to abandon his military ambitions and to give himself to Christ and the Church. His first step was to make a pilgrimage to the Benedictine Abbey at Montserrat, where he made a gesture in line with his chivalrous instincts: he stripped off his expensive garments and gave them to a poor beggar, and then he lay his sword and armor at the foot of a statue of the Blessed Mother and kept the entire night in vigil. Soon after this dedication, Íñigo gave himself to

a year of intense spiritual training, living in a cave near the little town of Manresa. He prayed for hours on end; he fasted; he engaged in intense introspection, trying to uncover the roots of his sin; he let his fingernails and hair grow, in an attempt to counteract the vanity that had so marked him in his youth. He passed through periods of terrible spiritual dryness, and at times he doubted the truth of the faith. Many of the townspeople, spying this odd loner with the unkempt appearance, assumed he was mad. In time, he came to moderate his behavior and lessen the intensity of his spiritual practices, but the Manresa experience was absolutely crucial to Íñigo, providing the basis for the *Spiritual Exercises* that would eventually become the cornerstone of his interior life and the inspiration for the work of his order.

After going through what amounted to a monastic novitiate, what Íñigo wanted most was to journey to Christ's own country—the Holy Land. Living hand to mouth, sleeping in doorways, begging for food, he eventually found the means to go to Palestine, and there he made a pilgrimage to the holy sites. (By the way, Jesuit novices to this day imitate their master by enduring a similar intense experience of begging, relying on the goodness of others, and trusting in God's providence.) Failing to secure permission to stay, he resolved to serve the Church by becoming a priest, and to be a priest he knew he had to study theology. And so he made his way to what had been from the twelfth century the intellectual capital of the Christian world: Paris. Though he was nearly forty, he signed up for some elementary classes in Latin rhetoric and grammar. His classmates were young boys, over twenty years his junior. The once proud courtier humbly sat among them for instruction. And through careless handling of a small burse that he had been given, Íñigo found himself penniless and was compelled, once again, to beg. Despite these difficulties, he was able to finish his studies in language and eventually in philosophy and theology, becoming in 1534 a certified master.

But even more important than his studies were the friendships that Íñigo developed with a number of fellow students at the university, including Francis Xavier from Spain and Peter Faber from the Savoy region. These men, it's fair to say, fell under Íñigo's spell, and under his direction they followed the *Spiritual Exercises*. In August of 1534, the band of brothers ventured to Montmartre, which at the time stood outside of the walls of Paris. There, in the crypt of the chapel of St. Denis, they vowed to a life of poverty and chastity, and they swore to make a pilgrimage to the Holy Land. If they were unable to fulfill that last promise, they resolved to offer themselves in obedience to the pope, all "for the good of souls." The brothers themselves later recognized this as the beginning of the Society of Jesus.

Shortly thereafter, Ignatius (the more Latinized version of his name, which he now adopted) and his brothers sought the formal approval of the pope. A number of obstacles stood in their way. From the 1520s, when he was first developing and teaching his manner of prayer, Ignatius was under suspicion by the Inquisition. Keep in mind that this was the era of Luther and the Reformation, and there was a general fear of upstart groups, especially those who advocated new forms of spirituality. Ignatius was, in fact, once imprisoned for seventeen days while officials investigated his thought. Others objected to the name that the little group of unknowns had adopted: the Company of Jesus. Wasn't this just a tad arrogant? There were Benedictines and Dominicans and Franciscans, all named for their founders. Who were these men to claim that they uniquely were the company of Jesus himself? I find it fascinating that Ignatius won over a number of his detractors not only through careful presentation of his point of view but precisely by leading them through the *Spiritual Exercises*.

Ignatius was ordained to the priesthood in 1537, when he was forty-six years old. He waited for over a year before celebrating his first Mass, both because he felt he had to prepare himself for this crucial event in his life and also because he hoped to do so in the Holy Land. When this proved impossible, he settled for the great church of St. Mary Major in Rome, which had—and has to this day—what is believed to be a relic of the crib of Christ.

In 1540, Pope Paul III formally approved the Company or Society of Jesus. Paul was a fascinating and indeed pivotal figure in the history of the Church. At a time of supreme crisis, when Western Christianity was falling apart at the seams, Pope Paul made two decisions that helped to knit things back together: he called the Council of Trent and he established the Jesuit order. Trent addressed many of the doctrinal and institutional issues that were at the heart of the Reformation protest, and the Jesuits, loyal soldiers of the pope, became the boots on the ground that concretized the formulas of the council. Ignatius made radical obedience to the pope perhaps *the* mark of his new order. The obedience of a Jesuit vis-à-vis the Holy Father, he wrote, should be as unresisting "as an old man's walking stick, or as a cadaver."

Resigning himself permanently to the fact that he would never make it to the Holy Land, Ignatius finally settled in Rome and commenced to give direction to his fast-growing company. Within his lifetime, the Society of Jesus spread from Rome and Italy to Spain, Portugal, Japan, and the New World. Though he continued to be a man of intense prayer and mystical contemplation, he was also a hardheaded administrator with

a soldier's sense of purpose. We have over seven thousand letters, all personally signed, that he sent to Jesuits all over the world, giving direction and offering encouragement. During these years in Rome, Ignatius labored over the *Constitutions* of his new order, and this work is recognized today as not only a model of clearheaded organization but also of distinctively Ignatian spirituality.

What was he like personally? He stood only about five foot one inch tall, and he had a slender, ascetic build. He dressed very simply, usually in a threadbare black cassock. The flowing locks of his youth abandoned him relatively early, and in all the portraits we have of him he is mostly bald. His style was informal. He encouraged everyone to call him Íñigo, and he didn't mind being made fun of. One of his young Jesuit charges used to walk behind the master, imitating his limp, and they say that Ignatius played the part of the straight man admirably.

It is said that Ignatius was so devoted in his prayer that he could rarely get through the Daily Office or the Mass without copious tears. In this, he reminds us of Thomas Aquinas. In point of fact, he received a dispensation from the Office, since it was felt that his weeping was damaging his eyes! He had a number of vivid mystical experiences in the course of his life. During the Manresa period, by the River Cardoner, he felt a sense of union with God that overwhelmed him. In his own words: "[I] understood and learned many things, both spiritual matters and matters of faith . . . and this was with so great an enlightenment that everything seemed new to [me]."

While on his way to Rome in 1537, Ignatius stopped to pray at a small chapel called La Storta. While he was in contemplation, he experienced a vision of Christ and the Father. Speaking to his Son and indicating Ignatius, the Father said, "I want you to take this man for your servant." Then the Father said, "I shall be propitious to you in Rome." The experience powerfully confirmed that the focus of the new order should be in Rome rather than Jerusalem. One of his contemporaries reported that he saw Ignatius sitting one night on the roof of his residence in Rome, gazing up at the silent stars, tears running down his face; and another said that when he heard Ignatius counseling the poor and the wayward, it was "the closest he would get to hearing the tones and spirit of Jesus echoing in a human voice."

Ignatius died on July 31, 1556. The day before his death, he had asked his secretary to go to St. Peter's and bring back the pope's blessing. Not understanding how sick his master was, the man replied that he would get it the next day, given all the work that had to be done. When they realized the next morning that he was in his death throes, the secretary raced to St. Peter's, but he returned too late with the blessing. The master was already dead.

Why is the difficult work of the Exercises *important?*

First, think of all the difficult work we do in other areas of life: the psychological measures we take to recover our mental health through counseling and therapy, or the physical work people go through with diet and exercise. But the deeper point is that while we tend to think of the spiritual as one more segment of our life, it is in fact what is deepest and most enveloping. Our spiritual life, in this sense, includes the physical and psychological: it is their deepest ground. Spiritual clarity leads to clarity at other levels of life. If we desire greater psychological and physical health, we should begin by attending first to our spiritual health.

THE *SPIRITUAL EXERCISES*

Unlike, say, the *Summa theologiae* of Thomas Aquinas or *The Divine Comedy* of Dante, Ignatius' masterpiece, the *Spiritual Exercises,* is not meant so much to be read as to be *done.* It is not really a treatise or a work of theology, but rather a manual, designed to guide both those who are directing and those who are following Ignatius' program. It grew, as we saw, out of the intensity and concentration of Ignatius' Manresa experience, and thus it is a radical and deeply challenging document. At the same time, since Ignatius tinkered with the text throughout his life, it reflects a good deal of very practical wisdom and spiritual prudence. And since it has profoundly shaped the minds and hearts of five centuries of Jesuits, who in turn have had a decisive influence on education and culture throughout the world, it would be difficult to overestimate its importance.

The overall purpose of the *Exercises* is to prepare one to make a decision regarding one's vocation or fundamental path in life. Though this has primarily to do with the determination to marry or to pursue priesthood or the religious life, it might be expanded to include the choice of job or career or project. They are meant to be done in the course of an intense thirty days, though Ignatius allows for adaptations to shorter periods—for example, the eight-day retreat.

The *Exercises* are divided into four major sections or "weeks"—namely, "the consideration and contemplation of sins"; a meditation on the life of Christ up to and including Palm Sunday; a meditation on the Passion of the Lord; and finally, a contemplation of the Resurrection and Ascension of Jesus. But the weeks are introduced by what Ignatius calls "the First Principle and Foundation." It behooves us to pay close attention to this cornerstone of Ignatius' thinking: "Man is created to praise, reverence, and serve God our Lord, and by this means to save his soul." We notice something that has roots in the Bible and that is reiterated by every major figure in the spiritual tradition: at the heart of the matter is orthodoxy or right praise (*ortho*, "right," *doxa*, "praise"). Ignatius insists that the ordering principle of any healthy life is the worship of God.

Once that idea is clear, everything else falls into place: "We must make ourselves indifferent to all created things." "Indifference" here does not denote carelessness or lack of interest—it means detachment. Once I know that God alone is to be worshiped, then I know that nothing else is of final or permanent importance to me. And this is why I can say with Ignatius: "We should not prefer health to sickness, riches to poverty, honor to dishonor, a long life to a short life." Worshiping God alone, I can be indifferent to wealth, praise, longevity—even life itself. The rest of the *Exercises* is designed to fulfill the requirements of the principle and foundation. Ignatius wants to produce soldiers, willing and able to follow the divine command, whatever it may be.

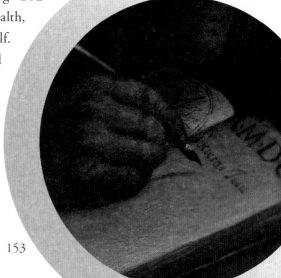

In the course of the first week, we will be compelled to come to terms both with the beauty of God's love and with those attachments of ours that prevent us from responding to that love. This opening move is particularly crucial in our time, when the instinct toward self-exoneration is so strong. The twelve-step programs, which are grounded in very healthy spiritual principles, require an addict to do a "searching moral inventory," to get to the bottom of his or her dysfunction. Ignatius is inviting us to do the same.

One feature of the first week that I should like to emphasize is what is known as the "consciousness examen." Though this sounds quite a bit like "the examination of conscience," Ignatius' practice is wider and deeper than a mere taking account of one's sins. It is a manner of calling explicitly to mind all of the ways in which God has been present to you throughout the day, all the ways in which he has offered his grace—and also the times when you resisted that grace, when your sin and attachments got the better of you. The overall attitude that ought to govern the examen is gratitude, not self-reproach. Nevertheless, when examining our sins, Ignatius urges us to be forthright and unflinching. He wants his retreatant to keep a careful notation of how many times he has succumbed to a particular sin throughout the day. In considering his day, he should review "one hour after another, one period after another. The thoughts should be examined first, then the words, and finally, the deeds." No easy letting-off-the-hook or self-exculpation here!

In the course of the first week, Ignatius asks his retreatant to engage in a series of meditations on sin: first the sin of the angels, then the sin of Adam and Eve, and finally the sin of an anonymous person who went to hell for committing just one mortal sin. He even invites us to see, smell, feel, and taste the horrors of hell. (Read the famous section of James Joyce's *Portrait of the Artist as a Young Man* to hear how an Irish Jesuit retreat master terrified the author with his particularly vivid commentary on this part of the *Exercises*!) Once again, for Ignatius, the purpose of all of this is not to depress the retreatant but rather to bring her to understand

and to feel the quality of sin, the texture of rebellion against God, the loss of friendship with the one who loves us.

After engaging in these intense spiritual practices, Ignatius urges the exercitant to engage in a colloquy with the crucified Jesus. Perhaps a word about this beautiful feature of the *Exercises* would be appropriate, for summonses to enter into such experiences abound throughout the text. A colloquy is a conversation between friends, but in the context of the *Exercises* this means between ourselves and our heavenly friends: the persons of the Trinity, the Blessed Mother, the saints, etc. We speak and we listen during a colloquy. In this first case, we acknowledge our sins before Jesus and express our deep sorrow that they contributed to his Crucifixion. We ask what we have done to Christ and what we now ought to do for him. Then we hear what the Lord has to say to us. For Ignatius says explicitly: "The colloquy is made by speaking exactly as one friend speaks to another."

Having come to terms with our sin, we are now ready for week two, which is an extended meditation on the life of Jesus, from the Annunciation and Nativity up to Palm Sunday. Having realized the problem, we are now meant to immerse ourselves in the solution.

The method is the "composition of place" and "application of the senses." What Ignatius means is that the retreatant should contemplate a scene from the life of Christ through a vivid imagining of the setting. Suppose we are considering the Annunciation to our Lady. How is the room arranged? Is Mary standing, sitting, kneeling? What does her garment look like? What is the tone of the angel's voice? Or suppose we are praying over the preaching of the Sermon on the Mount. Where is Jesus situated? Who is immediately around him? What is the quality of the light? What would we see if we were in the crowd? This practice is deeply incarnational in inspiration. It prevents prayer from becoming an exercise in mere abstraction, and it assures that the whole person—body, mind, senses, imagination, will—is involved in the communication with God. It constitutes one of the greatest gifts that Ignatius gave to the spiritual tradition.

One of the most memorable and powerful features of the second week is a contemplation inspired not directly by the Scriptures but by Ignatius' own military experience. It is called "A Meditation on Two Standards." Following his customary imaginative method, Ignatius invites the exercitant to see "a great plain, comprising the whole region about Jerusalem, where the sovereign Commander-in-Chief of all the good is Christ our

Lord; and another plain about the region of Babylon, where the chief of the enemy is Lucifer." We are to picture the devil on a fiery throne and in the process of summoning innumerable demons to send on mission to every corner of the world. We are to hear him giving them instruction as to how to seduce human beings with riches, honor, and pride. Then we are to picture Christ choosing "persons, apostles, disciples, etc., [sending] them throughout the whole world to spread His sacred doctrine." Then we overhear the speech of the Lord, recommending to all whom he summons to embrace the path of poverty, humility, and rejection. Finally, we are to have a colloquy with the Blessed Mother, asking for the grace to be received in Christ's great army and to do whatever the Lord commands us to do. Ignatius' point: we are involved, whether we know it or not, whether we like it or not, in a spiritual combat. What matters above all is to associate oneself with the right army and then to accept whatever role the Commander wants to give us.

In order to fight well in the right army, we have to be humble, and this is why Ignatius takes his followers through a meditation on the three degrees of humility. The first degree—requisite for salvation—is that one so subjects himself to the law of God that he would not commit a mortal sin, even if it meant he could become the Lord of all creation or save

Qui in electionis deliberatione versatur, præter naturam suam, diversorum quoque Statuum rationes, eorumque commoda juxta atque incommoda ad salutem finemque suum assequendum, debet habere explorata. Multos hominum ipsa pene natura atque ingenium rude determinat, & sine longa deliberatione ad certum statum, & per certa media, tanquam ad hoc solum natos, ded cit; ut sunt rustici, opifices, aliique, qui alias cogitationes nobilioris cujuspiam

his life on earth. As Jesus said, "What will it profit them to gain the whole world and forfeit their life?" (Mark 8:36). The second degree is greater, more intense. It is the path of indifference, total detachment from wealth or poverty, long life or short life, honor or dishonor. This is the availability of the dutiful soldier, ready to go in any direction the Lord might command. But there is a still greater type of humility: the third degree. This is the willingness to go beyond indifference and actively to choose to be poor with the poor Christ, to be accounted worthless and a fool with the despised Christ, to be insulted with the Christ mocked on the cross.

The meditation on the degrees of humility leads rather neatly into another dimension of Ignatius' spiritual method articulated in the *Exercises*—namely, the *agere contra* (to act against). Though hardly unique to Ignatius, the master mentions this principle often in his spiritual writings. The idea is simple: when the soul finds itself tempted toward one of the typical substitutes for God, it is best to run in the opposite direction. Thus, if one is drawn toward worldly honors, he should actively seek the lowest place; if he is lured by wealth, he should actively become poor; if he is filled with pride, he should actively walk the way of humility. Long ago, the philosopher Aristotle said that if a stick is bent in one direction, and you want to straighten it out, it is best to bend it back in the other direction. On Mt. Purgatory, Dante frequently has sinners doing the opposite of what they typically did in their lifetimes. Thus, the slothful are made to run, the gluttonous are starved, and the proud are made to carry great stones on their backs. This is the same idea that Ignatius develops under the rubric of the *agere contra*.

During week three of the *Exercises*, one contemplates the Passion and death of Jesus, and during week four, one focuses on the Resurrection of the Lord. As before, the imaginative method, the composition of place, and the employment of colloquies are central to the meditative process.

The entirety of the *Spiritual Exercises* is designed, as we saw, to bring a person to the point where she could utterly surrender to the will and purpose of God and be free from inordinate attachment to worldly goods. This is beautifully summed up in a prayer found near the very end of the *Exercises*, a prayer that has taken its name from its first word in Latin: *Suscipe* (take and receive): "Take, Lord, and receive all my liberty, my memory, my understanding, and my entire will, all I have and possess. Thou hast given all to me. To Thee, O Lord, I return it. All is Thine, dispose of it wholly according to Thy will. Give me Thy love and Thy grace, for this is sufficient for me."

As we learned from St. Thomas Aquinas, God is not a rival to us, not the enemy of our flourishing. Rather, the more we give to God, the more we receive. This idea informs the whole of Ignatius' prayer. Ignatius inherited from the Augustinian tradition the triplet of memory, understanding, and will; but what makes his prayer unique to him and distinctively modern is that he commences with liberty. We might say that for moderns, especially in the West, our freedom is what is most important to us, what we cling to most tenaciously. How wonderful that Ignatius makes of this most precious possession the first gift to the Lord. Here is the odd and deeply Christian paradox: only when I can give my liberty totally to Christ will I find real freedom.

MAIOR
GLO
QVICVNQ
IESV CHRI
TÆ NOMI
DERINT.
TEQVE SV
TI LVMBOS
TAM GRAN
BIT SOLVTION
MPTI ESSE E

160

WHY IS ST. IGNATIUS A PIVOTAL PLAYER?

At a crucial time in the history of the Church, when Western Christianity was coming apart, Ignatius established a religious order with the organization, zeal, and military discipline required to meet the challenge. The little band of brothers that he formed in the student dormitories of the University of Paris grew eventually into a religious family that has served the mission of the Church across the world for the past five centuries.

He was also a man who fell completely in love with Jesus Christ and endeavored, out of that love, to give himself totally. The *Spiritual Exercises* are conditioned, in every detail, by that intense friendship with Christ. And that document, originally designed to guide a handful of Ignatius' disciples, has set on fire the hearts of some of the greatest saints, missionaries, teachers, and writers in the history of the Church.

Ignatius is a Pivotal Player because he witnessed so radically to the *semper maior* principle; everything in him was devoted to giving God greater glory.

St. John Henry Newman

THE CONVERT

No serious student of Catholicism can ignore the massive and deeply influential figure of John Henry Newman. Newman has been characterized as perhaps the greatest Catholic theologian since Thomas Aquinas, and he was undoubtedly one of the most important theological influencers of the Second Vatican Council. His work represents the first and most notable attempt to place Catholic thought in dialogue with the Enlightenment. He was also one of the most elegant stylists in the English language. When James Joyce was told that he was the best ever writer of English, the great Irish novelist replied, "Nobody has ever written English prose that can be compared with that of a . . . prince of the only true church"—referring, of course, to Newman.

Newman was many things—controversialist, apologist, theologian, educator, poet—but through it all, he was a lover of the truth. At the close of his career, upon becoming a cardinal, he summed up his life's work this way: "For thirty, forty, fifty years I have resisted to the best of my powers the spirit of liberalism in religion"—by which he meant the view that religious statements are not matters of truth or falsity but only of subjective sentiment. Seeking the truth—especially the truth about God—was the principal passion of his life. And it remained so until his dying day, for he ordered that on his grave there should be inscribed the motto *Ex umbris et imaginibus in veritatem:* "From shadows and images into the truth."

John Henry Newman was born on February 21, 1801, in the heart of London. His father was a banker, and his mother was a descendant of French Huguenots. He came of age within the framework of Anglicanism, the national religion of England. At the age of fifteen, Newman underwent a sort of conversion experience that marked him for life. Through the influence of a preacher, he came to accept the basics of the Christian creed and to love Christian dogmas. Further, he felt in his bones that he had been justified, saved—destined for eternal life. In that same year of 1816, young Newman read a tract on Church history and was utterly captivated by the passages from Augustine and the other Church Fathers. This interest in the early Church would remain steady and deep throughout Newman's life.

In June of 1817, Newman enrolled at Oxford University, and it is scarcely possible to overestimate the role that Oxford played in Newman's life. It was the place of his greatest intellectual, personal, and spiritual formation. What Paris was for Thomas Aquinas, what Florence was for

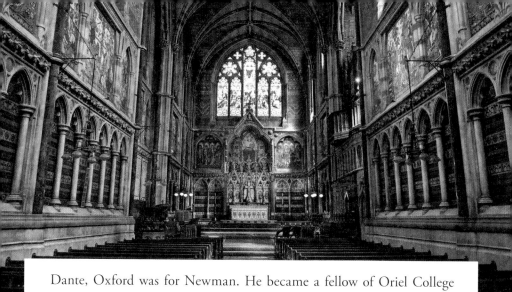

Dante, Oxford was for Newman. He became a fellow of Oriel College and fell under the influence of John Keble, the author of a book called *The Christian Year,* which presented a version of Anglicanism that was firmly rooted in the ancient Catholic tradition. What this meant more concretely was a rootedness in the sacramental view that "material phenomena are both the types and instruments of real things unseen."

In December of 1832, Newman set out with Richard Hurrell Froude, an Oxford friend, for a tour of southern Europe. While in Rome, they exulted in the various expressions of ancient Christianity that they found, but they were little charmed by Roman Catholicism, which they considered superstitious and unfaithful to the patristic consensus. Newman became increasingly convinced that his life's work would be to fight for a middle way between Protestantism and Catholicism.

Upon his return to England in early 1833, Newman banded together with a number of like-minded ecclesiastics and scholars and formed the so-called Oxford Movement. The various participants commenced to write essays or "tracts" on various aspects of Church life and theology. Hence the Oxford movement figures came to be called "tractarians." What precisely were they for? Newman laid it out in terms of three principles. First, the principle of dogma, which pitted the tractarians against all forms of liberalism—the view, as we saw, that dogma is but a derivative expression of feeling. Dogmas have intellectual substance, and they matter for the life of the Church.

Secondly, the tractarians believed in a visible Church with sacraments and rites, which are channels of invisible grace. This is the sacramental principle that Newman learned from Keble. Whereas the mainstream of Protestantism had internalized much of the spiritual life, the tractarians wanted to externalize and materialize it, in accord with an incarnational sensibility. The third principle, which Newman eventually repudiated, was the anti-Roman principle. Though they wanted to catholicize Anglicanism, the tractarians felt that Roman Catholicism had wandered from the Church of the Apostles and the Fathers. Newman went so far as to refer to the pope as "anti-Christ." Another principal complaint had to do with what they took to be an excessive devotion to Mary and the saints. In sum, he felt that Rome had substituted the authority of the Church for the authority of the Church Fathers.

In 1841, Newman composed what would prove to be his final tract, the infamous Tract 90. In this essay, he laid out his familiar *via media* position, but he also chose to focus on a particularly neuralgic point in British public life—namely, the holding of the 39 Articles. These were the basic statements of Anglican belief that had to be sworn to by anyone holding public office or a professorship at a major university. What Newman attempted to show in Tract 90 was that the articles could be given a "catholic" interpretation, according to his understanding of the term. Though the language of Tract 90 was fairly rarified and the intended audience more or less academic, the reaction was incendiary and widespread, for Newman had touched upon a cornerstone of the British establishment. He was condemned as a traitor "in every part of the country . . . through every organ and occasion of opinion, in newspapers, in periodicals, at meetings, in pulpits, at dinner-tables, in coffee-rooms, in railway carriages." In the wake of the Tract 90 controversy, Newman was compelled to resign his leadership of the Oxford Movement, and he entered into a period of intense study and prayer. He took up residence in the village of Littlemore, just outside of Oxford, living in a converted horse stable in great simplicity and under a quasi-monastic discipline. There he returned to the close reading of his beloved Church Fathers.

Why was Tract 90 so controversial?

While a modern reader might not see anything too controversial about Tract 90, in Newman's time, it was like a bomb going off. When Newman gave a very Catholic interpretation of the Articles, he was touching a sore point, since the great battles of Catholics and Protestants from the sixteenth century had left a lasting division in English society. This made Newman a controversial figure, which is something he did not enjoy. He was by nature a retiring figure, an academic, drawn to a life of reading and study. We don't always think of Newman as a model of courage, but we should. It took an enormous amount of courage for Newman to make this move. He was convinced that Catholicism was true and joined the Church even though it cost him greatly.

What he found took his breath away. As we have seen, Newman prided himself on staking out a *via media,* a middle way between Protestantism and Roman Catholicism. But when he examined the fierce arguments that raged in the fourth and fifth centuries concerning the identity of Christ, he found three positions, two extreme and one mediating. One extreme was heretical and so was the middle position, but the other extreme was orthodox—and that turned out to be the position of the Catholic Church up and down the centuries. He saw a devastating analogy between the ancient scenario and the present-day situation: Protestants seemed to be on the extreme left and Catholics on the extreme right, with Anglicanism taking up the middle position. Around this same time, Newman came across an article that cited an adage of the great St. Augustine: *Securus judicat orbis terrarum,* which roughly translates, "The whole world judges securely." This hit him like a thunderbolt. The adage implies that the entire Church, across space and time, best judges the truth of Christian doctrine. But the Anglican church was, by definition, the church of a particular country and culture. Moreover, antiquity (Newman's lodestar) was only one moment in the Church's history, not the whole of it.

Newman's conversion was not like Paul's; it was more like Augustine's—slow, meditative, unfolding over time. After much agonizing thought and prayer, Newman, on October 8, 1845, dramatically knelt before Fr. Dominic Barberi, a well-known Passionist priest, and asked to be received into the Catholic Church. After some hesitation, Newman decided to be ordained a Catholic priest and consequently made his way to Rome and seminary studies at the Propaganda Fide College. This period was a difficult and often awkward time for Newman—one of the greatest theological minds in Europe compelled to attend classes with seminarians.

It's fair to say that Newman was not overly impressed with the quality of the theological education he received in Rome. We must keep in mind that this was a fairly decadent period in the history of Catholic theology, scholasticism having ossified into something cramped, self-referential, and defensive.

While in Rome, Newman became acquainted with the Roman Oratory of St. Philip Neri. This was a community of secular priests living under a rule but not under vows. Newman was charmed by the urban setting of the oratories and by the intellectual discipline of the Oratorians—but most of all by the example of St. Philip Neri himself. After a good deal of prayer and thought, Newman joined the Oratorians and resolved to open an oratory in England upon his return. Newman was ordained to the Catholic priesthood on May 30, 1847, and then spent a few months in an Oratorian novitiate. He arrived in London on Christmas Eve of that same year and began the second half of his life. In 1849, Newman founded an oratory in the industrial city of Birmingham. His first major work as a Catholic was his *Lectures on the Present Position of Catholics in England,* a wonderful example of apologetic or "controversial" writing. Newman was a wicked satirist and polemicist, and nowhere are these gifts on fuller display than in these lectures.

In 1851, Newman was invited by Archbishop Paul Cullen of Armagh, the Primate of All Ireland, to become the rector of a new Catholic University the archbishop was forming in Dublin. In connection with his new position, Newman delivered, in Dublin, a series of lectures on the nature of university education. These were immediately and immensely popular and were later collected as a book, *The Idea of a University*—one of Newman's most important works. Unfortunately, Newman's administration of the Catholic University of Ireland was a somewhat rocky affair. From the beginning, he faced opposition from many of the bishops of Ireland, who were suspicious of him personally, but also suspicious of some of his novel ideas about university education. Deeply frustrated, Newman resigned the rectorship in 1858. It is fair to say that Newman's honeymoon as a Catholic was short lived. Most Anglicans, of course, viewed him as a traitor, and many English Catholics were suspicious of his work.

In March of 1859, Newman accepted the editorship of the *Rambler* magazine, a journal with a somewhat liberal reputation. He rode that horse for only a year, for a great controversy arose from an article that he penned for the *Rambler* called "On Consulting the Faithful in Matters of Doctrine." Conservative Catholics were unanimous in criticizing him. The years following his resignation from the editorship of the *Rambler* were, by all accounts, the worst of Newman's life. Of a somewhat depressive character by nature, Newman felt overwhelmed at this time by feelings of rejection and failure.

This period of depression and rejection ended in 1864 with the publication of Newman's spiritual autobiography called *Apologia Pro Vita Sua*. Prompted by sharp criticism from an Anglican controversialist named Charles Kingsley, Newman composed a beautifully written and compelling account of his conversion to Catholicism. People all over England lined up to read the chapters as they appeared in serial form. The *Apologia* made Newman once more a major figure in England, and he remained for the rest of his life in great demand as a speaker and writer. In 1879 Pope Leo XIII, who had succeeded Pius IX, named John Henry Newman a cardinal of the Catholic Church. This approbation was a triumph for Newman, whom Pope Leo characterized as *il mio Cardinale* (my Cardinal).

John Henry Cardinal Newman died on August 11, 1890, at the Birmingham Oratory. He was beatified by Pope Benedict XVI in September of 2010, and canonized by Pope Francis in October of 2019.

THE DEVELOPMENT
OF CHRISTIAN DOCTRINE

The first of Newman's major works that I would like to explore is his mid-career masterpiece, *An Essay on the Development of Christian Doctrine,* a work that he began when he was still an Anglican and finished as a Roman Catholic. The central argument is an anti-Protestant one. Luther and his disciples had claimed that much of Catholicism represented a deviation from or unwarranted addition to the biblical revelation. Hence a pruning was called for. Newman argued that these elements represented, not deviations from, but rather developments of the biblical revelation. Keep in mind that this text, written in the mid-nineteenth century, was

part of a general movement in thought called *Lebensphilosophie* (a philosophy of life), whose practitioners included Hegel and Darwin. Evolutionary theory was in the air.

Newman argues that doctrines, like living organisms, evolve over time, gradually revealing the fullness of their meaning. This is because any idea is, as he puts it, "commensurate with the sum total of its possible aspects." We can't know an idea fully until every dimension, face, and profile of that idea has disclosed itself, and that disclosure happens only over time. "There is no one aspect deep enough to exhaust the contents of a real idea." This process requires time, and it also requires the energy of a community of discourse. Ideas are mulled over, considered, compared and contrasted to other ideas, talked about, debated, tossed back and forth in lively argument—and in this way, they show forth their fullness. This development is not obscuring but clarifying.

Newman illustrates this point with a striking analogy: "It is indeed sometimes said that the stream is clearest near the spring. Whatever use may fairly be made of this image, it does not apply to the history of a philosophy or a belief, which on the contrary is more equable, and purer, and stronger, when its bed has become deep, and broad, and full." And only in light of this analogy can we properly grasp the meaning of one of Newman's most famous adages: "In a higher world it is otherwise, but here below to live is to change, and to be perfect is to have changed often." This is no celebration of change for its own sake or a call to permanent revolution; it is an affirmation that the development of doctrine that is on display in Catholicism is a sign of life and not of decadence.

One of the cleverest and most surprising moves that Newman makes in this text is to show that the affirmation of development, of the lively unfolding of doctrine, makes necessary the affirmation of an infallible authority within the Church. Ideas develop through the lively play of theologians, writers, critics, professors, etc. But developments can be accompanied by corruptions, which is plainly evident from the number of heresies that have sprung up throughout Church history. Therefore, in order to discipline, limit, and sanction the body of theologians, there needs to be an authority that stands above the fray and that can make a sort of umpiring judgment in regard to disputed questions. Newman's argument can be laid out in neat logical form: If revelation is part of the divine dispensation, and if the contents of revelation necessarily develop over time and space, then God must have desired that his Church be gifted with a living voice of authority.

Now, Protestants had held that the Bible itself played the role of infallible guide within the Church; but the sheer number of Protestant churches—each claiming the sure guidance of the Bible—gave the lie to that interpretation. Many Anglicans, including the young Newman himself, had held that the consensus of the Church Fathers played the umpiring role; but Newman came to realize that the Fathers' texts did not constitute a living voice that could actively determine truth and falsity in the here and now. The only Christian Church that claimed to have a *living* and infallible voice of authority, Newman conceded, was the Catholic Church, and this was one of the principal reasons that he crossed the Tiber. Keep in mind that he was writing this text precisely as he was making the move to Catholicism.

What makes this text so important for our time is the manner in which it brings together concerns of "liberals" and "conservatives." Newman nods strongly in the direction of a liberalism that insists on the legitimacy of change and development in the life of the Church, but at the same time, he nods strongly toward a conservatism that would insist on infallible authority. His peculiar genius was to have seen how the two are mutually implicative and not mutually exclusive.

What does it mean that doctrine develops?

Doctrine can be compared to a living thing like a tree. It begins as a seed, but a tree is actually a lot more interesting as it unfolds over decades and centuries into a richly complex thing. Additionally, a tree responds to its environment, assimilating to itself those things that deepen its life. We might also use the image of the river. You can jump over the source of the Mississippi, but think of the power and energy at the mouth of the river in New Orleans. All sorts of streams and tributaries come together, and the river is deepened and broadened. So, too, the doctrines of the Church have developed and deepened over time. Did St. Peter understand the doctrine of the Trinity better than Thomas Aquinas? Probably not. The Apostles were given the doctrine in seminal form, but it was only after many centuries, through the play of lively minds, that it developed into the richly complex doctrine of the Trinity.

THE IDEA OF A UNIVERSITY

We recall that this text is a compilation of nine lectures that Newman gave in Dublin in 1852 on the subject of university education. It constitutes one of Newman's best-loved works, and it is marked, through and through, by the master's incomparable prose style.

The central theme, addressed explicitly or implicitly throughout, is that theology properly finds a place within the circle of subjects in a university curriculum—that is to say, the study of the faith is truly an intellectual discipline. Another major concern of Newman's is to encourage Catholics to move out of an intellectual ghetto, to challenge them to engage the university world with greater confidence. Many in Newman's time held that religion, precisely as a private affair and a matter of feeling, had no place at a university. But Newman countered that such a subjectivization of religion is repugnant to the mainstream of the Christian tradition, which holds that religion speaks of an altogether objective reality who is the beginning and end of all things, who impinges on the whole of history, and who, as Creator, has to do with absolutely everything that exists. Therefore, a university, which by definition includes all disciplines, certainly ought to contain the discipline that speaks of God.

Given, in fact, the nature of its subject matter, religion ought to be not only in the circle of disciplines but at the center of it. In point of fact, the vacating of religion from the circle of university courses will lead inexorably to the supplanting of religion by some other discipline. This will take place because of a deep human instinct toward the philosophic, by which Newman means a passion for the whole, for a totalizing vision. And this will result in a skewing of every discipline. For example, if one of the physical sciences takes the central place, we will begin to see all reality through a scientific lens, which will distort or miss altogether huge swaths of reality. Similarly, if everything is read from the standpoint of economics—as it is, for instance, in all forms of Marxism—then the arts, philosophy, and culture are appreciated as but epiphenomena of an economic substructure. The permanent expulsion of religion from the university will result, Newman felt, in a constant succession of false pretenders to centrality and hence to a permanent destabilizing of the university.

In the fifth of his discourses, Newman defends the ancient Aristotelian idea that abstract knowledge is good in itself, even if it does not have a practical consequence. In the mid-nineteenth century, the view (now widespread indeed) that education should have, above all, a practical purpose was taking hold. Newman stood athwart this conception. He held that the highest kind of knowledge is useless—that is to say, pursued completely for its own sake as a good in itself. Philosophy, literature, the arts, etc., are "liberal" in the measure that they are free from utility—and this makes them specially sublime. He cites Aristotle in this context: "Of possessions, those rather are useful which bear fruit; those liberal which tend to enjoyment."

Newman wanted his audience to appreciate the beauty of a cultivated mind for its own sake and not to reduce it to another form of beauty, be it practical, political, moral, or even religious. The purpose of a university education was to produce a gentleman, a person with the philosophical frame of mind. Now, Newman knew perfectly well that the saint is something other than a gentleman. Whereas the gentleman tends to be balanced, equable, tolerant—or in Newman's terms, "like an easy chair or a good fire, which do their part in dispelling cold and fatigue"—the saint is typically edgy, extreme, impolitic. The Church's job is to make saints; the university's job is to make gentlemen.

THE GRAMMAR OF ASSENT

John Henry Newman's masterpiece was published in 1870, when he was sixty-nine years old. This book explored the theme dearest to Newman's heart, one that he had puzzled over all his life—namely, the relationship between faith and reason. More precisely, Newman wanted to know how we come to assent to religious propositions—what it is, precisely, that makes us say in regard to a religious doctrine, "This is true." What he came to see clearly—and the entire book really lays out this intuition—is that certitude, the obsession of most modern philosophers, was the wrong starting point. The right point of departure is *assent*, the psychological and intellectual act of accepting a proposition.

His first move is to distinguish between what he called "notional" assent and "real" assent. The first is the acquiescence we give to abstract propositions. By notional assent, we accept mathematical formulas and philosophical ideas. But by "real" assent, we come to accept concrete things, images, and impressions. So, for example, one might assent to the notion that slavery is a moral evil, but that conviction will float on the surface of one's intellectual life until he comes into vivid contact with the reality of slavery. In the American context, we might speak of the effect that *Uncle Tom's Cabin* had on the national psyche. In a similar way, the verses of Scripture, which one memorized as a child and to which one gave a sort of notional assent, take on enormous power as they are brought before the imagination as real objects. A basic contrast between the two types of assent is this: real assent affects action and behavior in a way that notional assent never can. Here is Newman: "Persons influence us, voices melt us, looks subdue us, deeds inflame us."

Now, in regard to religion, notional assent is given to the whole range of dogmas and doctrines, and Newman certainly held to the importance of this. But can real assent be given to God, who is essentially spiritual, immaterial, ethereal? The ground of real assent in matters of religion—and we come here to a central Newman theme—is conscience. Newman characterizes conscience in a vivid way: It is "a certain keen sensibility, pleasant or painful . . . attendant on certain of our actions which in consequence we call right or wrong." It is fascinating, he thinks, that we refer to conscience as a "voice," a word we would never use in connection with, say, an aesthetic sensibility. Somehow we know through conscience that we have pleased or offended a person by our actions, indeed a person powerful enough to see all of our acts and to press upon us unconditionally.

The section of the *Grammar of Assent* that is the most technical and the most influential is the one in which Newman takes on the thought of John Locke, the great English philosopher. Locke had said that the quality of one's assent ought to be in tight correlation to the quality of the inferential support that one can muster. In other words, if the inferential support is slight, the assent ought to be slight; if the argument is stronger, the assent ought to be stronger, etc. But Newman saw that, in point of fact, we often give total assent to propositions for which there is far less than clinching inferential support. In his famous example, no one hesitates even slightly in affirming that Great Britain is an island, though there is no absolute logical justification for that claim. Rather, the assent is based on a whole congeries of hunches, intuitions, testimonies, perceptions, and hints, none of which in themselves would constitute a "proof," but all of which, taken together, move the mind to assent. The upshot of all this is that assent, *pace* Locke, is not reducible to inference. That we live on a global planet covered with tracts of land and sea, that we had parents, that we cannot live without food, that one day we will die—none of it is known with apodictic certitude, but all of it is assented to without hesitation. We come to assent through an extremely subtle, indeed invisible, or largely unconscious, process of weighing converging probabilities. Newman invented a term for this feel, this intuition: *the illative sense.* Angels don't require an illative sense, but human beings do.

Why does all of this matter? If we are interested in bringing people to accept the truths of our religion—if we want, in a word, to evangelize—

then we have to use both formal and informal logic. We have to construct syllogisms, and we have to bear witness; we have to make arguments, and we have to stir up emotions; we have to appeal to both notional and real assent. There are lots of good arguments in support of the pro-life position, but sometimes real conversion comes more subtly through the illative sense. There is a scene in the movie *Juno* in which the main character is dissuaded from having an abortion, not because someone made a clever argument, but because a person observed to her, "Your baby has fingernails."

WHY IS ST. JOHN HENRY NEWMAN A PIVOTAL PLAYER?

At a time when modernity was posing a serious threat to Christianity, John Henry Newman did not shrink from the challenge. Rather, he went out to meet the modern objections with confidence, intelligence, and panache. His intellectual base was in the Fathers of the Church, but he understood Locke and Hume just as well. His thought represents a thrilling dialogue between the ancient faith and modernity.

At a time when subjectivism and sentimentalism—what he termed "liberalism"—were threatening classical Christianity from within, Newman responded with a bracing insistence on the objective integrity of the Church's dogmas.

And at a time when many felt that a self-respecting intellectual of the modern age could not believe in the biblical view of the world, Newman, by the witness of his life, proved this false.

G.K. Chesterton

THE EVANGELIST

Gilbert Keith Chesterton is one of the most sparkling and effervescent figures in the great Catholic tradition. A physically large man with an even larger intellect and imagination, he embodied the wealth and capaciousness of Catholicism. If one is ever tempted to see Catholic Christianity as something cramped, crabby, and puritanical, he should read even one paragraph of Chesterton. The distinctive mark of his style was a love for paradox, the crashing together of opposites that generates unexpected meaning and insight. He also delights in puns, plays on words, surprising reversals, etc. Reading Chesterton is a bit like opening a bottle of champagne: intoxicating, sparkling, and rare. Which words can best describe the Chestertonian take on the world? Joyful, playful, rambunctious, joking, realist, traditionalist, balanced, and sane. Chesterton felt that something had gone dreadfully wrong with the modern world and that classical Christianity would set it right.

At his death, Pope Pius XI sent a telegram to the archbishop of Westminster, in which he referred to Chesterton as a "devoted son" of the Church, and a "gifted Defender of the Catholic Faith." Chesterton remains the only Englishman besides Henry VIII to be called a *defensor fidei* (defender of the faith) by the pope. His writings, speeches, and radio addresses were recognized as powerful antidotes to the prevailing

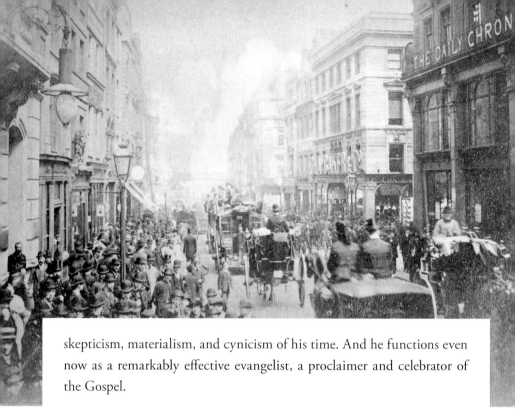

skepticism, materialism, and cynicism of his time. And he functions even now as a remarkably effective evangelist, a proclaimer and celebrator of the Gospel.

LIFE AND TIMES

Gilbert Keith Chesterton was born on May 29, 1874, in the Kensington neighborhood of London. His parents were comfortably middle class, and though they had their child baptized according to the formularies of the Church of England, their own convictions were Unitarian and progressive.

Gilbert was very close to his younger brother, Cecil. Upon his brother's birth, Gilbert remarked: "Now I shall always have an audience!" Once Cecil managed to speak, the two of them argued incessantly but good-naturedly, once sustaining an argument for eighteen hours straight. One of his earliest memories is of a toy theater that his father had assembled. It awakened in him a lifelong interest in theater and drama—and in what we might call serious play.

In his early school days, Chesterton was gawky and tall, and not very gifted at sports. He hid his passion for poetry behind a bland façade, hoping not to be noticed. Looking back on his youth, the chief impression he made on his teachers was, in his words, that "I was asleep." His gifts seemed to lie in the artistic direction and so, upon graduation, he did not proceed, as did most of his colleagues, to Oxford or Cambridge, but rather to the Slade School of Art, which was a constituent part of University College, London. All his life long, Chesterton loved to draw, usually in a playful or comic style. At the Slade School, he studied art formally but, it must be said, in a rather desultory way. He attended other lectures at the university, but never achieved a degree.

The dominant philosophical attitude at the university was, in Chesterton's words, "very negative and even nihilistic." This attitude threw a shadow over his mind and convinced him that the worthiest ideas were on the defensive. But in time, the young Chesterton became weary of this nihilism and, with the help of writers such as Browning and Stevenson and especially Walt Whitman, came to see existence itself as something wonderful, something for which we should be grateful—and gratitude for existence implied gratitude to someone. At the invitation of one of his Slade School classmates, Chesterton agreed to write some book reviews for a literary journal, and he thereby discovered his true calling. He was a remarkably perceptive reader and an even more remarkably expressive writer. He began to compose pieces for a number of journals and eventually for the *Daily News,* writing on Dickens, Blake, Browning, and many other personalities and topics.

By the turn of the twentieth century, Chesterton was becoming a well-known figure in London literary circles. He was noticed not only for his literary gifts but for his distinctive look and personality. He was a tall man, around six foot two inches, and though he had been slender in his youth, he had, by his late twenties, put on considerable weight. Once he was asked his height and weight. "Six foot two," he responded, "though my weight has never been successfully calculated." His large head was topped with an unruly mop of curly hair, and he typically wore large coats, capes, and floppy hats.

He was famously absent-minded, once stopping in the middle of a busy London street to consider an argument, while buses, trucks, and cars whirled around him and drivers shouted their dissatisfaction. Another time, he was arguing with a woman, who, apparently finding the discussion tiresome, fell sound asleep. Chesterton carried on, asking and answering his own questions! He was constantly getting lost, forgetting appointments, and riding trains to the wrong stations. Once he wired his wife, "Am at Market Harborough. Where ought I to be?"

One of his famous aphorisms, of course, is that absent-mindedness does not really mean absence of mind, but rather presence of mind elsewhere.

What Chesterton's mind was on, increasingly, were religious questions, for he discovered that the classical claims of Christianity corresponded remarkably to the truths of experience, that indeed the very paradoxes inherent in the Christian creedal system corresponded to the paradoxes of life. This kind of thinking led to the writing of the great masterpiece of apologetics known as *Orthodoxy*. This book appeared in 1908, the same year as Chesterton's best novel, a wild romp called *The Man Who Was Thursday,* the story of a band of anarchists actually made up entirely of undercover agents.

One of Chesterton's great friendships—and he was a man of friendship—was with the Irish dramatist and controversialist George Bernard Shaw. The two men could not have been more unalike in appearance and outlook: Chesterton was enormous and Shaw was thin as a rail; Chesterton loved to drink, while Shaw was a teetotaler; Chesterton was a devoutly orthodox Christian and Shaw was an atheist. Yet they bonded very deeply indeed. Across several decades, they argued both privately and publicly about everything, but their arguments ended with both men feeling enlivened. In one of their great exchanges, Chesterton reportedly said to Shaw, "To look at you, anyone would think that famine had struck England." Shaw responded: "And to look at you, Chesterton, anyone would think that you have caused it."

One of Chesterton's most delightful and enduring contributions to the literature of the twentieth century were the Father Brown mysteries. All his life long, Chesterton loved detective stories, and in 1910 he was inspired to compose a tale about a

mastermind detective—a near-sighted and mild-mannered priest who managed to solve crimes because of his remarkable insight into human depravity, derived from years of hearing confessions. There is, as many have observed, a good deal of Chesterton himself in Father Brown, most notably a love for simple and ordinary things—in fact, those things most often overlooked because of their insignificance (a useful trait in a detective). Chesterton wrote Father Brown stories until 1935, just a year before his death, and they have proved to be the most widely read of his books.

Chesterton made a trip to the United States in 1921. He was a barnstorming lecturer, barreling his way across the country from New York to Chicago, Philadelphia, Baltimore, Albany, Buffalo, Cleveland, Oklahoma City, and St. Louis. He was by all accounts a delightful speaker, though people said they were surprised by the somewhat high and piping voice that came out of such a lumbering body.

In 1922, after many years of thought and anguish, Chesterton became a Roman Catholic. When asked to explain his conversion, he said, "There are ten thousand reasons, all amounting to one reason: that Catholicism is true." Over and against the relativism and subjectivism of the time, "it is the only thing that talks as if it were the truth; as if it were a real messenger, refusing to tamper with a real message." Chesterton felt that there was something capacious, roomy, and expansive about Catholicism. It didn't take one idea and turn it into a monomania. "The Church is not a movement, but a meeting-place, the trysting-place of all the truths in the world."

In 1930, he undertook another lengthy lecture tour of the United States, covering in the course of many months more than twenty-five cities. The initial prompt for this visit was an invitation from the University of Notre Dame in South Bend, Indiana, then best known for its prodigious football team. The fathers of the university asked Chesterton to make a substantial commitment, functioning essentially as a visiting professor. Chesterton agreed to give thirty-six lectures on Victorian history and literature. Upon his arrival to the campus, Chesterton was taken to the football stadium to assist at its dedication. After speeches by the university's president and by Knute Rockne himself, Chesterton was introduced to the crowd, who gave him a standing ovation and commenced rhythmically to chant his name. The great author stayed with a local family and made his way by car each night of the week for his lecture. His exiting from the automobile—a lengthy and dramatic affair—was witnessed by scores of students, who applauded his successful extraction as they might the successful launch of a battleship!

At the height of his literary powers, Chesterton produced three truly great books: *St. Francis of Assisi, St. Thomas Aquinas,* and *The Everlasting Man.* He also continued to write his weekly column for the *Illustrated London News* and to edit a journal called *G.K.'s Weekly.* In the pages of this journal, he developed an economic theory in line with Catholic social doctrine. He called it "distributism," identifying it as a *tertium quid* (third way) beyond both capitalism and socialism. Critics have said that distributism was never carefully defined in Chesterton's writings. We might, however, distill some key features of the program. Distributists weren't against private property, but they wanted to see it dispersed and shared as widely as possible. In a word, they were against concentrations of money, power, and property in the hands of a few. This was in line with Catholic social teaching and out of step with both a socialism that would concentrate power in the state and a capitalism that would concentrate it in the hands of major corporations and economic institutions. One of the marks of distributists was an affection for the small, the local, the homemade. Think here of J.R.R. Tolkien's hobbits, living in their own homes, working with tools that they have made, producing goods and services for their own "shire." Think, too, of the destruction of nature wrought by Saruman in *The Lord of the Rings,* and you have some idea of what distributists thought about modern industrial capitalism.

Chesterton became quite ill in the spring of 1936, suffering probably from congestive heart failure. On June 13, his friend, the famous Dominican preacher Fr. Vincent McNabb, came to see him. After singing the *Salve Regina* over him, McNabb picked up Chesterton's pen, which was lying on the bed stand next to him, and kissed it. The next day, G.K. Chesterton died.

One of Chesterton's greatest books, and a master-piece of Christian apologetics, was published in 1908, when its author was only thirty-four. Though he was still fourteen years away from his formal conversion to Catholicism, *Orthodoxy* is filled with the Catholic spirit. He begins with a parable of an English yachtsman who lost his way and "discovered" England, thinking it was a South Sea island. To find the familiar as something strange—to rediscover Christianity as startling and new—is at the heart of his project in *Orthodoxy*.

Because people were increasingly uncomfortable with the idea of sin, Chesterton chose to begin by talking about sanity. Contrary to the common perception, he said, a madman is not someone who has lost his reason, but rather someone who has lost everything *but* his reason! He is characterizing as unhealthy any ideology that locks us into a narrow and all-explaining system. He was thinking especially of the materialism that was gaining strength at the turn of the twentieth century, the view that matter is all that there is. The problem, of course, is that the principle itself cannot be determined through empirical observation and so undermines itself. Moreover, it is a reductionism that leaves aside so much of life: beauty, morality, love, art, religion. Materialists claim to be infinitely reasonable, but that makes them, Chesterton said, like the coin that is "infinitely circular," turned in upon itself and turning around and around one dull idea. Chesterton wants to crack open the heads of materialists in order to let in some light and fresh air!

Another mark of his time—and of ours—is a suspicion of tradition. Much of modern politics and philosophy were predicated on a rejection of what came before. This cult of novelty amounted, Chesterton felt, to a denial of democracy, for it refused to listen to the voices of the dead. "All democrats object to men being disqualified by the accident of birth; tradition objects to their being disqualified by the accident of death." Tradition, he famously concluded, is the "democracy of the dead."

One of the most compelling of the chapters in *Orthodoxy* is called "The Ethics of Elfland." Here he turned David Hume, one of the most notorious of skeptics, on his head. Hume had said that there is no real logical ground for believing in causality, for all we can see is succession, not causal connection. Chesterton took this as true, but saw it as permission to throw off an oppressive determinism. Though it is necessary that 2 + 3 is equal to 5, it is by no means necessary that the sun come up every morning or that trees bear fruit. That these things happen is, in fact, always a delight and a surprise. One might suppose that a thing repeats itself because it is just a mechanical bit of clockwork. "Now, to put the matter in a popular phrase," Chesterton said, "it might be true that the sun rises regularly because he never gets tired of rising. His routine might be due, not to a lifelessness, but to a rush of life. . . . A child kicks his legs rhythmically through excess, not absence, of life." Staying with the analogy of the child—a favorite of his—Chesterton observes that just as a child delights in monotony, saying, "Do it again!" so God might say every morning to the sun "Do it again!" and every evening to the moon "Do it again!" The regularities of nature are not deterministic recurrence, but "a theatrical *encore*." And if it is permitted to view the world as magical, then it should be permitted to suppose there is a magician behind it. Or, to change the metaphor, if the world is like a story, we must suppose there is a storyteller responsible for it.

And this helps to explain, Chesterton felt, the complexity of the Church's creeds (something much mocked by moderns). The Christian creed is not a simple and streamlined affair—like the laws of nature—but is rather misshapen and odd, emphasizing one extreme and then another. It is not like a stick that might fit any hole by accident; it is more like a key, uniquely shaped to fit only one lock. When he was a young man, Chesterton tells us, he learned that Christianity was in possession of the worst vices. But the odd thing was that it seemed to have mutually exclusive vices. For example, many critics indicated that Christianity was hopelessly pessimistic, emphasizing a contempt for this world and the mortification of the flesh. But other critics said that it was wildly and irresponsibly optimistic, promising ultimate salvation and fulfillment. "Christianity could not at once be the black mask on a white world and also the white mask on a black world." Similarly, some critics claimed that Christianity was "timid, monkish, and unmanly," citing the craven imperatives of the Sermon on the Mount. (Think here of Nietzsche's exceptionally harsh characterization.) On the other hand, many critics, with the Crusades in mind, attacked Christianity for its bloodthirstiness and tendency toward warfare. Chesterton observed: "A thing might have these two opposite vices; but it must be a rather queer thing if it did." Or again, some critics maintained that Christianity was too monkish and austere, characterized by "naked and hungry habits." And other critics held, with equal vigor, that Christianity was too worldly, what with its pomp and ritual and ostentation. What began to occur to Chesterton was that of all the institutions in the world, Christianity must be the most depraved, the most purely evil. But then an odd alternative came to mind: perhaps Christianity was not so much oddly shaped as perfectly shaped, and perhaps those whose vision is distorted in various ways see it as, alternatively, too this and too that, just as various people might see one and the same man as too fat or too thin, too dark or too fair. "Perhaps (in short) this extraordinary thing is really the ordinary thing; at least the normal thing, the center. Perhaps, after all, it is Christianity that is sane and all its critics that are mad—in various ways."

It is exceptionally important to make, at this point, a clarification. It might seem that Chesterton is defending the view that Christianity represents the bland reconciliation of opposing points of view, the moderate middle ground between extremes. Nothing could be further from the truth. What he noticed was that there was nothing particularly moderate about Christian heroes. No one would ever accuse Thomas Aquinas of being moderately intellectual or Joan of Arc of being moderately militaristic or St. Antony of the Desert of being mildly committed to the ascetical life! Christianity is not a compromise, but rather a radical and confident putting together of mutually exclusive extremes, one wild excess balancing the other. And Chesterton felt that he had found the ground for this fact at the heart of the Christian creed, where it is boldly affirmed that Jesus Christ is not a demi-god, not half-human and half-divine, not a compromise between divinity and humanity, but fully human and fully divine. Paganism declared that virtue is found on the middle ground, but Christianity declared that it was found in a kind of conflict. Thus the symbol of the cross is especially illuminating, for it represents a collision of opposing forces.

A good example of this principle is the play between affirmation and negation in regard to human beings themselves. No philosophy or ideology has ever thought more highly of human beings than Christianity, which holds out deification as their proper end. And no philosophy or ideology has ever been more critical of the human project, for none of them can take account of how far we fall short of what we are meant to be. And thus, "St. Francis, in praising all good, could be a more shouting optimist than Walt Whitman," and "St. Jerome, in denouncing all evil, could paint the world blacker than Schopenhauer." In a similar vein, Chesterton notices the paradoxical ecclesial attitude toward marriage and children: "It is true that the historic Church has at once emphasized celibacy and emphasized the family; has at once (if one may put it so) been fiercely for having children and fiercely for not having children."

In sum, the Church has kept opposites "side by side like two strong colors red and white. . . . It has always had a healthy hatred of pink." As a final example, he gives us St. Thomas Becket, who "wore a hair shirt under his gold and crimson, and there is much to be said for the combination; for Becket got the benefit of the hair shirt, while the people in the street got the benefit of the crimson and gold."

THE EVERLASTING MAN

This text, published in 1925, three years after Chesterton's conversion to Rome, is his masterpiece. It is the richest expression of the themes closest to Chesterton's heart. It can legitimately be construed as an answer to H.G. Wells' best-selling *The Outline of History,* which had appeared in 1920. Wells' argument was that man had gradually evolved from his primitive state to his exalted modern and civilized form. In the process of his evolution, the human being had learned to slough off religion and embrace modern progress. This fully developed human being would now be in a position to bring peace and prosperity to the world. That such an argument could be made in the immediate wake of World War I struck Chesterton as beyond absurd.

The book has two major sections, the first dealing with the strangeness of man and the second with the even greater strangeness of the man called Christ. His target in the first section is the evolutionist who

sees the human being as simply a highly developed animal. Chesterton draws our attention to the mysterious and beautiful prehistoric paintings discovered in caves in the south of France. These are the only real evidence we have, he says, of what "cave men" were like. It shows that human beings did something that no other animal could do—namely, produce works of art: "The higher animals did not draw better and better portraits. . . . The wild horse was not an Impressionist and the race horse a Post-Impressionist." What the cave paintings reveal is that humans differ from other animals in kind and not merely in degree. Precisely as an artist, a creator, the human can mirror all other things, in some sense containing them all, and in this he is like God, the Creator of all. Here Chesterton is driving at something close to Newman's heart—namely, that the human being has a *capax Dei,* a capacity for God. He is ordered to union with his Creator; or, in biblical language, he is made in the image and likeness of God. And this is precisely what suits him to be open to the Incarnation— God becoming one of us.

And that Incarnation is the topic of the second major section of *The Everlasting Man,* called "The God in the Cave." If his conversation partner in the first section was the evolutionist, his interlocutor in this section is the comparative religionist, the one who tends to see Christianity simply as one religion among many and Christ as one religious founder among many.

Christianity begins, in a sense, with a sublime jest. The infinite and all-powerful God becomes a child born in a cave dug in the earth: "The hands that had made the sun and stars were too small to reach the huge heads of the cattle. Upon this paradox, we might almost say upon this jest, all the literature of our faith is founded." No other religion makes a claim anywhere near as radical and strange and wonderful as that. And whether we believe it or not, the very idea of the Incarnation has changed us.

When we turn to the figure of Christ presented by the Gospels, we find something unique and startling as well. Though the comparative religionist might suggest that the kind and simple moralist had been turned by centuries of dogma into a fearsome and inhuman character, precisely the reverse is in fact the case. Chesterton argues that the Christ presented in most churches is "almost entirely mild and merciful," whereas the real Jesus, on display in the Gospels, is fierce, often angry, given to puzzling and impenetrable sayings, and engaging in acts that confound us. Consider the sayings about nonresistance to evil, which are "rather too pacific for any pacifist." On the other hand, there is nothing that sheds any particular light on Christ's attitude toward organized warfare "except that he seems to have been rather fond of Roman soldiers." The statement that the meek would inherit the earth is anything but a meek statement. His conclusion is that the morality we are dealing with in the Gospel is not that of this or any other age, and certainly not like any of the ethical systems of the great philosophers or religious founders—though "it might be of another world." Chesterton suggests that, in every Catholic church, right next to the statue of the mild Christ, there should be a statue of the ferocious Christ, in full flight of anger!

The comparative religionist typically says that Jesus is like Mohammed or the Buddha, or Zoroaster or Confucius—but none of these figures ever came close to claiming about himself what Jesus did. Normally, we associate greatness with modesty: the greater the man, the humbler the claims he makes about his own person; concomitantly, the crazier or stupider the man, the more extravagant claims he tends to make for himself. "Nobody can imagine Aristotle claiming to be the father of gods and men, come down from the sky; though we might imagine some insane Roman Emperor like Caligula claiming it for him, or more probably for himself." The odd thing about Jesus is that he does indeed say the most extraordinary things about himself—"a strolling carpenter's apprentice [who] said calmly and almost carelessly, like one looking over his shoulder: 'Before Abraham was, I am.'" And, "whoever comes to me and does not hate father and mother, wife and children, brothers and sisters, yes, and even life itself, cannot be my disciple" (Luke 14:26). The Muslims have a saying, admirable in its clarity, that "God is God, and a great man knows he is not God, and the greater he is the better he knows it." But then there is Jesus, who is quite obviously great, and quite obviously sane, and who nevertheless speaks and acts in the person of God. To come to terms with this paradox is to begin to grasp the nettle of Christianity.

What is Chesterton's legacy?

Along with Newman, Chesterton gave an articulate defense of Christianity particularly at a time when it was under attack by the advocates of the Enlightenment. In this environment, Chesterton emerges with great joy and great clarity, precisely in opposition to these criticisms. This makes him very much an evangelist for our time, which is why he had such a lasting impact on individuals like C.S. Lewis, Fulton J. Sheen, and so many others evangelists of the modern world.

WHY IS G.K. CHESTERTON
A PIVOTAL PLAYER?

Christianity has long been haunted by the Gnostic or dualist temptation. This is the tendency to think of Christianity as something joyless, disembodied, and purely austere. By the sheer exuberance of his life and writing, G.K. Chesterton gives the lie to this sort of puritanism. He hearkens back to Irenaeus: "The glory of the God is a human being fully alive."

Another ancient and persistent danger to the Christian faith is a relativism that would turn Jesus into one inspiring religious founder among many. Like Athanasius, Newman, C.S. Lewis, and many others up and down the centuries, Chesterton insisted on the strangeness and distinctiveness of Jesus. In his own utterly unique voice, he sang the uniqueness of Christ.

Fulton J. Sheen

THE COMMUNICATOR

In the English-speaking Catholic world, in the mid-twentieth century, an extraordinary intellectual, literary, and spiritual revival took place. One thinks, for instance, of figures such as the novelists Evelyn Waugh, Flannery O'Connor, and Graham Greene, the social activist Dorothy Day, and the Trappist writer Thomas Merton. But by far the best known, and arguably most influential, of these mid-century players was a Catholic prelate, professor, writer, evangelist, and television personality named Fulton J. Sheen.

At the height of his fame, Sheen's radio program, *The Catholic Hour*, had an audience of four million, and his television show *Life Is Worth Living* was viewed by an estimated thirty million people every Tuesday night. A brilliant and classically trained Catholic academic, Sheen was also a mesmerizing public speaker, endowed with extraordinary oratorical gifts, a charming sense of humor, and a magnetic personal presence. When one watches video of Sheen today, one is especially struck by his eyes, which seem to gaze into the soul. Billy Graham himself referred to Sheen as, quite simply, "the great communicator."

What makes him more than merely a fine preacher of the Gospel was his willingness to embrace, with enthusiasm, the means of communication made possible by the technological advances of the modern age.

When many argued that the Christian message would be distorted, oversimplified, or compromised through the use of such methods, Sheen forged ahead, appreciating radio and television as the twentieth-century version of the parchment and ink and Roman roads that St. Paul had used to propagate the Gospel in his time.

LIFE AND TIMES

Fulton John Sheen was born on May 8, 1895, in the little town of El Paso, Illinois, located about thirty miles east of Peoria. His father and mother owned a hardware store in town, but just a few years after Fulton's birth, they moved to a farm. Young Fulton showed an extreme distaste for anything associated with farm work, much preferring books and the liturgy of the Catholic Church.

In his autobiography, *Treasure in Clay*, Sheen relates a story of his days as an altar server at the cathedral church in Peoria. At the age of eight, he found himself serving the morning Mass of the venerable Bishop John Spalding, himself a major player in the American Church of that time. In his nervousness, the young Sheen managed to drop a glass cruet to the marble floor in the presence of the bishop. Mortified, he was afraid even to look at Spalding when the Mass had ended. To his infinite surprise, the bishop put his arms around him and said, with rather unnerving precision, "Tell your mother that I said when you get big you are to go to Louvain [the site of a great Catholic University in Belgium], and someday you will be just as I am." Both predictions proved prophetic.

Sheen attended St. Viator's College in Bourbonnais, Illinois, and then was sent to St. Paul's Seminary in St. Paul, Minnesota, for his priestly preparation. On September 20, 1919, he was ordained to the priesthood in the Peoria Cathedral and was immediately dispatched to study for a doctorate in philosophy at the Catholic University of America in Washington, DC. Upon completion of his work at Catholic University, Sheen still didn't feel adequately prepared to meet the intellectual challenges of his time. Accordingly, he asked to be sent for advanced studies at the Catholic University of Louvain. "I should like to know two things," he explained to one of his professors. "First, what the modern world is thinking about; second, how to answer the errors of modern philosophy in the light of the philosophy of St. Thomas." This simultaneous interest in both the contemporary mind and the mind of Catholicism's greatest intellectual would characterize Sheen for the rest of his life. He proudly confessed to having read every word that Aquinas ever wrote. In 1925 he received, with highest possible honors, the prestigious *agrégé* degree from Louvain. His doctoral thesis bore the title *The Spirit of Contemporary Philosophy and the Finite God*, and this was later adapted as Sheen's first book, which boasted an introduction from G.K. Chesterton himself.

After a brief stint in parish ministry in the Peoria diocese, Sheen was given formal permission to undertake the academic career for which he had been prepared. He accepted an invitation from his alma mater, the Catholic University of America in Washington, DC, and commenced a nearly twenty-five-year career as professor of philosophy, theology, and apologetics.

Sheen said that, throughout his years as a professor, he relied on the advice given him by the great Cardinal Mercier—namely, that he should always keep up with the poetry, literature, architecture, art, and theater of the contemporary society, and that he should tear up his lecture notes at the end of every academic year, so as not to repeat himself. In fact, Sheen felt it was anomalous that football coaches don't have tenure but professors do. If even a great coach's work becomes inadequate, he loses his job, but if a tenured professor's work becomes tired and unproductive, he teaches on. He wondered what this said about our priorities.

In 1930, Fulton Sheen was invited by the bishops of the United States to be the host of a nationally broadcast radio program called *The Catholic Hour*. He proved to be an immediate hit, successfully competing against some of the most popular radio shows of the time. The characteristic Sheen style—intelligence, wit, awareness of the secular culture, a striking gift for analogies and apt illustrations—was on full display. The professor had found an audience far beyond the classroom. Sheen's outreach would become even wider when, in 1950, he was invited by the bishops of the United States to become director of the Society of the Propagation of the Faith, charged with raising funds for and encouraging the work of the foreign missions. The following year, Sheen was raised to the dignity of the episcopacy, becoming Auxiliary Bishop of the Archdiocese of New York, a position he would hold until 1966.

That same fateful year, Sheen was approached by representatives of commercial television and offered the opportunity to present a program in prime time. Many commentators, including some key figures in the Church, thought this was folly. How could a Catholic bishop compete against Milton Berle, Frank Sinatra, and Jackie Gleason, three of the most popular entertainers of the era? But not only did Sheen compete against them;

he beat them at their own game, becoming in short order one of the most successful personalities on television. His format could not have been simpler. He came out on stage in the formal dress of a Catholic bishop, including cassock, zucchetto, and cape. Using no notes whatsoever, he lectured for twenty-five minutes, occasionally writing some words or making a simple illustration on a blackboard. The entire country, by the way, learned that the initials JMJ, which Sheen invariably scrawled across the top of the board, stood for Jesus, Mary, and Joseph.

What appeared to be effortless, almost "off the cuff" speech was in fact painstakingly prepared. Sheen would write out the lecture in long-hand and then more or less commit it to memory. He would subsequently rehearse the speech in both French and Italian, just to make sure that the ideas were firmly in place. Professional orators wondered at his ease of communication and the high quality of his rhetoric, and professional comedians were amazed at his comic timing. He said that he typically spent thirty hours preparing for every telecast. Once, toward the end of his life, when asked how long he had worked on a sermon, Sheen replied, "Forty years." One of the great lessons we learn from Fulton Sheen is that the most effective popular communication of the faith is grounded in an extraordinary amount of research, thought, and culture.

Whereas on *The Catholic Hour* Sheen engaged in relatively straight-forward Catholic apologetics, taking on such issues as the divinity of Christ, the authority of the pope, and the efficacy of the sacraments, on the television program he used a more indirect approach. He generally commenced with a topic that a person of any religion or no religion might find intriguing—communism, art, science, humor, aviation, etc.—and then he would show connections between these themes and some basic truth of Christianity. And he certainly managed thereby to strike a chord, for his show appealed massively to Catholics and non-Catholics alike.

At the height of the program's popularity, Sheen was receiving, on average, twenty thousand letters a day, from all corners of American society. Both *Time* and *Life* magazines did lengthy features on him, and in 1952 he won an Emmy Award as Most Outstanding Television Personality. At the ceremony, he memorably thanked his writers: "Matthew, Mark, Luke, and John."

In his capacity both as head of the Society for the Propagation of the Faith and as evangelist extraordinaire, Sheen made numerous journeys across the country and around the world. In 1948, in the company of Cardinal Spellman of New York, Sheen toured Southeast Asia and Oceania. In Sydney, Australia, he addressed forty thousand people, and in Melbourne, one hundred thousand. He also spoke to throngs in Singapore, Hong Kong, Java, and Tokyo. On a missionary tour of Africa, he found himself in the little town of Buluba, Uganda, where the Catholic Church sponsored a leper colony. Sheen had brought a number of small silver crosses to give to the patients, and when the first sufferer presented his disfigured and diseased hand, the bishop pulled back and dropped the cross into the mangled palm. Ashamed of himself, Sheen resolved to press each gift in the hands of the remaining patients. Whenever he traveled to Europe, he always took the time to visit Lourdes, the lovely town in the Pyrenees where the Blessed Mother appeared to St. Bernadette. Sheen cultivated his whole life long a deep devotion to Mary, referring to her in his autobiography as "the woman I love."

Throughout his public life, Sheen was well known as a convert-maker. He had a number of famous converts, including the composer Fritz Kreisler, the journalist Heywood Broun, and Louis Budenz, the editor of the Communist *Daily Worker*. But the best-known person that he brought into the faith was the writer, congresswoman, and ambassador Claire Boothe Luce. After the death of her daughter in a tragic auto accident, Luce had fallen into a sullen antipathy to religion. Sheen asked for five minutes to speak to her of God. When he mentioned God's goodness, Luce got right in his face and shouted, "If God is good, why did he take my daughter?" Undaunted, Sheen responded, "In order that through that sorrow, you might be here now starting instructions to know Christ and his Church." That was the beginning of the process that led eventually to her enthusiastic embrace of the Catholic faith.

Fulton Sheen was a revered retreat director, especially for priests. He closed every one of these spiritual exercises with the same practical recommendation: spend an uninterrupted hour of prayer every day in the presence of the Blessed Sacrament. This steady devotion to Christ, he argued, would revolutionize the priest's spiritual life and invigorate his priesthood. Many of Sheen's colleagues testify that all his life, he remained faithful to this practice. I can personally testify that this teaching, which had been largely forgotten for a generation after his death, was massively embraced by the coterie of young men entering the seminary in the last years of the twentieth century and the first years of the twenty-first. The Holy Hour is now a staple spiritual discipline in most seminaries and in an increasing number of rectories and parishes around the country.

In 1966, Sheen was appointed Bishop of the Diocese of Rochester in upstate New York. Given his age—seventy-one—and his prominence as an evangelist and writer, it was a somewhat sur- prising appointment. Many speculate that it was due to the influence of Cardinal Spellman, with whom Sheen had had a falling out, and it is the general consensus that his time as diocesan bishop was less than successful. Practical administration was never his strong suit, and he took a number of positions, admirable in themselves, that were unpopular with both the priests and the people. After only three years in office, he resigned. A grateful Vatican gave him the title of archbishop and permitted him to spend his time in study, writing, and speaking. This he did until a series of surgeries sapped him of his strength.

He died on December 9, 1979, while praying in the presence of the Blessed Sacrament.

THE MYSTICAL BODY OF CHRIST

In 1935, when he was forty years old and firmly established as a professor at Catholic University, Sheen published a book entitled *The Mystical Body of Christ*. It is on the specific subject of ecclesiology (the study of the Church), but this text nevertheless contains many of the master themes of Sheen's teaching and preaching. It thus provides a helpful door for those seeking entry into the world of his thought.

Relying upon some of the masters of nineteenth-century Catholic thought as well as upon many of his most accomplished contemporaries, including Romano Guardini, Karl Adam, and Reynold Hillenbrand, Sheen insisted that participation in the *life* of Jesus is the key to Catholicism. More than a convincing teacher or an inspiring moral exemplar, Jesus is a field of force, an energy, a living person. His followers, accordingly, relate to him not from a distance but intimately, the way in which cells, molecules, and organs participate in the integrity of the body. Two thousand years ago, he argues, the second person of the Trinity took to himself a human nature and walked the hills and pathways of the Holy Land. After the Resurrection and the Ascension, that same divine person took to himself a new kind of Body: the Mystical Body of the Church.

Through this Body, he continues to do his work in the world: teaching, healing, forgiving, and reconciling. The Church, accordingly, is not the Jesus Christ Society—that is to say, a voluntary organization of those dedicated to preserving the memory of Jesus. No—it is something far stranger and more wonderful than that. It is not an organization, but an organism. With this master metaphor continually in mind, Sheen interprets the different dimensions of the Church's life.

The Head of the Mystical Body is, of course, Christ himself. He gives unity, integrity, direction, and purpose to the Church's activity. But in his heavenly state, Christ is invisible to us; therefore, it would seem fitting that there be a visible earthly representative of Christ the Head, and this is none other than the pope, who is called, quite properly, the "vicar of Christ."

But what is the vital principal that connects Head and members—the "soul," if you will, of the Church? This is the Holy Spirit. At the beginning of the Church's life, each of the Apostles of Jesus has his own individuality and personality and point of view, but they lacked what was needed to make them come together as a living thing. "They needed a soul, a spirit, a vivifying, simplifying, unifying principle which would make the cells of the mystical body cohere in unity under the headship of Christ." And this is what came to them on the day of Pentecost. It is the Holy Spirit who preserves the unity of the Church up and down the ages; it is the Holy Spirit who compels the Church to develop and unfold in an ordered manner; it is the Holy Spirit who prompts the musings of theologians, the outreach of missionaries, and the ardent prayer of monks and mystics.

Now we are in a position to understand a statement of Fulton Sheen that might seem counterintuitive, even scandalous, at first: the Church is the prolongation of the Incarnation across space and time. The same Christ who acted two thousand years ago acts today, but now through the

mediation of his Mystical Body. Though many of us, Sheen says, long to have Christ still with us as he was with the Apostles two millennia ago, didn't Jesus himself say to his disciples, "It is to your advantage that I go away" (John 16:7)? From his heavenly place, Jesus unleashes the Holy Spirit to animate the Church, so that now we can actively participate in the work and mission of the Lord. Indeed, Sheen says, "If he left them to go to His Father and sent His Spirit, then He would be, not an example to be copied, but a Life to be lived." Now he lives within the baptized "as the very Soul of our souls, the very Spirit of our spirit, the Truth of our minds, the Love of our hearts, and the Desire of our wills." Thus St. Paul can urge: "Let the same mind be in you that was in Christ Jesus" (Phil. 2:5), and he can exult, "It is no longer I who live, but it is Christ who lives in me" (Gal. 2:20). And St. John in his first letter could say, "We know that we abide in him and he in us, because he has given us of his Spirit" (1 John 4:13).

When we realize the full implications of this extraordinary teaching, says Sheen, we appreciate the disturbing truth of the parable recounted in the twenty-fifth chapter of Matthew's Gospel:

> "'I was hungry and you gave me no food, I was thirsty and you gave me nothing to drink, I was a stranger and you did not welcome me, naked and you did not give me clothing, sick and in prison and you did not visit me.' . . . 'Lord, when was it that we saw you hungry or thirsty or a stranger or naked or sick or in prison, and did not take care of you?' . . . 'Truly I tell you, just as you did not do it to one of the least of these, you did not do it to me.'" (Matt. 25:42–45)

The Church is not the Jesus Christ Club, but the Mystical Body of Jesus, stretching across space and time. This is a truth both marvelous and awful in its implications. In point of fact, Sheen continues, the Mystical Body stretches not just across space and time but beyond those dimensions as well. The Church of this world, currently engaged in the struggle to become more Christ-like, is called the "Church Militant," or the fighting Church. But it is connected to the "Suffering Church" and the "Triumphant Church." The Suffering Church is the community of those who have died in a state of insufficient readiness to be one with Christ and are accordingly undergoing the purifications of purgatory. Through prayer, the Church here below is connected vibrantly and intimately to this supernatural congregation. The Triumphant Church is that family of people who have attained full union with their Lord and hence experience perfect happiness. Sheen clearly delights in describing the "white-robed body of martyrs, confessors, virgins, pontiffs and Holy Women" who now inhabit the heavenly court. The salient point is that "these three divisions of the Mystical Body of Christ are not independent, but there is a constant flux and flow between each of them because all are filled by the same Spirit and crowned by the same Christ."

I find it fascinating that Sheen concludes this lyrical exploration of the mystical identity of the Church with a consideration of what was called in the years before the Second Vatican Council "Catholic Action." This was a movement made up almost completely of laypeople—lawyers, physicians, teachers, business leaders, parents, etc.—who had dedicated themselves to bringing their faith into the world. "Catholic Action," Sheen explains, "is Catholicism in action. It is Catholic because of its nearness to divinity; it is action because of its nearness to humanity. But there can be no divorce between the two." Making the market more just, providing care for the poor, evangelizing in the workplace, seeking the common good in the political order—all of these are the natural expressions in action of the Mystical Body. The life of Christ, which animates the sacramental, liturgical, artistic, and intellectual work of the Church, is meant finally to radiate outward so as to transform the whole of society.

Is the Church's charitable work the same as social work?

From the outside, the Church's charitable work might look a lot like social work. The difference is not only in the motivation but in the mystical animation. Behind the corporal and spiritual works of mercy is the reality of Christ continuing his work in and through his Mystical Body, the Church. Certainly, even an atheist of goodwill can serve the poor. But when a Christian serves the poor out of a deep sense of identity with Jesus Christ, the arms and eyes and hands of Jesus are mystically at work in the world.

LIFE IS WORTH LIVING

As I already mentioned, Fulton Sheen's extremely popular television presentations might have seemed spontaneous and conversational, but they were, in fact, grounded in substantial erudition. What is worth exploring is precisely how he managed to bring the wealth of the Church's intellectual tradition to bear on contemporary life. His program *Life Is Worth Living* is a kind of master class in evangelization.

Before looking at some of his particular talks, I might mention a few general qualities of Sheen's rhetoric. One is a breezy use of humor. At a time when a not inconsiderable number of Americans might have been suspicious of a Catholic bishop in full regalia, Sheen won over his audience with his punning and often self-deprecating remarks at the outset of his sermon. It has been observed that laughter can, as it were, turn the soil of the heart and make it more receptive to the planting of the Gospel seed.

A second feature of his speaking style is an extremely deft use of metaphor. Like all good teachers—and remember, he was a professor for more than twenty years when he began his television work—Sheen knew that it is best to move from the known to the unknown, finding a bridge, a connection, an analogy between the two. So, for example, in explaining the dynamics of the spiritual life, Sheen again and again draws comparisons with biological and psychological life. Whenever I return to Sheen's programs, I'm also struck by how often he draws on insights from Freudian psychology. He was critical of Freud to be sure, but frequently he finds something in Freud that serves as an illustration of a spiritual point.

A third quality is one that I believe every preacher and evangelist ought to imitate: Fulton Sheen's popular talks are invariably well constructed, marked by a discernible logic, moving coherently from beginning to middle to end. A student of classical rhetoric, Sheen understood that a significant reason why a talk becomes tiresome is precisely a lack of rational structure. If the mind is not engaged, it tends to drift. The bishop's hearers were certainly entertained and delighted, but they were also intellectually stimulated.

One of the first presentations that Sheen made on television was an explication of the title of his series and an extremly clever application of some pivotal questions in the second part of Thomas Aquinas' great *Summa theologiae*. He makes his thesis statement bluntly enough: "Life *is* monotonous if it is meaningless; it is *not* monotonous if it has a purpose." Imagine, says Sheen, a farmer who planted wheat one week, and then dug it up and planted barley, and then the next week dug that up and planted watermelon, and the following week dug that up and planted oats. In the autumn, there would be no harvest. And if this process were repeated year after year, the planter would go quite mad. So are many people today, who lack a fixed plan, a spiritual goal. Indeed, they tend to change philosophies with every book they read: now Marx, now Freud, now materialism, now idealism. They become, accordingly, addicted to motion and change for its own sake—and the result is boredom, frustration, deep anxiety.

So what is the purpose of human life? Following Aquinas, Sheen observes that we have something in common with the basic elements (namely, existence), something in common with plants (namely, life), and something in common with animals (namely, sensation and mobility)—and we do indeed desire existence, life, and mobility. But our proper end must be in regard to something peculiar to us—and this is the spiritual capacity to know and to will.

We want to know the truth, and thus we develop science and philosophy, we stubbornly ask and answer questions about the world, we restlessly seek wisdom. But the mind is never satisfied with a particular bit of knowledge or in exploring one subject, or in answering even a thousand questions. For finally it wants the Truth itself; it wants to know everything about everything; it won't rest until it finds pure Truth. And we want to possess the good, and thus we strive for justice, we seek to do what is right, we produce and appreciate beautiful things. But once again, our passion for goodness is not satisfied with any particular achievement of justice or act of righteousness or work of beauty. For finally we want Goodness itself, supreme Beauty. But Truth and Goodness in their unconditioned forms are precisely what we mean by the word "God." In a word, we are wired for God. "When are we most happy?" Sheen asks. "When we do that for which we are made." We are not meant to remain at the level of inanimate objects or plants or animals. We are meant to realize the deepest longing of our souls, to order our lives to God. When we do this, we are no longer bored, and "then there is a thrill and a romance to life."

Another of Sheen's broadcasts, entitled "Something Higher," is an extremely effective primer in the theology of grace, and it demonstrates that the great themes of his study of the Mystical Body were never far from his mind. He proposes that we consider the hierarchy of being on display in the natural world and the distinctive dynamic by which something moves from a lower to a higher level. So for example, "rain and phosphates and carbon and moisture and sunlight" can, as it were, be raised up to a higher level of existence precisely by being assimilated by a living plant. The plant has to lower itself and say to these fundamental elements, "Unless you die to your lower existence, you cannot live in my kingdom." And if plants are ever to live in a higher manner, they have to die to themselves. An animal, as it were, has to come down and assimilate the plant, taking it up into a higher organism. And if animals would come to a more intense pitch of existence, a human being must lower himself to their level, consuming them and taking them into the realm of the thinking and willing agent. In short, higher life never comes from the aspiration or effort of a lower form of life—rather the opposite.

And why, Sheen wonders, should this protocol cease in regard to the elevation of human beings? If they were to move into the more elevated realm of the divine life, God must come down and draw them into himself. The new life, in a word, must be offered as a gift, a grace. There is, of course, a significant difference in regard to human beings, for unlike chemicals, plants, and animals, we cannot be compelled to accept the offer of a higher life. No plant asks the permission of water or carbon; no animal seeks the cooperation of a plant; no human expects the animal to acquiesce in his own slaughter. But God is indeed constrained, for he must seek the free cooperation of his human creature in the process of elevation. God invites men and women to die to themselves, but they must say yes.

With this simple but telling illustration, we grasp the essential dynamics of the spiritual life. Grace, perforce, comes first; the higher life is a gift. But the gift must be accepted through a lifetime of free choices and acts of mortification, literally putting to death all that stands between us and God: "pride, covetousness, lust, anger, envy, gluttony, and sloth." This is why we characterize the authentic life of the Spirit as "supernatural." It is utterly beyond our capacities. "If a rose suddenly spoke, 'I think I will go to California for the winter, or to Florida,' that would be an act that does not belong to the nature and powers of a rose. If a dog should suddenly walk across a stage and begin to quote Shakespeare, that would be a very 'supernatural' act for a dog." Just as strange, anomalous, and wonderful it is when a human being becomes, through grace, a child of God, a partaker of the divine nature, an heir of the kingdom of heaven. At the same time, this grace awakens what is best in us, directs our powers, calls forth the response of our freedom. Under its influence, we become who we are meant to be.

If someone wants to begin to die to themselves, where do they start?

Engaging in even the simplest act of love is a form of dying to oneself, because to love is to will the good of the other as other—not to will my good through the other, but truly to want and will what is good for the other. To do this requires dying to oneself, dying to one's own ego and needs. This could be as simple as a parent helping a child with her homework, smiling and speaking a kind work when you're not in the mood, or reaching out to someone who's lonely. Start with the simplest act of love and you're participating in the divine life.

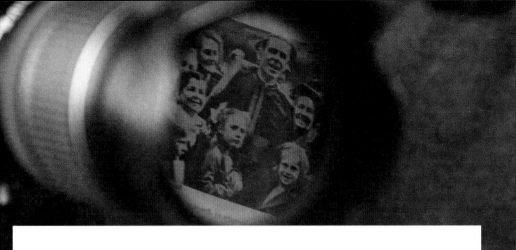

WHY IS FULTON J. SHEEN
A PIVOTAL PLAYER?

Though an exceptionally bright man, Fulton Sheen certainly would not rank with Augustine or Thomas Aquinas in regard to intellectual depth and creativity. Though certainly a man of prayer, he would not rival Catherine of Siena or Benedict for contemplative intensity. He would be closer to John Henry Newman or G.K. Chesterton—which is to say, someone who found a remarkably intelligent and winsome way to engage a world growing increasingly skeptical of Christianity.

What makes Fulton Sheen truly distinctive is that he had the courage and the imagination to use the new means of communication made available in the twentieth century. And this makes him a sort of patron saint for all those who would take up the challenge of the New Evangelization envisioned by Vatican II. Pope St. John Paul II said that the New Evangelization should be "new in its ardor, methods, and expression." One has only to watch a few minutes of a Sheen sermon or speech to see that he was filled with evangelical ardor, that he had found an original manner to speak the classic truths of the faith, and that he was a master of the new media.

At a truly pivotal moment in the history of communication, Fulton J. Sheen made his voice heard in service of Christ's Gospel.

Flannery O'Connor

THE STORYTELLER

One of the quirkiest and most intriguing of all the Pivotal Players was a twentieth-century Catholic writer of fiction from the American South, a woman whose macabre, puzzling, and luminous stories have had a transformative impact on both the Church and the wider culture. A somewhat mousy, retiring figure with a thick southern drawl and crippled by a serious disease for the whole of her adult life, Flannery O'Connor was the unlikely author of some of the most shocking, violent, and unnerving stories of our time. When discussing the grotesque quality of her fiction, she said, "To the hard of hearing you shout, and for the almost-blind you draw large and startling figures." She meant that in an age when most people had grown insensitive to the realities of the spiritual life, you had to get their attention any way you can.

James Joyce, a considerably less devout Catholic than Flannery O'Connor, commented that his art consisted in the reporting of "epiphanies"—that is to say, moments of sudden illumination and spiritual insight. O'Connor said of her writing that it had to do with "a moment of grace . . . a moment where it is offered, and is usually rejected." If "moment of grace" sounds rather benign, remember that it takes place in the midst of a fallen and compromised world. O'Connor masterfully shows, again and again, how wrenching, therefore, the experience of grace usually is. Even

the most superficial survey of the both the high and the popular culture today shows the mark of Flannery O'Connor. The comedian Conan O'Brien and the actor Tommy Lee Jones both composed Harvard theses on O'Connor's work, and her distinctive style has influenced the novelists Cormac McCarthy, Walker Percy, and Alice Walker. Bruce Springsteen has admitted that her work significantly impacted his songwriting. But perhaps nowhere is the O'Connor influence more evident than in the films of Joel and Ethan Coen. When I first saw their masterpiece *Fargo*, with its alarming blend of the absurd, the religious, the comical, and the shockingly violent, I immediately thought of Flannery O'Connor. I have since remarked the influence in any number of their movies, from *A Serious Man* and *True Grit* to *Raising Arizona* and *The Big Lebowski*.

LIFE AND TIMES

Mary Flannery O'Connor was born March 25, 1925, in the lovely city of Savannah, Georgia. Her parents, Edward and Regina O'Connor, were fairly well-to-do members of an Irish Catholic community that, in that time and place, still experienced a good deal of marginalization. The young girl received a solid religious formation from the Sisters of Mercy, and she remained all her life a devout if not ostensibly pious Catholic. When she was six years old, she failed to attend the required children's Sunday Mass, for her family had decided to worship at a different time. When confronted by one of the sisters, she stood her ground: "The Catholic Church does not dictate to my family what time I go to Mass." Around the same age, she was, curiously enough, filmed by the Pathé newsreel company, for the word had gotten all the way to New York that she had successfully trained a chicken to walk backward. Though the filming didn't go very well, this early encounter with the extraordinary bird signaled the commencement of a lifelong fascination with exotic birds, especially peafowl.

When Flannery was thirteen, her family moved to Milledgeville, a sleepy town in the center of the state, which had been the capital of Georgia during the Civil War years. This would be her home base for the rest of her life. When she was fifteen, her beloved father died of lupus, an autoimmune disease that Flannery herself would eventually contract. Devastated by the loss, the young girl moved increasingly into an interior world of fantasy and imagination. She attended the Georgia State College for Women and proved an able student as well as a gifted editor of *The Corinthian*, the school's literary magazine. It was in this capacity that

221

her writer's gifts first became apparent—as well as a flair for the artistic. Somewhat in the manner of Chesterton, she contributed a cartoon to every edition of the journal, and even covered the walls of the student lounge with her drawings.

In 1945, Flannery received a scholarship in journalism from the State University of Iowa. During the first semester, she transferred to the well-respected program in creative writing at the university, called the Iowa Writers' Workshop. Paul Engle, the director of the program at the time, recalls his first meeting with Flannery O'Connor. A shy young woman approached his desk and stood for some time without saying a word. When she finally spoke, her accent was so impenetrable to his Midwestern ear that he asked her to repeat herself. When a second attempt failed, Engle handed her a pad and pencil. She wrote down, "My name is Flannery O'Connor. I am not a journalist. Can I come to the Writers' Workshop?" In the heady atmosphere of the workshop, where her teachers included Robert Penn Warren and some of the other most important writers and critics of the era, she honed her craft. Her master's thesis was a collection of short fiction called *The Geranium*, the title story of which became her first published work.

After receiving her MFA degree, she was accepted at Yaddo, a prestigious writers' colony in Saratoga Springs, New York, a sort of haven where writers and other artists could do their work in peace and in a supportive atmosphere. Over the years, John Cheever, Aaron Copland, Leonard Bernstein, Philip Roth, Katherine Anne Porter, and Truman Capote all spent time at Yaddo. While she was there, Flannery became friends with the poet Robert Lowell and labored to bring her first novel,

Wise Blood, to completion. In 1949, she moved into an apartment over the garage at the home of Robert Fitzgerald, a scholar of the classics, and his wife Sally. These kind, intelligent, and devoutly Catholic friends provided a nurturing environment for the aspiring author. More importantly, Sally would become one of Flannery's principal correspondents—O'Connor was, like John Henry Newman, a prolific letter-writer—and eventually the editor of the magnificent collection of O'Connor's missives called *The Habit of Being.*

It was around this time that the shy but promising writer received a dinner invitation from the author Mary McCarthy and her husband. In the course of a lengthy supper at McCarthy's New York apartment, O'Connor said barely a word. Finally, McCarthy, attempting to draw her out, commented that though she was an ex-Catholic, she had a great admiration for the Eucharist as a symbol. To which Flannery O'Connor responded in a shaky voice: "Well, if it's a symbol, to hell with it." Nowhere in the great theological tradition is there a better defense of what the Church means by the "Real Presence" of Christ in the Eucharist, coming as it does from an exquisite master of symbolic literature.

In 1950, O'Connor was diagnosed with lupus, the disease that had killed her father, and she was compelled to return to Milledgeville, settling into the family farm, called Andalusia, on the outskirts of the town. Under her mother's care and surrounded by her beloved peacocks, Flannery lived a simple and quiet life, usually managing to work rather intensely for two or three hours a day on her writing. Despite her physical limitations—both the lupus itself and the medications she took to control it left her worn out much of the time and on crutches—she produced a fairly substantial body of work. *Wise Blood*, her first novel, appeared in 1952, followed in 1955 by a collection of short fiction entitled *A Good Man Is Hard to Find*, the title story of which is generally regarded as one of the literary gems of the twentieth century, and which we will consider in due course. In 1960, she published a second novel called *The Violent Bear It Away*, and in 1965, a posthumous collection of short stories called *Everything That Rises Must Converge* appeared.

Even on crutches, she made a surprising number of journeys to give lectures on themes both literary and theological. Many of these surface in the marvelous letters that we will look at in a moment. One of my favorite of her one-liners was delivered on a speaking trip. "Everywhere I go," she said, "I'm asked if I think the universities stifle writers. My opinion is that they don't stifle enough of them."

In the summer of 1964, the lupus, which had gone mostly into remission, returned with a vengeance. Flannery O'Connor died in Milledgeville on August 3, 1964, at the age of thirty-nine.

LETTERS AND OCCASIONAL PROSE

I have often encouraged those who are looking into Flannery O'Connor for the first time to begin with her letters rather than with her stories. In these wonderful missives, she appears a woman in full: smart, wickedly funny, and as spiritually alert as any Catholic of the twentieth century. In fact, her comments on her Catholic faith, in the words of her friend Sally Fitzgerald, "shed light in every direction."

A few examples might suffice to give some sense of her wit. To the poet Robert Lowell, she writes, "I have bought me some peafowl and sit on the back steps a good deal studying them. I am going to be the World Authority on Peafowl, and I hope to be offered a chair some day at the Chicken College." To Sally Fitzgerald, she reported this exchange between herself and her mother regarding some books that Flannery had ordered:

"She: Mow-by Dick. The Idiot. You would get something called Idiot. What's it about? Me: An Idiot." And this pithy assessment of some of her fellow writers: "Mr. Truman Capote makes me plumb sick, as does Mr. Tennessee Williams. Of foreigners living I like Frank O'Connor. I keep waiting for some club lady to ask me if I am kin to Frank O'Connor. At which I hope to reply, 'I am his mother.'"

A theme to which she returns over and again is that of the Catholic writer. An ardent student of St. Thomas Aquinas—in fact, she refers to herself as a "hillbilly Thomist"—she holds that grace builds on nature. This means that the first obligation of the Catholic writer is to represent the truth of things—that is to say, the world as it is, not as one might wish it to be. But the doctrine of the Church opens up new and unexpected horizons. It doesn't shut down the mind of the writer; on the contrary, it frees it to see what is really there. The Catholic writer describes the human condition, but this means a human condition marked by the fall, addressed by grace, and destined for eternal life. Again and again in her letters, Flannery says that she writes the way she does, not despite her Catholicism, but because of it.

Another consistent preoccupation in her letters and essays is the Incarnation, the master idea of Catholicism. She notices that fiction writing—unlike, say, philosophical or theological writing—has to do with particulars: with this person, this town, this manner of speech. The moment storytellers become preoccupied with abstractions, they lose their way. This gives the Catholic writer an advantage, for the doctrine of the Incarnation positively encourages a concrete, embodied approach to life. Like another Catholic novelist, David Lodge, Flannery exults in the fact that Catholic doctrine takes the physical so seriously. One thinks, for example, of the grittiness of the sacraments, as well as feasts that celebrate conception, circumcision, and bodily assumption.

She also delights in the way that revelation turns things upside down. It was a commonplace among the intellectuals of her time that Catholic talk of Incarnation, virgin birth, walking on water, and Resurrection was naïve, a holdover from a period innocent of science and hard thinking. But these miracles, she held, were not so much violations of the laws of nature as they were the disclosure of the way things really are: "For me, it is the virgin birth, the Incarnation, the resurrection which are the true laws of the flesh. Death, decay, destruction are the suspension of these laws."

"REVELATION"

One of the most important motifs in the stories of Flannery O'Connor is the awakening to sin and hence to one's need for a Savior. She intuited that, in the twentieth century, perhaps the greatest block to Christianity was precisely a spiritual complacency, a sense that all in us is basically in order. But when this attitude is internalized, Jesus necessarily devolves to the level of teacher or inspiring hero and ceases to be Savior. Hence the moment—necessarily painful—when grace breaks through the defenses we have built around ourselves is an epiphany worth describing. To my mind, the best presentation of this breakthrough in O'Connor's writing is the pithy, funny, and deeply troubling story called, appropriately enough, "Revelation."

The narrative begins with the entry of Mr. and Mrs. Turpin into a doctor's crowded waiting room. The place is filled with sick people, but the plump and self-possessed Mrs. Turpin is not one of them: she is quick to tell everyone that it is her husband who has the appointment. As the story progresses, Flannery allows us to hear two conversations: the outer one that Mrs. Turpin is having with those in the waiting room and the inner one that she is carrying on with herself. On the outside, everything is pleasant, warm, and generous. But on the inside, Mrs. Turpin is fiercely judging everyone in the room. When a lady tells her that she had bought some "joo-ry" with green stamps, Mrs. Turpin says to herself, "Ought to have got you a wash rag and some soap." When a young woman, slouching in the corner, is described as having been to college up north, Mrs. Turpin thinks to herself, "Well, it hasn't done much for her manners."

All of this comes to a head when Mrs. Turpin utters a soliloquy of gratitude for all the gifts that God has given her: "If it's one thing I am, it's grateful. When I think who all I could have been besides myself and what all I got . . . I just feel like shouting, 'Thank you, Jesus, for making everything the way it is!'" With that, a book hits her directly over her left eye. It had been thrown by the scowling college girl who was now on Mrs. Turpin, her fingers digging into the soft flesh around our hero's throat. The doctor, nurses, and other attendants scramble into action, pulling the girl off of Mrs. Turpin and administering a sedative. But before drifting into unconsciousness, the young woman fixes Mrs. Turpin with a fierce stare, and the older woman realizes that this frightening figure knows her in some intense and personal way. Both fascinated and terrified, Mrs. Turpin sputters, "What you got to say to me?" Continuing to stare into Mrs. Turpin's face with awful concentration, the girl says, "Go back to hell where you came from, you old wart hog." Despite the horrified protests of the denizens of the waiting room, Mrs. Turpin realizes, in some uncanny but definitive way, that the girl is right. The words of the unmannered college student carried the force of a revelation. As the unconscious girl is being carried away, we understand the power of her name: Mary Grace.

Very much like the Pharisee in Jesus' famous parable, who publicly thanked God for not making him like other men, Mrs. Turpin exulted in her moral superiority. And it was upon this sense that her relationship with God was based. Like a terrapin (how like Turpin!), she had encased herself in a carapace of self-righteousness. What was needed was a breakthrough—and this is precisely what happened through the ministrations of Mary Grace. In a fallen world, God's love is often experienced as unnerving, disorienting, painful. In O'Connor's stories, we are usually being invited to look with the eyes of faith directly at the most violent and disturbing scenes.

What we see at the close of the story is that Mrs. Turpin's revelation has in fact prompted a decisive change. Standing alongside the hog pen on her farm—how like the prodigal son who had fallen to the point of working among the pigs—Mrs. Turpin looks up into the evening sky and spies a curious purple streak. As a visionary light sparkles in her eyes, "she saw the streak as a vast swinging bridge extending upward from the earth. . . . Upon it a vast horde of souls were rumbling toward heaven. There were whole companies of white-trash, clean for the first time in their lives . . . battalions of freaks and lunatics shouting and clapping and leaping like frogs." And taking up the rear of the procession of the blessed were people like her husband and herself—proper, dignified, sure of themselves. But she saw—and the story concludes with this luminous observation—"by their shocked and altered faces that even their virtues were being burned away."

We recall Jesus' admonition to the chief priests and elders: "Truly I tell you, the tax collectors and the prostitutes are going into the kingdom of God ahead of you" (Matt. 21:31). He doesn't mean that the self-righteous won't get in, but he is certainly suggesting that those who feel the need for salvation walk the privileged path.

Are we meant to recognize ourselves in Mrs. Turpin?

Flannery O'Connor intuited something that you find in the teachings of Jesus himself—namely, that those who are in the worst spiritual shape are not sinners who know it, but sinners who don't know it. Sinners who think they are righteous are in a much more dangerous spiritual condition than a sinner who knows it and approaches the divine mercy. Think of Jesus' parable of the Pharisee and the publican. The Pharisee is convinced of his own righteousness, and offers a prayer of pity for "poor sinners." But the publican, who does not even look up, humbly admits his sin and asks God for mercy. It is the publican, Jesus tells us, who went home justified. Mrs. Turpin is a version of the Pharisee: she is convinced of her own righteousness, and spends her time looking down on other people and judging them. This is, in fact, a temptation for all spiritual people, which is part of the universal relevance of "Revelation." As we come to better understand the law of God, we can begin to use that law to judge other people. And this is why Mrs. Turpin needs this breakthrough of grace, a moment that shocks her out of her hardened self-righteousness.

"A GOOD MAN IS HARD TO FIND"

The story generally regarded as Flannery O'Connor's masterpiece is called "A Good Man Is Hard to Find." Moody, suspenseful, darkly comic, violent, and brimming with theological and spiritual wisdom, this tale is a pure distillation of her distinctive art. There is a recording of Flannery herself reciting this story aloud, and once you've heard her voice, I would defy you to un-hear it as you read the tale.

It commences with a warning. A grandmother tells her son Bailey and his family that they oughtn't to go on a planned trip to Florida because the paper says that an escaped convict, called "The Misfit," is headed there and has been known to do terrible things. They ignore her—as it seems they usually do—and set out on the journey. The grandmother dressed carefully for the trip, decking herself out in a jaunty hat and elegant navy blue dress so that, "in case of an accident, anyone seeing her dead on the highway would know that she was a lady." Arriving at an eating establishment run by a certain "Red Sammy Butts," they settle into their lunch. When June Star, one of her grandchildren, says something rude to Red Sammy's wife, the grandmother hisses, "Aren't you ashamed?" The proprietor commiserates with her and both conclude "a good man is hard to find." In a few deft strokes, Flannery has sketched the character of the grandmother. She's not unlike Mrs. Turpin: sure of her own righteousness and pretty convinced of the depravity of the world around her; good people are just pretty thin on the ground.

As they continue on their journey, the grandmother recalls a lovely house that she had known in her youth, and she waxes so lyrically about it that she convinces her son, against his better judgment, to go off the road and search it out. On the way down a bumpy country lane, the grandmother, to her horror, suddenly remembers that the house in question is in fact in another state. Alarmed, she kicks her valise, which upsets a basket in which their cat had been snoozing. The animal leaps up onto Bailey's shoulder and he loses control of the car, sending them all into a somersault and landing them in a ditch by the side of the road.

This entire drama has been witnessed from a distance. Soon a car approaches and three men emerge, apparently to offer help. When the grandmother sees the bespectacled man with no shirt, she is convinced that she knows him but she can't quite place him. Then, in a flash, she realizes who it is, and before she can catch herself, she blurts out, "You're The Misfit. I recognized you at once!" With a dreadful matter-of-factness, he drawls, "It would have been better for all of you, lady, if you hadn't of reckernized me." As her son, daughter-in-law, and grandchildren are led one by one into the forest to be shot, the grandmother and The Misfit engage in a deadly serious theological conversation. "Do you ever pray?" she asks him. He shakes his head no. When he speaks of years of mistreatment in prison, including solitary confinement, she eagerly suggests, "That's when you should have started to pray. If you would pray, Jesus would help you." He agrees with her in principle, but he adds, "I don't want no hep. I'm doing alright by myself." Here we see that, despite their enormous differences at the superficial level, the grandmother and The Misfit are in the same spiritual space: secure in their conviction of self-sufficiency.

Then their conversation takes a decisive and finally salvific Christological turn. Hearing the gunshots in the distance and knowing that her family is being put to death, the grandmother stands in the ditch muttering, "Jesus, Jesus." And The Misfit takes the cue: "Yes'm, Jesus thrown everything off balance." This is the profoundest theological remark in the story and the hinge upon which the narrative turns. The hardened criminal is acknowledging something that the Christian tradition has always held to be of central importance—namely, that Jesus is the judge of the sinful world, the one who threw an unbalanced world off balance. And The Misfit demonstrates even more striking theological acumen, commenting: "Jesus was the only One that ever raised the dead, and He shouldn't have done that. He thrown everything off balance." Jesus' victory over sin and death has made all the difference. If you believe in it, you live in a transformed world. Therefore, Jesus compels a choice. Here again is the remarkably profound Christology of The Misfit: "If He did what He said, then it's nothing for you to do but throw away everything and follow Him, and if He didn't, then it's nothing for you to do but enjoy the few minutes you got left the best way you can—by killing somebody or burning down his house or doing some other meanness to him. No pleasure but meanness."

In her shock and confusion, the old lady mutters, "Maybe He didn't raise the dead," and the killer pounces on the suggestion with enthusiasm: "I wasn't there so I can't say He didn't. I wisht I had of been there. It ain't right I wasn't there because if I had of been there I would have known . . . and I wouldn't be like I am now." In uttering those words, The Misfit signals a major spiritual transformation. Just moments earlier, he had assured the grandmother that he needed no help, but now he acknowledges that all is far from right with him. And he further admits that it is Jesus' conquest of death that would make all of the difference in his life, changing him from someone who finds pleasure in cruelty to someone able to throw everything away and follow Christ. When he spoke those words "his voice seemed about to crack," and in that moment "the grandmother's head cleared for an instant." Looking The Misfit directly in the eye, she murmured, "Why you're one of my babies. You're one of my own children!" At the outset of the story, one couldn't have imagined a less likely scenario; but now, in the awful pressure of the moment and having heard The Misfit confess his weakness, she realizes her own frailty and that both of them are sinners in need of mercy. Overcome with a feeling of compassion, the old lady reaches out and touches The Misfit on the shoulder. But the killer reacts violently to this touch, springing back "as if a snake had bitten him," and shooting the grandmother three times through the chest.

This climactic resolution of the conversation is not, all indications to the contrary notwithstanding, one-sidedly tragic. In Flannery O'Connor's universe, death is hardly the worst of fates. Having seen what she needed to see—her solidarity in sin with even the worst of sinners—and having thereby opened herself to grace, the grandmother was ready for heaven. Indeed, in death, she sits in "a puddle of blood with her legs crossed under her like a child's and her face smiling up at the cloudless sky." She has recovered her innocence and found her joy.

Having shot the old woman, The Misfit "put his gun down on the ground and took off his glasses and began to clean them." Just as the old lady's head had cleared in her moment of identification with the killer, so now The Misfit's vision is being clarified. But what does he see? As Bobby

Lee, one of The Misfit's associates, comes to take away her body, he says, "She was a talker, wasn't she?" And The Misfit responds, in undoubtedly the most famous line in the story: "She would of been a good woman if it had been somebody there to shoot her every minute of her life." First he sees that she understood something of enormous significance—that grace, in the typically terrible O'Connor manner, had broken through. But then Bobby Lee, still exulting in the excitement of the killing, exclaims, "Some fun!" And The Misfit, in the grace-filled final line of the story, responds, "Shut up, Bobby Lee. It's no real pleasure in life." Earlier, The Misfit had proposed the stark Kierkegaardian either/or: either you give your whole life to Christ, or you find whatever pleasure you can in killing or other acts of meanness. In admitting that there is no pleasure in the life he's leading, The Misfit, perhaps, is signaling his openness to the only other option that remains.

Was it the grandmother's evocation of the holy name? Was it her outreach to him in compassion? Who knows? But grace was offered. Grace is always offered. But we need clear eyes to see it.

How did Flannery O'Connor's battle with lupus affect her work?

Think of the line in "A Good Man Is Hard to Find": "She would of been a good woman if it had been somebody there to shoot her every minute of her life." The point is, if the grandmother was constantly brought to this place of ultimate concern and ultimate decision, she would have been a good woman. And in a certain sense, O'Connor herself lived most of her adult life with someone holding a gun to her head. She knew she had lupus. She knew the disease would kill her sooner rather than later. But that gave great intensity to her life and writings. Her writings are in a certain way Kierkegaardian, because there is the either/or, the decision for or against grace, which is finally what matters. Everything else is a footnote.

WHY IS FLANNERY O'CONNOR
A PIVOTAL PLAYER?

In the middle of the twentieth century, which witnessed more death, despair, and tyranny than any other century on record, Flannery O'Connor had the courage to show just how dark are the hearts of fallen human beings. But at the same time, she had the incomparable grace to demonstrate how God continues to work even on that bleak and blasted ground. If I might make bold to compare her to Dante, she manages, within the confines of her carefully crafted short stories, to take the reader through hell, purgatory, and heaven. It was precisely because she believed so passionately in the mercy of God that she was able to gaze so unblinkingly at human depravity. And perhaps here we see why she was such a great comic writer. If, as Chesterton argued, the essence of humor is the coming together of incongruous things, then there is nothing funnier than the juxtaposition of sin and grace that she was able to describe with such deftness of touch.

Thomas Merton, just months after O'Connor's death, wrote a lovely elegy, which contains these lines: "When I read Flannery, I don't think of Hemingway, or Katherine Anne Porter, or Sartre, but rather of someone like Sophocles. What more can be said of a writer? I write her name with honor, for all the truth and all the craft with which she shows man's fall and his dishonor."

IHS
FLANNERY O'
DAUGHTER OF
REGINA LUCILLE
AND
EDWARD FRANCIS
BORN IN SAV

Becoming Pivotal Players Today

HOLLY ORDWAY

What can we learn from these Pivotal Players? We have seen how their lives reflected their love of God, and how their devotion to Christ decisively influenced the Church. We have recognized the way that these figures embodied the Church's mission to evangelize the culture. We have admired them, learned from them, been surprised and challenged by them.

But we should not stop there. We should ask: What next? How can we carry on their work of evangelization? That question may seem daunting or even prideful. After all, these are truly great figures! Who are we to emulate someone like St. Ignatius, St. Catherine of Siena, or Michelangelo? It might seem more fitting and more humble to view these men and women as set apart, bigger and better than ordinary Catholics like us. Let others who have great spiritual gifts do great things, right? No: that's not right, and I daresay that any of these Pivotal Players would speak up to say so.

When we look at the lives of these great figures, we see again and again the truth that they recognized: their lives were not about them. From St. Benedict to St. John Henry Newman, from G.K. Chesterton to Flannery O'Connor, we see that these figures had tremendous intellectual, spiritual, pastoral, and creative gifts—and they used them with great humility to pursue the beautiful, the good, and the true; that is, to love and serve God in his Church.

237

In our own day, the idea of humility has gotten mixed up with ideas about self-deprecation and pretending to be less accomplished than we really are. This is false humility, actually a kind of pride, which is captured best, perhaps, in the odious 'humblebrag.' True humility does not mean pretending that one doesn't have any talents or downplaying the value of one's gifts. Rather, it means recognizing that these are precisely gifts from God, and focusing on how they can be put to service for the kingdom. The Pivotal Players we have encountered were gifted in many ways, and their humility is grounded in their outward focus: how to serve Christ with talents that God gave them.

So it is right and fitting—and indeed vitally important—that we should ask the question: How can we do what they did in our own day and with our own gifts and talents?

In order to answer that question, we first need to discern the shape of the culture. 'Culture' in its broadest sense means 'our way of life': the ideas, attitudes, habits, and values of our day-to-day lives, and the way that these are embodied in specific behaviors, material objects, and artistic expressions. This includes everything from large-scale concerns (what is marriage? what is a person?) to the smallest ordinary details (what clothing we wear, what we eat and drink). It also includes a whole range of material and aesthetic expressions of what the culture values, from architecture to interior decorating, from sports to children's toys, and all the varied forms of entertainment and artistic expression (music, television, film, books, video games). Culture can be healthy or unhealthy, and in varied ways; it can have specific weaknesses and particular strengths; it is complex, because human beings are complex.

Every age and every culture presents particular opportunities and challenges for evangelization. Certain aspects of the human experience are perennial: People have always faced the problem of suffering, and struggled with issues of justice and mercy. Individual people have grappled with questions about the existence of God, the truth of the Resurrection, the nature of sin, and so on. But the way that these issues are experienced is profoundly shaped by the culture. The culture influences which questions are asked and which are left unasked; it subtly dictates which issues are considered important and which are secondary. Perhaps most important-ly, the culture shapes the assumptions that people bring to their questions and to their experience of the faith. These hidden assumptions create obstacles to evangelization, because they cause people either to reject the truth or to misunderstand what they are told.

Evangelizing the culture, then, requires being able to 'read the signs of the times': to discern the underlying issues, questions, and misun-derstandings of one's own day, and to respond accordingly. All of our Pivotal Players had that ability, whether consciously or intuitively: from St. Benedict discerning that he needed to leave the decadent urban culture of sixth-century Italy and set up a monastic community, to Bartolomé de las Casas in the fifteenth century recognizing that he must challenge the inhumane treatment of indigenous people in the Americas, to St. John Henry Newman engaging in the intellectual life of nineteenth-century Oxford. Closer to our own day, we find Flannery O'Connor responding to the spiritual deafness of twentieth-century America with her fiction, and Fulton Sheen recognizing the potential of television for evangelization. These figures presented the same truth in distinctive ways that met the needs of their times.

One of the things that we can learn from the Pivotal Players is how to observe the culture and really see it, to discern the underlying patterns and not just react to the surface disturbances. This is a skill akin to an athlete sensing the way that an opponent is responding in the moment, or to a teacher assessing the comprehension of a group of students as they listen to a lecture. It is like a farmer or sailor recognizing a change in the weather; or like a mother sensing that her infant is unwell; or like an artist discerning where the next brushstroke should fall. What all these analogies have in common is that they require a holistic response, a recognition of patterns and meaning that is more than mere data. And in the Pivotal Players, we can get some hints both of how they developed this 'evangelizing intuition' and how they put it to good use.

Many of the figures we have encountered are famous for some

particular gift, whether it's preaching, teaching, prayer, or the arts. But consider how we've seen, as well, the way that they are integrated Catholics. St. John Henry Newman is rightly honored for his brilliant intellect and ability to express the faith in his writing—and he also played the violin. Flannery O'Connor was a storyteller, gifted in her imagination and creative expression—and she was well versed in the philosophy of St. Thomas Aquinas (who, himself, also wrote hymns). St. Francis of Assisi was a preacher who founded a religious order—and he wrote poetry. St. Augustine was a profound theologian—and also, as a bishop, a working pastor.

They had particular callings, to be sure, but they didn't allow that to make them into isolated specialists, interested only in what was immediately and obviously relevant. Rather, they cultivated different ways of engaging with the world: philosophical, artistic, pastoral, imaginative. This approach not only helped them to more clearly discern the patterns of the culture, whether intuitively or consciously, but it also gave them more avenues to present the beautiful, the good, and the true in ways that resonated with their times.

We can emulate them by expanding the scope of our own engagement with the culture. This doesn't mean becoming an expert on everything—that's neither possible nor desirable! Rather, it means cultivating different ways of seeing. That may, for instance, mean venturing to learn something of philosophy to sharpen our intellect; it may mean exploring the writings of Christian contemplatives to deepen our prayer lives. The arts are particularly needful if we are to evangelize in this secular, materialist age, when the default attitude is that if it's not measurable, it doesn't matter. Stories, music, visual arts, architecture . . . these communicate knowledge in distinctive ways, and expand our ability to take in, not just facts, but meaning. When we are able to 'read' the culture in this way, we will be better placed to make a difference with the use of our own gifts and efforts.

What do you have to offer for the service of Christ's kingdom? That is a question that each of us must ask for ourselves—but not by ourselves, because God has made us to live in relation with each other. Friends, family, colleagues, pastors, and fellow Catholics in our communities (whether in person or online) can help us identify our God-given talents. And we must pray—always, always, we must offer up our gifts in prayer so that God can guide us to see the ways that our gifts meet the needs that we have prayerfully and thoughtfully discerned in our culture.

Here we must have the humility to look for what we can do, whether or not it seems especially important by the criteria of our modern culture, or fits with our preconceived ideas about what 'evangelization' looks like. Who would have thought that St. Benedict going off into a cave to pray would eventually help preserve Christianity in the West? Who would have seen G.K. Chesterton's first newspaper articles and detective stories and realized that they were looking at one of the great Catholic apologists of the twentieth century? And we must learn our craft and be patient. No one becomes a philosopher by reading one book, or a writer by writing one story. Every calling requires patience, diligence, and humility, and we may never see, in this life, the fruits of it—but we will in the next.

Whatever particular gifts any one of us may have, one thing we do all have, for certain: a vocation to holiness. We are all called to be saints, and to witness with our lives to the truth of the faith. We have seen in our Pivotal Players how their witness, their passionate love of Christ, and their urgent seeking after holiness was transformative for others. There are new saints being raised up right now, who in future generations will be recognized as pivotal players of the twenty-first century. It might be you or me, in God's providence—it might be someone whom you or I help to come into the Church, or someone we encourage, or teach, or pray for, or serve. Each and every one of us is a pivotal player for someone in our lives. Let us live out that calling, with God's help and the help of all the saints!

NOTES

Chapter 1: *St. Augustine*

2   **"prayer overheard":** Thomas Prufer, "A Reading of Augustine's Confessions, Book X," in *Recapitulations: Essays in Philosophy* (Washington, DC: Catholic University of America Press, 1993), 29.

3   **"Lord, you have made us for yourself; therefore, our heart is restless until it rests in you":** Augustine, *Confessions*, 1.1 (author's translation).

4   **"with suspicions and fears and tempers and quarrels":** Augustine, *Confessions*, 3.1 (Park Ridge, IL: Word on Fire, 2017), 42.

7   **"stuck fast in flesh and blood":** Augustine, *Confessions*, 8.8, p. 196.

8   **"put ye on the Lord Jesus Christ and make not provision for the flesh in its concupiscences":** Augustine, *Confessions*, 8.12, pp. 194–195.

Chapter 2: *St. Benedict*

23   **"a religious house, a farm, an abbey, a village, a seminary, a school of learning, and a city":** John Henry Newman, *Historical Sketches,* vol. 2 (New York: Longmans, Green, and Co., 1906), 410, http://www.newman-reader.org/works/historical/volume2/index.html.

24   **only real light during the Dark Ages was the Church:** G.K. Chesterton, *Orthodoxy* (Park Ridge, IL: Word on Fire, [1908] 2017), 149–150.

24   **"We are waiting not for a Godot, but for another—doubtless very different—St. Benedict":** Alasdair MacIntyre, *After Virtue: A Study in Moral Theory* (New York: Bloomsbury Academic, 2013), 305.

25   **"please God alone":** St. Gregory the Great, *The Life of Saint Benedict,* trans. Terrence G. Kardong, OSB, in *St. Benedict Collection* (Park Ridge, IL: Word on Fire, 2018), 111.

29   **"noble weapons of obedience to do battle for the true King, Christ the Lord":** St. Benedict, *The Rule,* ed. Timothy Fry, OSB, in *St. Benedict Collection,* Prologue, 1, p. 7.

29   **"Let us open our eyes to the light that comes from God":** Benedict, *Rule,* Prologue, 9, p. 7.

29   **"the buffered self"**: Charles Taylor, *A Secular Age* (Cambridge, MA: The Belknap Press of Harvard University Press, 2007 [2018]), 37–42.

30   **"a school for the Lord's service"**: Benedict, *Rule,* Prologue, 45, p. 9.

30   **"combat of the desert"**: Benedict, *Rule,* 1.5, p. 11.

30   **"slaves to their own wills and gross appetites"**: Benedict, *Rule,* 1.11, p. 11.

32   **"the Lord often reveals what is better to the younger"**: Benedict, *Rule,* 3.3, p. 16.

32   **"He will have to give an account of all his judgment to God"**: Benedict, *Rule,* 3.11, p. 16.

33   **"tools of the spiritual craft"**: Benedict, *Rule,* 4.75–78, pp. 19–20.

35   **"not speaking unless asked a question"**: Benedict, *Rule,* 7.56, p. 27.

35   **"Only a fool raises his voice in laughter"**: Benedict, *Rule,* 7.59, p. 27.

35   **"We absolutely condemn in all places any vulgarity and gossip and talk leading to laughter"**: Benedict, *Rule,* 6.8, p. 23.

35   **"but without raising his voice"**: Benedict, *Rule,* 7.60, p. 27.

36   **"nothing is to be preferred to the Work of God"**: Benedict, *Rule,* 43.3, p. 68.

37   **"goods of the monastery as sacred vessels of the altar"**: Benedict, *Rule,* 31.10, p. 54.

37   **"specified periods for manual labor as well as for prayerful reading"**: Benedict, *Rule,* 48.1, p. 74.

38   **"This evil practice [of private ownership] must be uprooted and removed from the monastery"**: Benedict, *Rule,* 33.1, p. 57.

38   **"nothing at all—not a book, writing tablets or stylus—in short, not a single item"**: Benedict, *Rule,* 33.3, p. 57.

38   **"*Omniaque omnium sint communia*"**: Benedict, *Rule,* 33.6, p. 57.

38   **common ownership is impossible to achieve at the political level, but remains a monastic ideal**: Thomas Merton, "Marxism and Monastic Perspective," in *The Asian Journal of Thomas Merton* (New York: New Directions, 1975), 326–343.

38 **"All guests who present themselves are to be welcomed as Christ":** Benedict, *Rule,* 53.1, p. 80.

Chapter 3: *St. Francis of Assisi*

45 **"Then why follow the servant, instead of the master":** Quoted in Omer Englebert, *St. Francis of Assisi: A Biography* (Cincinnati, OH: Franciscan Media, 2013), 26.

45 **"so good that none of you ever saw her like":** Quoted in Engelbert, *St. Francis of Assisi,* 27.

46 **"Francis, go repair my house, which is falling in ruins":** Quoted in Englebert, *St. Francis of Assisi,* 35.

47 **"saying in truth no longer: my father, Peter Bernardone, but: our Father who art in heaven":** Quoted in Englebert, *St. Francis of Assisi,* 39.

50 **"Go find your pigs instead. You can preach all the sermons you want to them":** Quoted in Englebert, *St. Francis of Assisi,* 69.

51 **"and so to blaspheme Christ, its Author":** Quoted in Englebert, *St. Francis of Assisi*, 74.

51 **"spiritual joy is as necessary to the soul as blood is to the body":** Quoted in Englebert, *St. Francis of Assisi*, 94.

51 **"hardly a citizen of the city of God":** Englebert, *St. Francis of Assisi*, 94.

51 **"You can see that we couldn't find a better place anywhere than this":** Quoted in Englebert, *St. Francis of Assisi*, 98.

53 **"Stay here by the road and wait for me, while I preach to our sisters the birds":** Quoted in Englebert, *St. Francis of Assisi*, 151.

53 **"God sustains you without your having to sow or reap":** Quoted in Englebert, *St. Francis of Assisi,,* 151.

54 **"My brother wolf here promises never to harm you again if you will promise to feed him as long as he lives":** Quoted in Englebert, *St. Francis of Assisi*, 154–156.

55 **whether they were the heretical band that had already wreaked havoc in Italy, they innocently responded, "Ja":** Englebert, *St. Francis of Assisi*, 187.

55 **"carrying stones and mortar like a mason's apprentice":** Englebert, *St. Francis of Assisi*, 192.

55 **"Now I can truly say that I have five Friars Minor":** Quoted in Englebert, *St. Francis of Assisi*, 206.

56 **"write down that at last I have found perfect joy":** Quoted in Englebert, *St. Francis of Assisi*, 198.

57 **"feel for you the same love that made you sacrifice yourself for us":** Quoted in Englebert, *St. Francis of Assisi*, 281.

57 **"with bent points extruding from the back of the hands and the soles of the feet":** Quoted in Englebert, *St. Francis of Assisi*, 281.

59 **"The Christian ideal has not been tried and found wanting. It has been found difficult; and left untried":** G.K. Chesterton, *What's Wrong with the World* (London: Cassell and Co., 1910), 39.

Chapter 4: *St. Thomas Aquinas*

65 **"bellowing that it will echo throughout the entire world":** Quoted in Jean-Pierre Torrell, *Saint Thomas Aquinas*, vol. 1, *The Person and His Work*, trans. Robert Royal, rev. ed. (Washington, DC: The Catholic University of America Press, 2005), 26.

68 **"he suspended his writing instruments":** William de Tocco, quoted in Placid Conway, OP, *Saint Thomas Aquinas of the Order of Preachers: A Biographical Study of the Angelic Doctor* (New York: Longmans, Green and Co., 1911), ch. 7.

68 **"Everything I have written seems to me as straw in comparison with what I have seen":** Recorded in the proceedings for the process of canonization of St. Thomas Aquinas, quoted in Torrell, *Saint Thomas Aquinas*, 289.

70 **to be God is "to be to-be":** David B. Burrell, *Aquinas: God and Action* (Notre Dame, IN: University of Notre Dame Press, 1979), 26.

74 **"The whole human soul is in the whole body, and again, in every part, as God is in regard to the whole world":** St. Thomas Aquinas, *Summa theologiae*, 1.93.3, New Advent, 1920, https://www.newadvent.org/summa/.

74 **"The soul is in the body as containing it, not as contained by it":** St. Thomas Aquinas, *Summa theologiae*, 1.52.1.

74 **"we ought to love our bodies also":** St. Thomas Aquinas, *Summa theologiae*, 2-2.5.5.

74 **"No, it will resume a human body made up of flesh and bones":** St. Thomas Aquinas, *Compendium theologiae*, 1.153, trans. Cyril Vollert (London: Herder, 1947), https://isidore.co/aquinas/Compendium.htm.

77   **"the glory of God is a human being fully alive"**: St. Irenaeus of Lyon, *Adversus Haereses*, 4.20.7 (author's translation).

Chapter 5: *St. Catherine of Siena*

85   **"You are she who is not and I AM HE WHO IS"**: Quoted in Raymond of Capua, *The Life of Catherine of Siena*, trans. C. Kearns (Wilmington, DE: Glazier, 1980), 85.

85   *mare pacifico* **(a peaceful sea)**: See, e.g., St. Catherine of Siena, *The Dialogue*, no. 79, trans. Suzanne Noffke (Mahwah, NJ: Paulist Press, 1980), 147.

85   **"fish in the sea"**: St. Catherine of Siena, *Dialogue*, 211.

87   **"steeped and kneaded with his divinity into the one bread"**: St. Catherine of Siena, *Dialogue*, 52.

87   **"I became a man and humanity became God through the union of my divine nature with your human nature"**: St. Catherine of Siena, *Dialogue*, 205.

87   **"cellarer"** with the **"keys of the blood"** of Christ: St. Catherine of Siena, *The Letters of Catherine of Siena*, vol. 3, trans. Suzanne Noffke (Tempe, AZ: ACMRS, 2007), 213. Quoted in Matthew Levering, *The Feminine Genius of Catholic Theology* (London: T&T Clark, 2012), 84.

88   **"This bridge [is] my only begotten Son"**: St. Catherine of Siena, *Dialogue*, 64–65.

90   **"every time and place is for them a time and place of prayer"**: St. Catherine of Siena, *Dialogue*, 145.

90   **"sweet tears shed with great tenderness"**: St. Catherine, *Dialogue*, 161.

91   **"that would be the greatest of joys for me"**: Quoted in Hans Urs von Balthasar, *Dare We Hope "That All Men Be Saved"?* (San Francisco: Ignatius Press, [1988] 2014), 172.

92   **"To attain charity you must dwell constantly in the cell of self-knowledge"**: St. Catherine, *Dialogue*, 118.

92   **"where there is earth as well as water"**: Catherine to Tommaso della Fonte, Letter T41, quoted in Thomas McDermott, OP, *Catherine of Siena: Spiritual Development in Her Life and Teaching* (Mahwah, NJ: Paulist Press, 2008), 121.

92   **Catherine refers to this process as "discernment":** St. Catherine, *Dialogue*, 40–44.

92   **"the soul is as obedient as she is humble and as humble as she is obedient":** St. Catherine, *Dialogue*, 328.

92   **"with well-ordered charity, it seeks everyone's salvation":** *The Prayers of Catherine of Siena*, trans. and ed. Suzanne Noffke, 2nd ed. (Lincoln, NE: Author's Choice Press, 2001), no. 15, 155. Quoted in Grazia Mangano Ragazzi, *Obeying the Truth: Discretion in the Spiritual Writings of Saint Catherine of Siena* (New York: Oxford, 2014), 96.

93   **"When love grows, so does sorrow":** St. Catherine, *Dialogue*, 33.

94   **"she finds and enjoys you, high eternal fire, the abyss of charity":** St. Catherine, *Dialogue*, 273.

94   **"one thing" with God:** See, e.g., St. Catherine, *Dialogue*, 25.

96   **"than are dreamt of in your philosophy":** William Shakespeare, *Hamlet*, 1.5.187–188 (New York: Simon & Schuster, 2012), 195.

Chapter 6: *Michelangelo*

101   **"I sucked in with my nurse's milk the chisels and hammer with which I make my figures":** Quoted in Giorgio Vasari, *Lives of the Most Eminent Painters, Sculptors, and Architects*, vol. 9, trans. Gaston du C. De Vere (London: Macmillan/Medici Society, 1915), 4.

104   **"Do you not know that chaste women retain their fresh looks much longer than those who are not chaste":** Quoted in Ascanio Condivi, *The Life of Michael Angelo Buonarroti*, trans. Charles Holroyd (New York: Charles Scribner's Sons, 1903), 26.

104   **"Virgin Mother, daughter of your Son, humbler and loftier past creation's measure":** Dante, *Paradise*, trans. Anthony Esolen (New York: Modern Library, 2007), 33.1–2, p. 351.

105   **she is like a great mountain, and his body is like a river flowing down:** *Sister Wendy's Grand Tour*, episode 3, "Rome," aired March 21, 1994, on BBC.

107   **"What a man":** Kenneth Clark, *Civilisation*, episode 5, "The Hero as Artist," aired March 23, 1969, on BBC.

108   **that Adam is a prototype of Jesus:** Andrew Graham-Dixon, *Michelangelo and the Sistine Chapel* (New York: Skyhorse Publishing, 2009), 69–70.

108 **"O happy fault that earned so great, so glorious a Redeemer":** The Easter Proclamation (Exsúltet), *Roman Missal: Third Edition* © 2010, International Commission on English in the Liturgy Corporation (ICEL).

109 **which seem as rounded as a woman's breasts:** Graham-Dixon, *Michelangelo and the Sistine Chapel*, 73.

110 **It is, as Kenneth Clark said, at once sublimely great and universally accessible:** Kenneth Clark, *Civilisation*, episode 5, "The Hero as Artist."

111 **"the finger of God is God's spirit through whom we are sanctified":** St. Augustine, *The Spirit and the Letter*, in *Later Works*, ed. John Burnaby (Philadelphia: Westminster Press, 1955), 216. See Graham-Dixon, *Michelangelo and the Sistine Chapel*, 83.

112 **"God is seen with arm and hand outstretched as if to impart to Adam the precepts as to what he must and must not do":** Quoted in Graham-Dixon, *Michelangelo and the Sistine Chapel*, 85.

115 **Traditionally, figs are associated with sexuality:** Graham-Dixon, *Michelangelo and the Sistine Chapel*, 95.

117 **Could that sermon [of Savanarola] have been echoing in Michelangelo's mind as he composed this scene:** Graham-Dixon, *Michelangelo and the Sistine Chapel*, 103–105.

118 **What is the significance of The Last Judgment:** See Graham-Dixon, *Michelangelo and the Sistine Chapel*, 159–176.

Chapter 7: *Bartolomé de las Casas*

125 **"Perhaps it was a nightmare. I can hardly believe it myself":** Bartolomé de las Casas, *A Short History of the Destruction of the Indies*, quoted in Lawrence A. Clayton, *Bartolomé de las Casas: A Biography* (New York: Cambridge University Press, 2012), 39–40.

126 **"You are killing them to get the gold you so crave":** Fr. Antonio de Montesinos, quoted in Clayton, *Bartolomé de las Casas*, 57–58.

126 **"I think the devil got into them":** Quoted in Clayton, *Bartolomé de las Casas*, 72.

127 **"Greed, Your Majesty, unvarnished greed. The thirst and hunger for gold":** Quoted in Clayton, *Bartolomé de las Casas*, 176–177.

129 **"Where in the law, or in Rights, natural, human, or divine, is it a given that these people should be plunged into a service so awful for the sake of Spaniards":** Quoted in Clayton, *Bartolomé de las Casas*, 250.

129 **"New Laws," promulgated in 1542 by King Charles:** Clayton, *Bartolomé de las Casas*, 270–284.

132 **"are by nature a servile and barbarous people":** Quoted in Clayton, *Bartolomé de las Casas*, 355.

133 **"And, if they are made submissive, it is easier and more expedient to preach the faith":** Quoted in Clayton, *Bartolomé de las Casas*, 355.

133 **"the injuries they cause each other, killing men for sacrifices and even to cannibalize them":** Quoted in Clayton, *Bartolomé de las Casas*, 355.

134 **"the work commends the craftsman":** Quoted in Clayton, *Bartolomé de las Casas*, 357.

134 **"Indeed I cannot say enough about the things which were there before me":** Quoted in Clayton, *Bartolomé de las Casas*, 357.

135 **"and heard with my own ears while living a great many years among these peoples":** Quoted in Clayton, *Bartolomé de las Casas*, 357.

136 **"What does the herald of the gospel have to do with armed thieves":** Quoted in Clayton, *Bartolomé de las Casas*, 361–363.

138 **"it will easily be determined that justice was being rendered on account of the destruction of the Indies":** Quoted in Clayton, *Bartolomé de las Casas*, 461.

139 **"We shall see" about it:** Quoted in Clayton, *Bartolomé de las Casas*, 462.

Chapter 8: *St. Ignatius*

144 **"great and foolish desire to win fame":** St. Ignatius of Loyola, *The Autobiography*, in *Ignatius of Loyola: The Spiritual Exercises and Selected Works*, ed. George E. Ganss, SJ (Mahwah, NJ: Paulist Press, 1991), 68.

144 **"atrocious crimes carried out . . . with premeditation and involving ambush and treachery":** Quoted in Malachi Martin, *Jesuits* (New York: Simon and Schuster, 1987), 154.

145 **In the *Autobiography*, he referred to all of this, with admirable laconicism, as "butchery":** St. Ignatius, *Autobiography*, 69.

149 **"as an old man's walking stick, or as a cadaver":** Quoted in Martin, *Jesuits*, 161.

150 **they say that Ignatius played the part of the straight man admirably:** Martin, *Jesuits*, 168.

151   **"and this was with so great an enlightenment that everything seemed new to [me]":** Ignatius, *Autobiography*, 81.

151   **"I shall be propitious to you in Rome":** Recorded by Diego Lainez, SJ, quoted in *Ignatius of Loyola: The Spiritual Exercises and Selected Works*, 42.

151   **"the closest he would get to hearing the tones and spirit of Jesus echoing in a human voice":** Quoted in Martin, *Jesuits*, 168.

153   **a contemplation of the Resurrection and Ascension of Jesus:** St. Ignatius of Loyola, *Spiritual Exercises*, in *Ignatian Collection* (Park Ridge, IL: Word on Fire, 2020), no. 4.

153   **"Man is created to praise, reverence, and serve God our Lord, and by this means to save his soul":** Ignatius, *Spiritual Exercises*, no. 23.

153   **"We should not prefer health to sickness, riches to poverty, honor to dishonor, a long life to a short life":** Ignatius, *Spiritual Exercises*, no. 23.

154   **"consciousness examen":** See George Aschenbrenner, "Consciousness Examen," *Review for Religious*, no. 31 (January 1972), available online at https://www.ignatianspirituality.com/ignatian-prayer/the-examen/consciousness-examen/.

154   **"The thoughts should be examined first, then the words, and finally, the deeds":** Ignatius, *Spiritual Exercises*, no. 43.

155   **"The colloquy is made by speaking exactly as one friend speaks to another":** Ignatius, *Spiritual Exercises*, no. 54.

156   **the "composition of place" and "application of the senses":** Ignatius, *Spiritual Exercises*, nos. 121–126.

157   **"where the chief of the enemy is Lucifer":** Ignatius, *Spiritual Exercises*, no. 138.

157   **"throughout the whole world to spread His sacred doctrine":** Ignatius, *Spiritual Exercises*, no. 145.

159   **"Give me Thy love and Thy grace, for this is sufficient for me":** Ignatius, *Spiritual Exercises*, no. 234.

Chapter 9: *St. John Henry Newman*

163   **"Nobody has ever written English prose that can be compared with that of a . . . prince of the only true church":** James Joyce to Harriet Weaver, May 1, 1935, in *Letters of James Joyce*, ed. Stuart Gilbert (New York: Viking Press, 1957), 365–366.

163   **"For thirty, forty, fifty years I have resisted to the best of my powers the spirit of liberalism in religion":** John Henry Newman, "Biglietto Speech," in *Addresses to Cardinal Newman with His Replies*, ed. Rev. W.P. Neville (New York: Longmans, Green, and Co., 1905), 64, http://www.newmanreader.org/works/addresses/file2.html.

165   **"material phenomena are both the types and instruments of real things unseen":** John Henry Newman, *Apologia Pro Vita Sua* (New York: Oxford, 1913), 186, http://www.newmanreader.org/works/apologia/part4.html.

166   **"in newspapers, in periodicals, at meetings, in pulpits, at dinner-tables, in coffee-rooms, in railway carriages":** Newman, *Apologia*, 89.

172   **"commensurate with the sum total of its possible aspects":** John Henry Newman, *An Essay on the Development of Christian Doctrine* (Park Ridge, IL: Word on Fire, [1845] 2017), 28.

172   **"There is no one aspect deep enough to exhaust the contents of a real idea":** Newman, *Essay on the Development of Christian Doctrine*, 28.

172   **"when its bed has become deep, and broad, and full":** Newman, *Essay on the Development of Christian Doctrine*, 32–33.

172   **"to be perfect is to have changed often":** Newman, *Essay on the Development of Christian Doctrine*, 33.

176   **"Of possessions, those rather are useful which bear fruit; those liberal which tend to enjoyment":** Aristotle, *Rhetoric*, 1.5, quoted in John Henry Newman, *The Idea of a University* (New York: Longmans, Green, and Co., 1907), 109, http://www.newmanreader.org/works/idea/discourse5.html.

177   **"like an easy chair or a good fire, which do their part in dispelling cold and fatigue":** Newman, *Idea of a University*, 209.

178   **"Persons influence us, voices melt us, looks subdue us, deeds inflame us":** John Henry Newman, *An Essay in Aid of a Grammar of Assent* (New York: Longmans, Green, and Co., 1903), 93, http://www.newmanreader.org/works/grammar/index.html.

179   **"attendant on certain of our actions which in consequence we call right or wrong":** Newman, *Grammar of Assent*, 105.

Chapter 10: *G.K. Chesterton*

184   **"Now I shall always have an audience":** G.K. Chesterton, *The Autobiography of G.K. Chesterton* (San Francisco: Ignatius Press, 2006), 191.

185   **the chief impression he made on his teachers was, in his words, that "I was asleep":** Chesterton, *Autobiography*, 74.

185   **"very negative and even nihilistic":** Chesterton, *Autobiography*, 96.

186   **"though my weight has never been successfully calculated":** Ian Ker, *G.K. Chesterton: A Biography* (Oxford: Oxford University Press, 2011), 632.

186   **while buses, trucks, and cars whirled around him and drivers shouted their dissatisfaction:** Ker, *Chesterton*, 94.

186   **Chesterton carried on, asking and answering his own questions:** Ker, *Chesterton*, 96.

186   **"Am at Market Harborough. Where ought I to be":** Chesterton, *Autobiography*, 320.

188   **"as if it were a real messenger, refusing to tamper with a real message":** G.K. Chesterton, "Why I Am a Catholic," in *The Collected Works of G.K. Chesterton*, vol. 3 (San Francisco: Ignatius, 1990), 127.

189   **"The Church is not a movement, but a meeting-place, the trysting-place of all the truths in the world":** Chesterton, "Why I Am a Catholic," 132.

190   **After singing the *Salve Regina* over him, McNabb picked up Chesterton's pen, which was lying on the bed stand next to him, and kissed it:** Randall Paine, Introduction to Chesterton, *Autobiography*, 17.

191   **like the coin that is "infinitely circular":** G.K. Chesterton, *Orthodoxy* (Park Ridge, IL: Word on Fire, [1908] 2017), 21.

192   **"democracy of the dead":** Chesterton, *Orthodoxy*, 43.

192   **"A child kicks his legs rhythmically through excess, not absence, of life":** Chesterton, *Orthodoxy*, 56.

192   **"Do it again! . . . a theatrical encore":** Chesterton, *Orthodoxy*, 56.

193   **"the white mask on a black world":** Chesterton, *Orthodoxy*, 84.

193   **"timid, monkish, and unmanly":** Chesterton, *Orthodoxy*, 85.

193   **"A thing might have these two opposite vices; but it must be a rather queer thing if it did":** Chesterton, *Orthodoxy*, 85.

193   **"naked and hungry habits":** Chesterton, *Orthodoxy*, 88.

194   **"Perhaps, after all, it is Christianity that is sane and all its critics that are mad—in various ways":** Chesterton, *Orthodoxy*, 89.

195   **"St. Jerome, in denouncing all evil, could paint the world blacker than Schopenhauer"**: Chesterton, *Orthodoxy*, 95.

195   **"fiercely for having children and fiercely for not having children"**: Chesterton, *Orthodoxy*, 96.

195   **"It has always had a healthy hatred of pink"**: Chesterton, *Orthodoxy*, 96.

195   **"the people in the street got the benefit of the crimson and gold"**: Chesterton, *Orthodoxy*, 98.

196   **"The wild horse was not an impressionist and the race horse a Post-impressionist"**: G.K. Chesterton, *The Everlasting Man* (San Francisco: Ignatius Press, 2008), 35.

196   **"all the literature of our faith is founded"**: Chesterton, *Everlasting Man*, 169.

197   **"almost entirely mild and merciful"**: Chesterton, *Everlasting Man*, 187.

197   **"except that he seems to have been rather fond of Roman soldiers"**: Chesterton, *Everlasting Man*, 191.

198   **"some insane Roman Emperor like Caligula claiming it for him, or more probably for himself"**: Chesterton, *Everlasting Man*, 202–203.

198   **"like one looking over his shoulder: 'Before Abraham was, I am'"**: Chesterton, *Everlasting Man*, 198.

Chapter 11: *Fulton J. Sheen*

202   **much preferring books and the liturgy of the Catholic Church:** Fulton J. Sheen, *Treasure in Clay: The Autobiography of Fulton J. Sheen* (New York: Image, 2008), 10.

202   **"someday you will be just as I am":** Sheen, *Treasure in Clay*, 14.

203   **"in the light of the philosophy of St. Thomas":** Sheen, *Treasure in Clay*, 25.

204   **He wondered what this said about our priorities:** Sheen, *Treasure in Clay*, 52–56.

205   **professional comedians were amazed at his comic timing:** Sheen, *Treasure in Clay*, 344.

205   **communication of the faith is grounded in an extraordinary amount of research, thought, and culture:** Sheen, *Treasure in Clay*, 72–73.

206   he memorably thanked his writers: "Matthew, Mark, Luke, and John": Sheen, *Treasure in Clay*, 318.

206   the lovely town in the Pyrenees where the Blessed Mother appeared to St. Bernadette: Sheen, *Treasure in Clay*, 109–177.

206   "the woman I love": Sheen, *Treasure in Clay*, 333.

207   "In order that through that sorrow, you might be here now starting instructions to know Christ and his Church": Sheen, *Treasure in Clay*, 274–275.

207   This steady devotion to Christ, he argued, would revolutionize the priest's spiritual life and invigorate his priesthood: Sheen, *Treasure in Clay*, 197–206.

208   This he did until a series of surgeries sapped him of his strength: Raymond Arroyo, Foreword in Sheen, *Treasure in Clay*, xi–xiii.

209   none other than the pope, who is called, quite properly, the "vicar of Christ": Fulton J. Sheen, *The Mystical Body of Christ* (Notre Dame, IN: Ave Maria Press, 2015), 117.

209   "cells of the mystical body cohere in unity under the headship of Christ": Sheen, *The Mystical Body of Christ*, 72.

210   "not an example to be copied, but a Life to be lived": Sheen, *Mystical Body of Christ*, 18.

210   "the Love of our hearts, and the Desire of our wills": Sheen, *Mystical Body of Christ*, 183.

211   "white-robed body of martyrs, confessors, virgins, pontiffs and Holy Women": Sheen, *Mystical Body of Christ*, 195.

211   "all are filled by the same Spirit and crowned by the same Christ": Sheen, *Mystical Body of Christ*, 196.

211   "But there can be no divorce between the two": Sheen, *Mystical Body of Christ*, 281.

213   "it is *not* monotonous if it has a purpose": Fulton J. Sheen, *Life Is Worth Living* (San Francisco: Ignatius, 1999), 15.

214   "When we do that for which we are made": Sheen, *Life Is Worth Living*, 19.

214   "then there is a thrill and a romance to life": Sheen, *Life Is Worth Living*, 19–20.

215   **"Unless you die to your lower existence, you cannot live in my kingdom":** Sheen, *Life Is Worth Living*, 114.

215   **"pride, covetousness, lust, anger, envy, gluttony, and sloth":** Sheen, *Life Is Worth Living*, 116.

216   **"that would be a very 'supernatural' act for a dog":** Sheen, *Life Is Worth Living*, 117.

217   **"new in its ardor, methods, and expression":** John Paul II, Address to CELAM (Opening Address of the Nineteenth General Assembly of CELAM, March 9, 1983, Port-au-Prince, Haiti), *L'Osservatore Romano* English Edition 16/780 (April 18, 1983), no. 9.

Chapter 12: *Flannery O'Connor*

219   **"To the hard of hearing you shout, and for the almost-blind you draw large and startling figures":** Flannery O'Connor, "The Fiction Writer & His Country," in *Flannery O'Connor Collection* (Park Ridge, IL: Word on Fire, 2019), 412.

219   **his art consisted in the reporting of "epiphanies":** See, e.g., James Joyce, *Stephen Hero*, ed. Theodor Spencer (New York: New Directions, 1963), 211.

219   **"a moment where it is offered, and is usually rejected":** Flannery O'Connor to Andrew Lytle, February 4, 1960, in *The Habit of Being: Letters of Flannery O'Connor*, ed. Sally Fitzgerald (New York: Vintage, 1980), 373.

221   **"The Catholic Church does not dictate to my family what time I go to Mass":** Brad Gooch, *Flannery: A Life of Flannery O'Connor* (New York: Little, Brown and Company, 2009), 34.

222   **"My name is Flannery O'Connor. I am not a journalist. Can I come to the Writers' Workshop":** Gooch, *Flannery*, 117.

223   **"Well, if it's a symbol, to hell with it":** Flannery O'Connor, "On 'A Temple of the Holy Ghost' and the Eucharist," in *Flannery O'Connor Collection*, 157; see also Gooch, *Flannery*, 174.

224   **"My opinion is that they don't stifle enough of them":** Flannery O'Connor, *Mystery and Manners: Occasional Prose*, ed. Sally and Robert Fitzgerald (New York: Farrar, Straus & Giroux, 1970), 84.

224   **"shed light in every direction":** Sally Fitzgerald, Introduction in *Habit of Being*, xi.

224   **"I hope to be offered a chair some day at the Chicken College":** Flannery O'Connor, "On Her Peafowl," in *Flannery O'Connor Collection*, 126.

225 **"She: Mow-by Dick. The Idiot. You would get something called Idiot. What's it about? Me: An Idiot":** O'Connor, "On Literature and Poetry," in *Flannery O'Connor Collection*, 121–22.

225 **"At which I hope to reply, 'I am his mother'":** Flannery O'Connor to "A.," December 8, 1955, in *Habit of Being*, 121.

225 **she refers to herself as a "hillbilly Thomist":** Flannery O'Connor, "On Being a 'Hillbilly Thomist,'" in *Flannery O'Connor Collection*, 23.

226 **"Death, decay, destruction are the suspension of these laws":** Flannery O'Connor, "On Truth and Emotion," in *Flannery O'Connor Collection*, 64–65.

227 **"Ought to have got you a wash rag and some soap":** Flannery O'Connor, "Revelation," in *Flannery O'Connor Collection*, 422.

227 **"Well, it hasn't done much for her manners":** O'Connor, "Revelation," 428.

227 **"Thank you, Jesus, for making everything the way it is":** O'Connor, "Revelation," 429.

227 **"Go back to hell where you came from, you old wart hog":** O'Connor "Revelation," 431.

228 **"battalions of freaks and lunatics shouting and clapping and leaping like frogs":** O'Connor, "Revelation," 439.

228 **"by their shocked and altered faces that even their virtues were being burned away":** O'Connor, "Revelation," 440.

230 **"anyone seeing her dead on the highway would know that she was a lady":** Flannery O'Connor, "A Good Man Is Hard to Find," in *Flannery O'Connor Collection*, 45.

230 **"a good man is hard to find":** Flannery O'Connor, "A Good Man Is Hard to Find," 48–49.

230 **"It would have been better for all of you, lady, if you hadn't of reckernized me":** O'Connor, "A Good Man Is Hard to Find," 53–54.

231 **"I don't want no hep. I'm doing alright by myself":** O'Connor, "A Good Man Is Hard to Find," 56–57.

231 **"Yes'm, Jesus thrown everything off balance":** O'Connor, "A Good Man Is Hard to Find," 58.

231   **"No pleasure but meanness":** O'Connor, "A Good Man Is Hard to Find," 59.

232   **"and I wouldn't be like I am now":** O'Connor, "A Good Man Is Hard to Find," 59.

232   **"Why you're one of my babies. You're one of my own children":** O'Connor, "A Good Man Is Hard to Find," 59.

232   **"as if a snake had bitten him":** O'Connor, "A Good Man Is Hard to Find," 59–60.

232   **"her face smiling up at the cloudless sky":** O'Connor, "A Good Man Is Hard to Find," 60.

233   **"Shut up, Bobby Lee. It's no real pleasure in life":** O'Connor, "A Good Man Is Hard to Find," 60.

234   **"for all the truth and all the craft with which she shows man's fall and his dishonor":** Thomas Merton, "Flannery O'Connor—A Prose Elegy," in *The Literary Essays of Thomas Merton*, ed. Patrick Hart (New York: New Directions, 2005), 161.

ART & PHOTOGRAPHY

Introduction

The Collegiate Basilica of Santa Maria, Manresa, Spain, photo by Word on Fire.

Chapter 1: *St. Augustine*

11   **(Detail)** Philippe de Champaigne, *Saint Augustine*, c. 1446–82, oil on canvas, 30.9 x 24.4 in. (78.7 x 62.2 cm), Metropolitan Museum of Art, New York, Wikimedia Commons, public domain (PD-US).

12-13   Tempio del Divo Claudio, Rome, Italy, photo by Nicole Reyes, Unsplash.

14   **(Detail)** Peter Paul Rubens, *Romulus and Remus,* 1615, oil on oak, 51.6 x 37 in. (131.2 x 94.2 cm), Capitoline Museums, Rome, Wikimedia Commons, public domain.

15   Peter Paul Rubens, *Cain Slaying Abel,* 1608. University of London, Courtauld Institute of Art. Accessed June 1, 2020. Wikimedia Commons, public domain (PD-US).

16   Albrecht Dürer, *Adoration of the Trinity,* 1511, oil on panel, 53.1 × 48.4 in. (135 × 123 cm) Kunsthistorisches Museum, Vienna, Wikimedia Commons, public domain (PD-US).

17   **(Detail)** Philippe de Champaigne, *Saint Augustine*, c. 1446-82, oil on canvas, 30.9 x 24.4 in. (78.7 x 62.2 cm), Metropolitan Museum of Art, New York, Wikimedia Commons, public domain (PD-US).

18   Bartolomé Esteban Murillo, *San Agustín entre Cristo y la Virgen,* 1664, oil on canvas, 107.8 x 76.7 in. (274 x 195 cm), Museo Nacional del Prado, Madrid.

20   **(Detail)** Philippe de Champaigne, *Saint Augustine*, c. 1446–82, oil on canvas, 30.9 x 24.4 in. (78.7 x 62.2 cm), Metropolitan Museum of Art, New York, Wikimedia Commons, public domain (PD-US).

20   Ibid.

Chapter 2: *St. Benedict*

22   Gerard David, *Poliptych of Cervara, St. Benedict*, c. 1506–1510, oil on oak wood, 100.3 x 85.8 in. (255 x 218 cm), New York, Metropolitan Museum of Art, Wikimedia Commons, Sailko / CC BY-SA (https://creativecommons.org/licenses/by-sa/3.0), (PD-US).

23   **(Detail)** Gerard David, *Poliptych of Cervara, St. Benedict*, c. 1506–1510, oil on oak wood, 100.3 x 85.8 in. (255 x 218 cm), New York, Metropolitan Museum of Art, Wikimedia Commons, Sailko / CC BY-SA (https://creativecommons.org/licenses/by-sa/3.0), (PD-US).

25   The sacred cave of St. Benedict, Subiaco, Italy, photo by Leemage/Universal Images Group via Getty Images.

26   Master of Meßkirch, *Saint Benedict of Nursia in Front of His Cave in Prayer,* c. 1535–1540, oil on canvas, St. Martin's Church in Meßkirch, Wikimedia Commons, public domain (PD-US).

27   (**Detail**) Master of Meßkirch, *Saint Benedict of Nursia in Front of His Cave in Prayer,* c. 1535–1540, oil on canvas, St. Martin's Church in Meßkirch, Wikimedia Commons, public domain (PD-US).

27   Abbey of Monte Cassino, Italy, photo by Mattis, Wikimedia, CC BY-SA 4.0 (https://creativecommons.org/licenses/by/4.0).

28   Il Sodoma, *Life of St Benedict, Come Benedetto appare a due monaci lontani e loro disegna la costruzione di uno monastero,* c. 1505–1508, Italy, Abbey of Monte Oliveto Maggiore, Wikimedia Commons, Sialko / CC BY-SA 3.0 (https://creativecommons.org/licenses/by/3.0).

31   Philippe Sauvan, *Saint Benoît,* c. 1749, oil on canvas, Vaucluse, France, Transfiguration church in Sorgues, Wikimedia Commons, public domain.

32   (**Detail**) Philippe Sauvan, *Saint Benoît,* c. 1749, oil on canvas, Vaucluse, France, Transfiguration church in Sorgues, Wikimedia Commons, public domain.

34   Lorenzo Monaco, *Saint Benedict Admitting Saints into the Order*, c. 1407–1409, London, National Gallery, Wikimedia Commons, public domain (PD-US).

36   Benedictine monk in prayer, Le Mont-Saint-Michel, France, photo by Word on Fire.

36   Interior of chapel in Le Mont-Saint-Michel, France, photo by Word on Fire.

38   Crucifix on altar in side chapel in Le Mont-Saint-Michel, France, photo by Word on Fire.

39   Detail of interior of chapel in Le Mont-Saint-Michel, France, photo by Word on Fire.

40-41   Le Mont-Saint-Michel vu du ciel au lever du soleil, France, photo by Amaustan, Wikimedia Commons, CC BY-SA 4.0 (https://creativecommons.org/licenses/by/4.0).

41   (**Detail**) The entrance cloister of Monte Cassino Abbey and the death of Saint Benedict statue. Italy. Photo by Wieslaw Jarek, Alamy.com, ID: PE83AP.

Chapter 3: *St. Francis of Assisi*

57 Giovanni Bellini, *Saint Francis in the Desert,* c. 1480, oil and tempura on poplar wood, 48.9 × 55.5 in. (124.4 × 141 cm), The Frick Collection, New York, Wikimedia Commons, public domain.

58 Unknown artist, formerly attributed to Giotto di Bodone, *Legend of St. Francis, Death and Ascension of St. Francis,* 1300, fresco, 270 x 230 cm, Basilica of Saint Francis of Assisi, Assisi, Italy, Wikimedia Commons, public domain (PD-US).

59 Exterior of Basilica of St. Francis, Assisi, Italy, photo by Word on Fire.

Chapter 4: *St. Thomas Aquinas*

60 Antonio del Castillo y Saavedra, *Santo Tomás de Aquino*, c. 1600–1649, oil on canvas, 88.5 x 45.2 in. (225 x 115 cm), Museum of Fine Arts of Córdoba, Spain, Wikimedia Commons, public domain.

62 Roccasecca, *Torre e mura del castello,* photo by Pietro Scerrato, Wikimedia Commons, CC BY-SA-3.0 (https://creativecommons.org/licenses/by/3.0).

62 (**Detail**) Abbey of Monte Cassino, photo by Mattis, Wikimedia Commons, CC BY-SA-4.0 (https://creativecommons.org/licenses/by-sa/4.0/deed.en).

63 The bust of Aristotle, a Greek philosopher and polymath in the old book the Aristotle's life, by E. Litvinova, 1892, St. Petersburg, https://www.istockphoto.com/vector/the-bust-of-aristotle-a-greek-philosopher-and-polymath-in-the-old-book-the-gm1219546214-356769583.

64 Diego Velázquez, *Temptation of St. Thomas*, 1632, oil on canvas, 96 x 79.9 in. (244 x 204 cm), Museo Diocesano de Arte Sacro, Spain, Wikimedia Commons, public domain (PD-US).

65 Notre Dame Cathedral along River Seine, Paris France, photo by Norimages, Alamy.com, ID: EAJHG0.

67 Open text of the *Summa contra Gentiles*, Vatican Library, Vatican City, photo by Word on Fire.

68 Nicklaus Manuel, *St. Thomas Aquinas (1214–74) and Louis IX (1215–70)*, c. 1516–18, tempura on panel, 61.1 x 46.6 in. (156 x 118 cm), Basel, Kunstmuseum, Alamy.com, ID: 2A2NW20.

69 Carlo Crivelli, *The Demidoff Altarpiece: Saint Thomas Aquinas*, 1476, tempura on poplar, 24 x 15.7 in. (61 x 40 cm), National Gallery, London / Art Resource, NY.

70 Photo mid-fifteenth century manuscript of the *Summa Theologica,* donated to Brandeis by Peter H. Brandt, courtesy of the Robert D. Farber University Archives & Special Collections Department, Brandeis University.

72　　Francisco de Zurbarán, *The Apotheosis of St. Thomas of Aquino,* 1631, oil on canvas, 15.5 x 12.3 ft. (475 cm x 375 cm), Museum of Fine Arts of Seville, Wikimedia Commons, public domain (PD-US).

72　　(**Detail**) Francisco de Zurbarán, *The Apotheosis of St. Thomas of Aquino,* 1631, oil on canvas, 15.5 x 12.3 ft. (475 cm x 375 cm), Museum of Fine Arts of Seville, Wikimedia Commons, public domain (PD-US).

75　　Santi di tito, *Vision of St. Thomas Aquinas,* 1593, oil on panel, 141.6. x 91.7 in. (362 x 233 cm), San Marco, Florence, Wikimedia Commons, CC BY-SA-3.0 (https://creativecommons.org/licenses/by/3.0).

76　　Titian, *Salvator Mundi,* c. 1570, oil on canvas, 96 x 80 cm, Hermitage Museum, St. Petersburg, Wikimedia Commons, public domain (PD-US).

77　　Bartolomé Esteban Murillo, *Santo Tomás de Aquino,* 1650, oil on canvas, 37.7 x 26.7 in. (96 x 68 cm), photo by Amuley, Wikimedia Commons, CC BY-SA-3.0 (https://creativecommons.org/licenses/by/3.0).

Chapter 5: *St. Catherine of Siena*

78　　Baldassare Franceschini, *St. Catherine of Siena,* 17th century, oil on canvas, 34.48 x 40.74 in. (87.6 x 103.5 cm), Dulwich Picture Gallery, London, Wikimedia Commons, pubblic domain, PD-US.

81　　Gaetano Marinelli, *Nozze mistiche di S. Caterina* (The Mystical Marriage of St. Catherine), c. 1896, Sanctuary of the Casa di Santa Caterina, Siena, Italy, photo by Word on Fire.

81　　(**Detail**) Gaetano Marinelli, *Nozze mistiche di S. Caterina* (The Mystical Marriage of St. Catherine), c. 1896, Sanctuary of the Casa di Santa Caterina, Siena, Italy, photo by Word on Fire.

82　　Eugène Delacroix, *Christ on the Cross,* c. 1846, oil on canvas, 31.4 x 25.2 in. (80 x 64.2 cm), Walters Art Museum, Baltimore, Wikimedia Commons, public domain (PD-US).

83　　Marco Benefial, *St Catherine Trying to persuade the Pope to move from Avignon to Rome,* 18th century, oil on canvas, 34.2 x 28.7 in. (87 x 73 cm), Nationalmuseum, Stockholm, Sweden, Wikimedia Commons, public domain (PD-US).

85　　Unknown Artist, *Mosaic of marine life,* c. 100 BC, 34.65 x 34.65 in. (88 x 88 cm), National Archaeological Museum, Naples, Italy, Wikimedia Commons, CC BY-SA-2.0 (https://creativecommons.org/licenses/by-sa/2.0/deed.en).

Chapter 6: *Michelangelo*

108   Michelangelo's Sistine Chapel ceiling, Saint Peter's Basilica, Vatican City, Wikimedia Commons, photo by Antoine Taveneaux, CC BY-SA 3.0 (https://creativecommons.org/licenses/by/3.0/deed.en).

109   (**Detail**) Michelangelo's Sistine Chapel ceiling, *The Creation of the Sun and the Moon,* Saint Peter's Basilica, Vatican City, Wikimedia Commons, public domain (PD-US).

110   (**Detail**) Ibid.

110   Michelangelo's Sistine Chapel ceiling, *The Creation of Adam*, Saint Peter's Basilica, Vatican City, Wikimedia Commons, public domain (PD-US).

112   (**Detail**) Ibid.

113   Michelangelo's Sistine Chapel ceiling, *The Creation of Eve*, Saint Peter's Basilica, Vatican City, Wikimedia Commons, public domain (PD-US).

113   (**Detail**) Ibid.

114   Michelangelo's Sistine Chapel ceiling, *The Fall and Expulsion from Paradise*, Saint Peter's Basilica, Vatican City, Wikimedia Commons, public domain (PD-US).

116   (**Detail**) Micelangelo's Sistine Chapel ceiling, *The Sacrifice of Noah*, Saint Peter's Basilica, Vatican City, Wikimedia Commons, public domain (PD-US).

116   Michelangelo's Sistine Chapel ceiling, *The Deluge*, Saint Peter's Basilica, Vatican City, Wikimedia Commons, public domain (PD-US).

117   (**Detail**) Michelangelo's Sistine Chapel ceiling, *The Drunkenness of Noah*, Saint Peter's Basilica, Vatican City, Wikimedia Commons, public domain (PD-US).

118   Michelangelo's Sistine Chapel, *The Last Judgment*, Saint Peter's Basilica, Vatican City, Wikimedia Commons, Public domain (PD-US).

120   (**Detail**) Daniele da Volterra, *Michelangelo Buonarroti*, c. 1544, oil on panel, 34.7 x 25.2 in. (88.3 x 64.1 cm), New York, Metropolitan Museum of Art, Wikimedia Commons, public domain (PD-US).

120   Duomo, Florence, Italy, photo by Word on Fire.

Chapter 7: *Bartolomé de las Casas*

122   Félix Parra, *Fray Bartolomé de las Casas*, 1875, oil on canvas, 11.69 ft. x 103.54 in., Museo Nacional de Arte, Mexico City, 2020, Wikimedia Commons, public domain (PD-US).

125   Joos van Winghe, Theodor de Bry, *Hanging, Burning and clubbing of Indians by Spanish soldiers.* Folio 1., 1665, wood engraving, Collection Peace Palace Library, The Hague, The Netherlands, Wikimedia Commons, public domain.

127   Eugène Delacroix, *The Return of Christopher Columbus,* 1839, Oil on canvas, 35.5 x 46.5 in., Toledo Museum of Art, Ohio, United States, Wikimedia Commons, public domain.

128   Santiago, Dominican Republic, photo by Siednji Leon, Unsplash.

128   The shores of the Dominican Republic, photo by Word on Fire.

131   Unidentified Painter, *Portrait of Bartolomé de Las Casas*, c. 16th century, oil on canvas, General Archive of the Indies, Seville, Spain, Wikimedia Commons, public domain (PD-US).

132   Unknown artist, *Portrait of Juan Ginés de Sepúlveda (1490–1573), Spanish humanist*, 11.6 x 16.3 in. (29.5 x 41.3 cm), Biblioteca Colombina, Sevilla, Alamy.com, ID: P4NRWB.

133   Antonio del Castillo y Saavedra, *Santo Tomás de Aquino*, c. 1600–1649, oil on canvas, 88.5 x 45.2 in. (225 x 115 cm), Museum of Fine Arts of Córdoba, Spain, Wikimedia Commons, public domain.

134   Albrecht Dürer, *Self-portrait*, 1500, oil on lime, 26.4 x 19.2 in., Alte Pinakothek, Munich, Germany, Wikimedia Commons, public domain.

135   Unknown Artist, *Bartolomé de las Casas, c. 1484–1566. 16th-century Spanish historian, social reformer and Dominican friar,* from *La Ilustracion Española y Americana*, published 1892, Alamy.com, ID: E9JKBH.

136   Domincan Republic, photo by Word on Fire.

138   Unknown artist, *Bartolomé de las Casas, Spanish historian and missionary, visited on his deathbed by Native Americans who valued his sympathy for them,* 21 x 14.8 in. (53.3 x 37.6 cm), Alamy.com, ID: G39XPC.

139   Miguel Noreña, *Fray Bartolomé de las Casas, converting an Aztec Family,* relief, 50.9 x 70.4 in., photograph by Alejandro Linares Garcia, Wikimedia Commons, CC BY-SA 4.0 (https://creativecommons.org/licenses/by/4.0/deed.en).

141 Constantino Brumidi, *Bartolomé de las Casas,* 1876, oil on plaster, Senate Wing, US Capitol, https://www.flickr.com/photos/uscapitol/6238653364, public domain.

Chapter 8: *St. Ignatius of Loyola*

142 Francisco de Zurbarán and workshop, *St. Ignatius Loyola*, 17th century, oil on canvas, 39.7 x 35.1 in., Royal Collection, Kensington, England, Wikimedia Commons, public domain (PD-old-auto; PD-US).

144 Photo by Nik Shuliahin, Unsplash.

145 Photo by Clarisse Meyer, Unsplash.

147 Cave of Saint Ignatius, Manresa, Spain, photo by Word on Fire.

149 Church of the Gesù, Rome, Italy, photo by Word on Fire.

150 Saint Petersburg, Russia, photo by Jan Zhukov, Unsplash.

150 Death mask of St. Ignatius of Loyola, Rome, Italy, photo by Word on Fire.

151 Domenichino Zampieri (called Domenichino), *Saint Ignatius of Loyola's Vision of Christ and God the Father at La Storta*, c. 1622, oil on canvas, 65 3/8 × 38 5/8 in. (166.05 × 98.11 cm), Los Angeles County Museum of Art, public domain.

153 Painting of St. Ignatius writing, the House of Ignatius, Rome, Italy, photo by Word on Fire.

155 Unidentified painter, *The Vision of Ignatius of Loyola*, c. 1622–1630, oil on canvas, 50 x 77.5 in. (127 x 197 cm), Unknown collection, Wikimedia Commons, public domain (PD-US).

156 *A Page from Ignatius of Loyola's Spiritual Exercises*, 2014, photograph, Wikimedia Commons, CC BY-2.0 (https://creativecommons.org/licenses/by/2.0/deed.en).

158 Church of the Gesù, Rome, Italy, photo by Word on Fire.

159 Photo by Hussain Badshah, Unsplash.

160 Peter Paul *Rubens, Saint Ignatius of Loyola*, c. 17th century, 87.9 x 54.4 in., Norton Simon Museum, Pasadena, California, Wikimedia Commons, public domain (PD-US).

162   Unknown artist, after a drawing by George Richmond, *John Henry Newman,* 13 x 15.5 in. (33 x 39.3 cm), Lebrecht Music & Arts, Alamy.com, ID: ERH248.

164   Oxford University, photo by Word on Fire.

164   (**Detail**) William Charles Ross, *Portrait Miniature of Cardinal Newman,* 1904, Keble College, Oxford, United Kingdom, Wikimedia Commons, public domain.

165   John Bower, Chapel of Keble College, Oxford, Alamy.com, ID: AFJXR2.

166   Fra Angelico, *Coronation of the Virgin* (Cell 9), 1440–1442, fresco, 67.3 x 59.4 in., Museum of San Marco, Florence, Italy, Wikimedia Commons, public domain (PD-US).

167   Chatsworth House, Bakewell, United Kingdom, photo by Thomas Kelley, Unsplash.

168   St. John Henry Newman's reading glasses, photo by Word on Fire.

169   Oxford, United Kingdom, photo by Alex Motoc, Unsplash.

169   (**Detail**) Carlo Dolci, Saint Philip Neri, 1645–46, oil on canvas, 17.2 x 14.2 in., Metropolitan Museum of Art, New York, Wikimedia Commons, CC BY 1.0 (https://creativecommons.org/licenses/by/1.0/deed.en).

170   John Henry Newman Reading a Book, 1890, from Sermon Notes of John Henry Cardinal Newman by Henry J. Whitlock, Wikimedia Commons, public domain.

172   Frits Thaulow, La Dordogne, 1903, oil painting, Wikimedia Commons, public domain (PD-US).

173   Photo by Nathan Dumlao, Unsplash.

174   Photo by Sean Brown, Unsplash.

175   Oxford, United Kingdom, photo by Word on Fire.

176   Lower Library, Worcester College, Oxford University, United Kingdom, photo by Nabeel Hussein, Unsplash.

177   Newman's desk in the Birmingham Oratory, photo by Lastenglishking, Wikimedia Commons, public domain.

178   Newman's pen and ink, photo by Word on Fire.

181   Photo of John Henry Newman, c. 1904, photo by Herbert Rose Barraud, Alamy.com, ID: K9R3TP.

Chapter 10: *G.K. Chesterton*

183   Unknown photographer, G.K. Chesterton at work, Wikimedia Commons, public domain (PD-US).

184   Bain News Service, Fleet St., London, 1910, Library of Congress, United States, public domain.

185   Unknown photographer, G.K. Chesterton at the age of 17, 1908, Wikimedia Commons, public domain (PD-US).

186   Unknown photographer, Cheapside, with the Church of Saint Mary le Bow in the background, 1909, Wikimedia Commons, public domain (PD-US).

186   (**Detail**) E.H. Mills, *G.K. Chesterton*, bromide print, published 1909, 7 3/4 in. x 6 1/8 in. (198 mm x 156 mm), Given by Terence Pepper, 2011, Photographs Collection, National Portrait Gallery, London.

187   Davart Company, *George Berard Shaw*, 1934, Library of Congress, United States, Wikimedia Commons, public domain (PD-US-expired).

188   Keystone Pictures, *Father Brown*, Alias Alec Guinness, 1953, Alamy.com, ID: E0M6C1.

189   Tichnor Brothers, The Stadium, Notre Dame, Indiana, c. 1930-1945, Boston Public Library, United States, Wikimedia Commons, public domain (PD-US).

190   G.K. Chesterton's grave, Beaconsfield, South Bucks District, Buckingham-shire, England, photo by Word on Fire.

190   (**Detail**) Jacksonville, Florida, US, Glasses with book, photo by Debby Hudson, Unsplash.

191   John S. Johnston, Seawanhaka Corinthian Yacht Club, 1894, Library of Congress, United States, Wikimedia Commons, public domain.

193   Vintage keys of various kinds on the same ring, photo by Susan Holt Simpson, Unsplash.

194   Craig Franck, *Joan of Arc*, 1907, Alamy.com, ID: MX7G0C

196   *Aurochs, Horses and Deer*, Lascaux cave painting, photo by @profsaxx, CC BY 3.0 (https://creativecommons.org/licenses/by/3.0/deed.en) (PD-US).

197 El Greco, *Christ Cleansing the Temple*, oil painting, 25.7 x 32.7 in. (65.4 x 83.2 cm), Samuel H. Kress Collection, National Gallery of Art, Washington, DC, Wikimedia Commons, public domain (PD-US).

197 (**Detail**) El Greco, *Christ Blessing ('The Saviour of the World')*, c. 1600, oil painting, 28.7 x 22.2 in. (73 x 56.5 cm), National Galleries of Scotland, Wikimedia Commons, public domain.

199 James Craig Annan, *G.K. Chesterton*, carbon print, 1912, 7 3/4 in. x 6 in. (197 mm x 151 mm), given by Richard Miles, 1974, Photographs Collection, National Portrait Gallery, London.

Chapter 11: *Fulton J. Sheen*

200 Bishop Fulton J. Sheen, full-length portrait, standing, facing right, 1952, *World Telegram & Sun,* photo by Fred Palumbo, Library of Congress, https://www.loc.gov/pictures/item/99471669/.

202 Anahuac Norte, Lomas Anahuac, Naucalpan de Juárez, Méx., México, photo by Luis Ángel Espinosa, Cathopic, https://www.cathopic.com/photo/18846-tomen-beban-todos-el, CC0 1.0.

203 Catholic University of America sign, Washington, DC, photo by Word on Fire.

204 *Bishop Fulton Sheen writing on blackboard during the broadcast of his TV show, Life Is Worth Living,* 1954, photo by Everett Collection, Alamy.com, ID: F2B0G2.

205 Blackboard at Catholic University of America, Washington, DC, photo by Word on Fire.

206 Film strip, Peoria, Illinois, photo by Word on Fire.

207 Exposición Santísimo Sacramento, photo by ArqTI, Cathopic.com, CC0 1.0 (https://creativecommons.org/licenses/by/1.0/deed.en).

209 Holy Spirit dove detail, Washington, DC, photo by Word on Fire.

210 Fra Angelico and Benozzo Gozzoli, *Christ in Judgment,* c. 1447, San Brizio Chapel, Orvieto Cathedral, Orvieto, Italy, photo by Word on Fire.

211 San Brizio Chapel, Orvieto Cathedral, Orvieto, Italy, photo by Word on Fire.

213 Film canister, Peoria, Illinois, photo by Word on Fire.

216   Adoracion Eucaristica, photo by Juan Pablo Arias, Cathopic.com, CC0 1.0 (https://creativecommons.org/licenses/by/1.0/deed.en).

217   Sheen through a lens, Washington, DC, photo by Word on Fire.

Chapter 12: *Flannery O'Connor*

218   Yearbook photo of Flannery O'Connor in her childhood home in Savannah, Georgia, photo by Word on Fire.

220   Images of Flannery O'Connor's parents in her childhood home in Savannah, Georgia, photo by Word on Fire.

221   Peacock at Flannery's O'Connor's family farm in Milledgeville, Georgia, photo by Word on Fire.

222   Entrance to Yaddo, a residential artists' colony in Saratoga Springs, New York, where Flannery O'Connor lived from 1948–49, photo by Word on Fire.

223   Flannery's prescription bottle at her family farm in Milledgeville, Georgia, photo by Word on Fire.

224   Fountain pen on stationery, photo by Álvaro Serrano, Unsplash.

225   Francisco de Zurbarán, *The Apotheosis of St. Thomas of Aquino,* 1631, oil on canvas, 15.5 x 12.3 ft. (475 cm x 375 cm), Museum of Fine Arts of Seville, Wikimedia Commons, public domain (PD-US).

226   Micah Brenner, sketch of scene from Flannery O'Connor's short story "Revelation," image courtesy of Word on Fire.

227   Micah Brenner, sketch of scene from Flannery O'Connor's short story "Revelation," image courtesy of Word on Fire.

230   Hagg Wood Community Wood, York, United Kingdom, photo by Thom Holmes, Unsplash.

231   **(Detail)** Photo by Owtana, Unsplash.

234   Framed photo of Flannery O'Conner from her family home in Milledgeville, Georgia, photo by Word on Fire.

235   Flannery O'Conner's grave, Milledgeville, Georgia, photo by Word on Fire.

Afterword: *Becoming Pivotal Players Today*